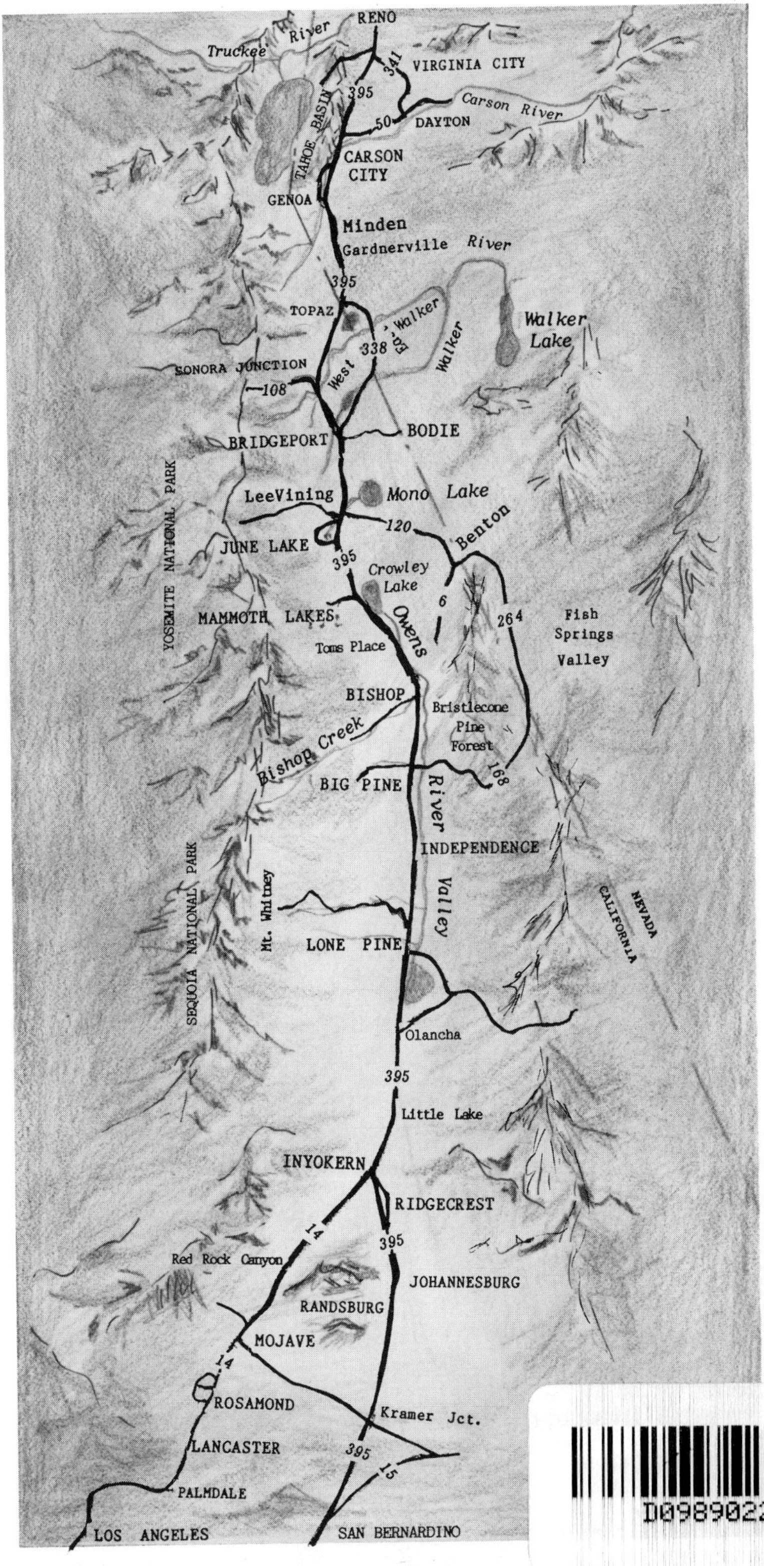
RENO
Truckee River
VIRGINIA CITY
341
395
TAHOE BASIN
Carson River
50
DAYTON
CARSON CITY
GENOA
Minden
Gardnerville
River
395
TOPAZ
East Walker
Walker Lake
338
West
Walker
SONORA JUNCTION
108
BODIE
BRIDGEPORT
YOSEMITE NATIONAL PARK
LeeVining
Mono Lake
120
Benton
JUNE LAKE
395
Crowley Lake
6
MAMMOTH LAKES
Owens
264
Fish Springs Valley
Toms Place
BISHOP
Bristlecone Pine Forest
Bishop Creek
168
BIG PINE
River
INDEPENDENCE
SEQUOIA NATIONAL PARK
Mt. Whitney
Valley
NEVADA
CALIFORNIA
LONE PINE
Olancha
395
Little Lake
INYOKERN
RIDGECREST
14
395
Red Rock Canyon
JOHANNESBURG
RANDSBURG
MOJAVE
14
ROSAMOND
Kramer Jct.
LANCASTER
395
15
PALMDALE
LOS ANGELES
SAN BERNARDINO

WESTERN TRAILS PUBLICATIONS

guide to
HIGHWAY 395
los angeles to reno

ginny clark

Western Trails Publications
P.O. Box 1697
San Luis Obispo, CA 93406

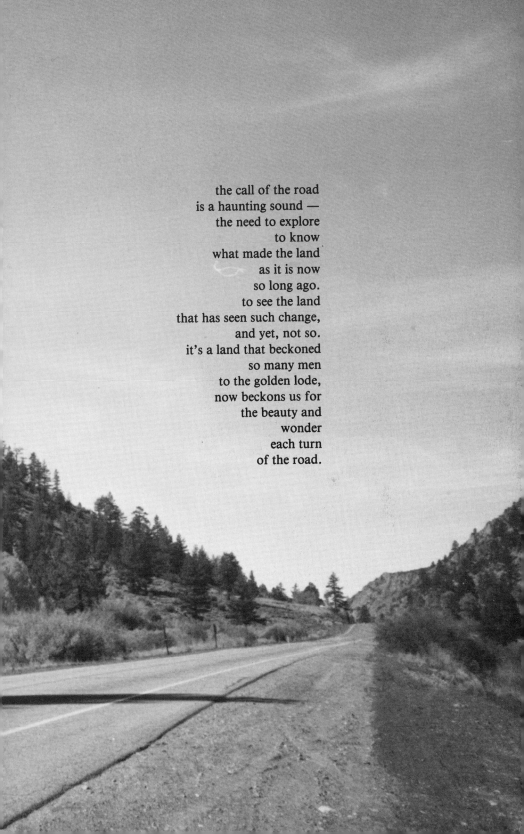

the call of the road
is a haunting sound —
the need to explore
to know
what made the land
as it is now
so long ago.
to see the land
that has seen such change,
and yet, not so.
it's a land that beckoned
so many men
to the golden lode,
now beckons us for
the beauty and
wonder
each turn
of the road.

TABLE OF CONTENTS

INTRODUCTION 8-9

ELEVATION CHART 10-11

FIRST INHABITANTS 12-15

MOJAVE DESERT
    Highway 395 - Ridgecrest 16-33
    Highway 14 to Inyokern 34-49
    Inyokern to Owens Valley 50-53

OWENS VALLEY
    Owens Lake Area .54-61
    Lone Pine Area 62-70
    Independence 71-85
    Big Pine to Bishop 86-95
    Bishop Area 96-110

MONO COUNTRY
    Sherwin Summit to Mammoth Lakes . . .111-130
    "Burnt Land" 131-139

YOSEMITE NATIONAL PARK AREA
  Tuolumne Meadows Country 140-144
  LeeVining, Lundy, Virginia Lakes 145-149

UPPER MONO COUNTY
  Bodie, Bridgeport, Walker River 150-161

HISTORIC CORRIDOR
  Carson Valley 162-171
  Carson City Area 172-181
  Tahoe Basin 182-183
  Virginia City Area 184-187
  Reno Area 188-192

CHRONOLOGICAL TABLE 193-194

CAMPGROUND & TRAILER PARK
DIRECTORY 195-201

INDEX 202

The Mono Craters sign reads:

MONO CRATERS

THE MONO CRATERS ARE A CHAIN OF VOLCANIC MOUNTAINS. WHEN THEY BEGAN TO FORM DURING THE ICE AGE, THIS BASIN WAS COVERED BY ANCIENT LAKE RUSSELL. MONO LAKE IS A REMNANT OF LAKE RUSSELL.
INITIALLY, A SERIES OF EXPLOSIONS CREATED HIGH, BOWL-SHAPED CONES OF PUMICE. LATER, GREAT DOMES OF OBSIDIAN (VOLCANIC GLASS) AROSE IN THE CRATERS. THE OBSIDIAN, AS CHAOTIC, STEEP-SIDED JUMBLES OF BOULDERS, USUALLY OVER TOPPED THE PUMICE RIMS AND ADVANCED ONTO THE PLAIN. SUCH AN ADVANCE, CALLED A COULEE, IS SEEN HERE. PUMICE, BLASTED OUT AND CARRIED BY THE WIND, COVERS THIS VALLEY TO A DEPTH OF 20 OR MORE FEET. BENEATH THE PUMICE MANTLE ARE SEDIMENTS OF ICE AGE LAKE RUSSELL.

INYO NATIONAL FOREST

INTRODUCTION

MAC

Highway 395 leading north off I-15 climbs gently through the Mojave desert to skirt the snow-capped Sierra Nevada along Owens Valley. It rises over the Sherwin Summit, descending through Long Valley to Mammoth Lakes, then crosses the June Lake and Mono Lake country to ascend Conway Summit. It wanders through the rangelands around Bridgeport reaching the white water tumble of West Walker River, and leads northward to historic Carson City and glittering Reno in the Lake Tahoe region. This picturesque route through a most beautiful recreation and vacation land captures the imagination and entices a visitor to fully explore its many facets and wonders.

Evidences of the ancient violent volcanic action that helped shape the land can be seen everywhere: colorful cinder cones, fossil falls, earthquake faults that tore holes in the landscape, unusual rock formations, cooled lava fields, hot springs and creeks that boil and steam, and craters that silently rest on pumice flats.

The Sierra Nevada was not formed solely by volcanic action, however. Its spectacular ridges and peaks were block-faulted from gigantic folds in Earth's crust. Glaciation, too, has left characteristics visible from the highway: moraines that run west to east down into the valley; eroded cirques and basins; high serrated ridges; erratic boulders; and existing glaciers. Palisade Glacier, west of Big Pine is the largest living glacier in California. (It cannot be seen from the highway.) There are 12 areas of existing glaciers in the Sierra Nevada today, comprising about 60. John Muir, in 1870, claimed there were some 65.

Visitors will also find history-haunted hamlets, pioneer and cattle towns and old mines where one can sense and be made aware of days gone by. There are historical markers and museums that display artifacts and preserve remnants of the early Indian civilization, and of the extensive mining activities that took place throughout the region. Well-known ghost towns such as Randsburg, Bodie, and Virginia City can be visited as well as the smaller, now weed-studded sites scattered over the canyons and desert slopes where only rubble remains.

Many side roads lead into wilderness areas, including the vast Sierra Nevada backcountry of the Pacific Crest and John Muir Trails. There are lake-filled basins and trout-filled streams where excellent fishing can be enjoyed in unspoiled scenery. Dirt and gravel roads off the highways afford the bicyclist many opportunities to ride away from the more popular areas to seek solitude.

Special events such as parades, fireworks, fairs, rodeos, fishing tournaments, Motocross Races, and winter activities add pleasure to young and old. Services along the highway are available to satisfy all of a visitor's needs.

Because of the extended use of the highway by an increasing number of vehicles each year, Caltrans has diligently repaired the weather damage spots, made wider shoulders for easier passing on the two-lane sections, added more passing lanes on hills, and made four lanes instead of two wherever feasible.

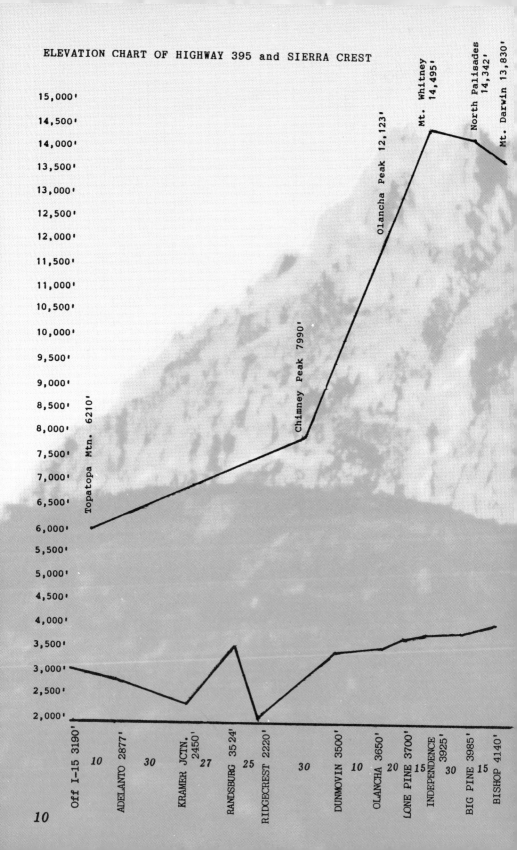

ELEVATION CHART OF HIGHWAY 395 and SIERRA CREST

15,000'
14,500'
14,000'
13,500'
13,000'
12,500'
12,000'
11,500'
11,000'
10,500'
10,000'
9,500'
9,000'
8,500'
8,000'
7,500'
7,000'
6,500'
6,000'
5,500'
5,000'
4,500'
4,000'
3,500'
3,000'
2,500'
2,000'

Mt. Whitney 14,495'
North Palisades 14,342'
Mt. Darwin 13,830'
Olancha Peak 12,123'
Chimney Peak 7990'
Topatopa Mtn. 6210'

Off I-15 3190'
ADELANTO 2877'
KRAMER JCTN. 2450'
RANDSBURG 3524'
RIDGECREST 2220'
DUNMOVIN 3500'
OLANCHA 3650'
LONE PINE 3700'
INDEPENDENCE 3925'
BIG PINE 3985'
BISHOP 4140'

10   30   27   25   30   10   20   15   30   15

10

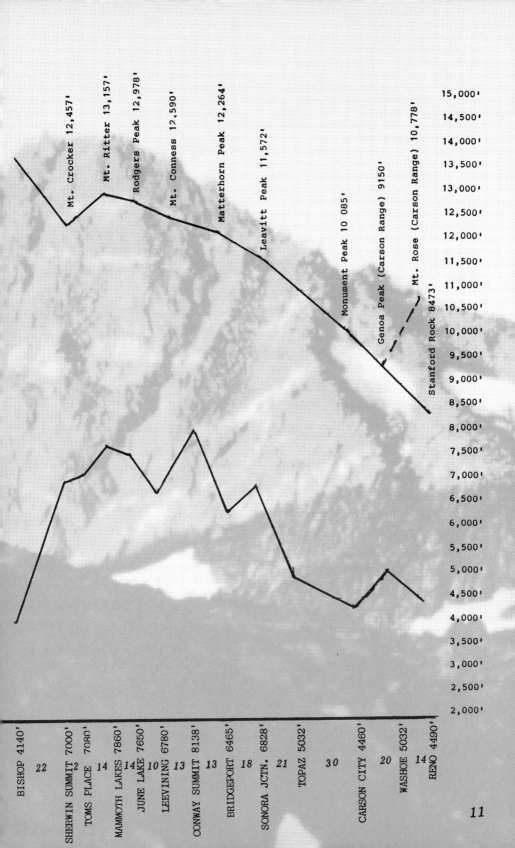

- Mt. Crocker 12,457'
- Mt. Ritter 13,157'
- Rodgers Peak 12,978'
- Mt. Conness 12,590'
- Matterhorn Peak 12,264'
- Leavitt Peak 11,572'
- Monument Peak 10 085'
- Genoa Peak (Carson Range) 9150'
- Mt. Rose (Carson Range) 10,778'
- Stanford Rock 8473'

15,000'
14,500'
14,000'
13,500'
13,000'
12,500'
12,000'
11,500'
11,000'
10,500'
10,000'
9,500'
9,000'
8,500'
8,000'
7,500'
7,000'
6,500'
6,000'
5,500'
5,000'
4,500'
4,000'
3,500'
3,000'
2,500'
2,000'

- BISHOP 4140'
- SHERWIN SUMMIT 7000'
- TOMS PLACE 7080'
- MAMMOTH LAKES 7860'
- JUNE LAKE 7650'
- LEEVINING 6780'
- CONWAY SUMMIT 8138'
- BRIDGEPORT 6465'
- SONORA JCTN. 6828'
- TOPAZ 5032'
- CARSON CITY 4460'
- WASHOE 5032'
- RENO 4490'

22   2   14   14   10   13   13   18   21   30   20   14

11

THE FIRST INHABITANTS

MAC

After the great Sierra bloc was formed, ocean waters receded, the blanketing glaciers melted, and firey spewing of lava from volcanic upheavels ceased. The eastern Sierra country became a habitable environ for man and wildlife. At first prehistoric animals roamed and foraged in the lush tropical climate. As conditions changed with each epoch, so did the wildlife and the development of man. Scratched and carved petrogylphs found on rocks in many canyons depict such changes. Early man first made simple markings of lines and swirls on rocks. But later, as in the Coso Range, more elaborate stylized drawings were made.

The western Shoshoni people settled in the lands of eastern California, Nevada, Idaho and Arizona, which is known as the Basin and Range country. Coso Range Shoshoni, the Washoe Indians of the Reno-Carson City-Lake Tahoe area, Mono Indians of Mono Lake and the Owens Valley Paiutes all belonged to the basic Western Shoshoni people. Generally these Indians lived similar lives, although the desert Paiute tribes were not as advanced and were more nomadic within their territories than other Paiute or Shoshoni who lived farther north.

For centuries the Paiutes, Monos and Washoes were able to endure in the dry, high desert lands. These scantily-clad natives were termed "savages" when first encountered by the white man. In a land of dry soil with high evaporation of moisture, and cold, stormy winters, it is surprising that they could exist at all. To live throughout the centuries without "civilized" comforts or even the small conveniences that the white men who first met these Indians enjoyed, was remarkable. Under such poor conditions, it is no wonder they found no time to enrich their lives in a higher material culture that many other Western tribes enjoyed.

But they were a happy, unwarlike people, seeking food, nurturing young, living with customs and ceremonies that were handed down. They were hunters and harvesters, living together as families or in small bands, gathering food in continual nomadic movement through their respective hunting and gathering territories. Routes were determined by streams or other water sources, and seasonal plant growth. They had to carry all their domestic implements, bows and arrows, baskets of supplies and stored foods. Material possessions were limited.

With so little (if any) clothing, their skin was adapted to climate. Layers of fat protected them from the freezing weather in winter. What clothing they did wear consisted of loin or breech cloths for men and a double apron woven from plant fibers for women.

In the warm summer months simple shade structures were built, but for winter use, more substantial dwellings were required. Pits were dug in a circle, then poles made from willow trees were formed into a cone shape and covered with tule, aspen limbs, grass and brush, or a kind of bulrush found in swamps and marshlands.

The staple food was mainly nuts from the pinyon pines, ground into flour for gruel. The food stored during the summer and fall seasons had to last through the winter. Their diet varied from spring to fall as the seasons changed. Roots and bulbs were dug. Seeds found in marshland plants were dried in the summer sun and ground, then stored for the cold winter months. They planted seeds from wild plants that produced the food they enjoyed in the marshlands and devised an irrigation system to increase their yearly crop. This was an important communal activity. Frogs, rodents, deer, and rabbits were caught or trapped, but one animal they did not eat was the coyote. Actually in all Indian cultures there was an avoidance of coyote eating. This was due to the Indian's regard for the crafty, mischievous coyote and his place in their legends.

The water of Mono Lake was too alkaline for fish life, but it did support the larva worm of the *Kutsavi* fly which is oily and rich in protein. From salt marshes along the shores of Mono Lake the pupa of the tiny fly flourished and it was relished as a food. The flies bred in large numbers out on the briny lake and as winds swept across the watery expanse the tiny pupa were carried to the shore. The Mono women and girls collected them and separated the hard carapace from the edible small fat body of the fly inside by rubbing the pupa between their hands.

Caterpillars of the Pandora moth found in the yellow pine trees were another source of food. Because the caterpillars usually were high up in the tall trees and unreachable, the Indians would build a fire under the tree to smoke them out. As they dropped to the ground they were gathered to be roasted, dried and stored. A method of trapping grasshoppers on the ground was to build a fire and produce coals in the middle of a field infested with the insects. The Indians would then spread out in a wide circle around the coals and beat the ground to make the insects jump toward the coals. After they were sufficiently roasted they were taken out and eaten. Left-overs were stored for future use.

The women in each band, with the help of daughters, brought in wood and sagebrush for the fires, dried all the fish the men and boys caught, dressed the game, gathered the seeds and nuts and ground them into flour or dried them in the sun, and made the many types of baskets needed to carry and hold their food and tools. The baskets, made from willows, dragon claw and Joshua, were used for seed beaters, water vessels, food containers and cradles for the very young. Baskets made by the Washoe were constructed by a single-rod coiling method that had a distinctive decorating style. With lattice and a unique openwork diagonal twining and feathering, aesthetic as well as useful baskets were made.

In their basket designs, the dark brown, almost black color is from dragon claw; the brown from Joshua trees, and the tan from willows. The baskets are woven so tightly they are waterproof. If the tan of a basket rots out, it is because the willow was green and undried when woven. Dried willow doesn't rot.

Boys learned how to hunt deer and mountain sheep, trap rabbits and rodents and catch fish by the men in their band. All the children were taught the particular traits of each animal, about plants, and tribal knowledge of their world. They heard stories of creation, the good wolf, mischievous coyotes and sources of life power. The men made strong sinew-backed bows that were highly prized by other Indian tribes. Men enjoyed gambling and spent a great deal of time at it. Games were made up and played by the men and children, and even the women ran races for fun. Women played a game of ball toss at Pinenut Harvest Festivals.

14

They abided by the established customs and rules of the land and family. They paid tribute to plants and animals, and when food was given them by nature or other tribes it was blessed before eating. Any clothing offered was also blessed before wearing. Special rites and behavior were observed for important milestones of life such as birth, child-naming, puberty, marriage, and death. Sweathouses were made by all three of these Indian tribes. These small earth-covered structures had a narrow entry, or a dome of willows covered with mats, large enough for the men of the tribe to sit in. They were used as club houses for male members, and for ceremonial quarters.

The Paiutes were quick to learn new ways and adapt new methods introduced by other tribes or the white men. They were basically a moral, friendly, social people who enjoyed visiting other tribes. Trading was done with Indians who lived east and west of Owens Valley. They traveled up into the White Mountains via Silver Canyon, just east of Bishop, to reach Fish Lake Valley. The gravel road used today follows their old route. Other trails eastward went out of Marble Canyon. And further south, trails went from Big Pine over the Westgard Pass, and across the Inyo Mountains to Eureka Valley. Obsidian chips and arrowheads have been found along the old paths, especially in Wyman Canyon.

Well established routes were made over Kearsarge Pass west of Independence, down Woods Creek and Bubbs Creek to the west where they entered Cedar Grove and met the San Joaquin Indian tribes who summered there. Other routes were made over Walker, Cottonwood, Piute and Nine Mile Canyon Passes. Most of the backcountry trails follow these same routes today. Obsidian from Owens Valley was traded for black oak acorns, berries, arrow shafts and buck skins. Pinyon pine nuts, baskets, bows, rabbit skin blankets and salt were also traded. Studies in the languages of the San Joaquin Valley tribes and that of the Owens Valley Paiutes show that they were significantly similar in their word descriptions. Furthermore, the need for one another in both economical and social affairs provided for a consistent and peaceful interchange.

When the first white men entered Paiute, Mono and Washoe territory in 1827 and met these desert people, understanding and respect for their way of life were not considered. This was, of course, true with most of the white men who met the Indians of the west. From that date on, their peaceful, nomadic days were numbered. After Jedediah Smith, Fremont, Walker, and the other frontier men, came the settlers who entered the valleys, brought in their livestock, took over the land, and ruined the Indians' food supply. Later the cattlemen and sheepherders came to furnish the miners with meat. Miners took over the water supply, which destroyed the game that Indians depended on. The war for survival brought soldiers and guns until the Indians were defeated. In the space of 38 years, the civilization of a people was ultimately wiped out. Settlers were freed from the worry of "fearful-looking dirty Indians" attacking their homes for revenge, or killing their cattle for food. Retaliation killing on both sides ensued after each offense.

COYOTE

Similar to the gray fox, the coyote is heavier and larger weighing about 25 lbs. and is 3' long. He has round eyes; long erect pointed ears and nose; and a gray body with white belly and throat. Feet, legs, and ears are a light rust color. The end of the bushy tail is dark.

THE MOJAVE DESERT

Descending the large, almost level alluvial fan from the Cajon Pass between San Bernardino and the San Gabriel Mountains, I-15 travels in a straight line towards Victorville. Jedediah Smith first blazed this route when he crossed what is known as the Cajon Pass in 1827. He made his westward trek from the Utah country in search of the Buenaventura River. He followed well-used Indian trails across the Mojave Desert, which later became known as the Old Spanish Trail. It was the slave trade route used by the Ute Indians, a Shoshoni tribe living in Utah that kidnapped Paiute women, girls and young boys. The Ute's took them to Utah where they sold them to the Spaniards, who transported them down to Mexico City. After 1847 it was renamed the Mormon Trail when the first Mormon Battalion came from Salt Lake City to reach California and was one of the most important routes of the west.

Highway 395 branches off towards the north near Hesperia and into Victor Valley lying within the Mojave Desert. The road leads through the western part of the arrowhead-shaped or triangular wedge of this great desert region. Mojave desert is the southern portion of the Great Basin and Range Region that covers eastern California, parts of Nevada, Utah, Arizona and New Mexico. The entire area makes up much of the western part of the United States and derives its name from the many mountain ranges alternating with basins and valleys.

These ranges are uplifted fault blocks while the valleys have become sediment-filled *gabens* — land that subsided between uplifted blocks. During the Ice Age, these interconnecting depressions between the ranges filled with deep fresh water lakes. Then as the glaciers receded, the lowest places became collection basins for salts, nitrates, and borates, in depths of more than 1000 feet. Upon these minerals, muds and rocky debris were washed down from the mountain sides. Sloping alluvial fans were built up by these run-off deposits, and subsequent drainage from the mountain ranges had created saline lakes and dry lake beds, or *playas* in these basins and valleys. Some of the playas are rough with crunchy salt or smooth and hard like Rogers Dry Lake at Edwards Air Force Base where the layers deposited through centuries have built up to such a hard surface that the Space Shuttle is able to land on it.

The many hills, buttes, and mountains rising up from the desert floor were not formed at the same time. For instance, on the north slope of Rand Mountain the mica, quartz and schists are Precambrian — the oldest rocks from the beginning of time. Shadow Mountain, just south of Kramer Junction, was formed from the Upper Precambrian Era to the Permian Period and is made up mostly of dolomite, quartzite, schist, and marble. From the Miocene Epoch, Gem Hills just west of Rosamond has rhyolite tuff, volcanic agglomerate and conglomerate some 1200 feet thick. The northwest side of neighboring Soledad Mountain has white-pink to brown porphyrite quartz from the Middle Miocene Epoch. The newest rocks found at Red Buttes and Saddleback Mountain near Kramer are made up of black quartz-bearing basalt from the Pliocene Epoch. The extraordinary diversity of minerals found in these mountains and valleys throughout the Mojave Desert has prompted geologists and prospectors to comb the land for its vast wealth, and the scientists for the fascinating information it provides.

The land is semi-desert. Precipitation from the Pacific Ocean is intercepted by the extreme height of the Sierra Nevada. Humidity is low with a rainfall of 4″ to 15″ annually. Temperatures are moderate in winter and high in summer during the day, yet refreshingly cool at night. Winds can be strong coming from the Sierra Nevada at certain times of the year. In this semi-desert and desert environment all plants and animals have learned to adapt in their own unique way.

16

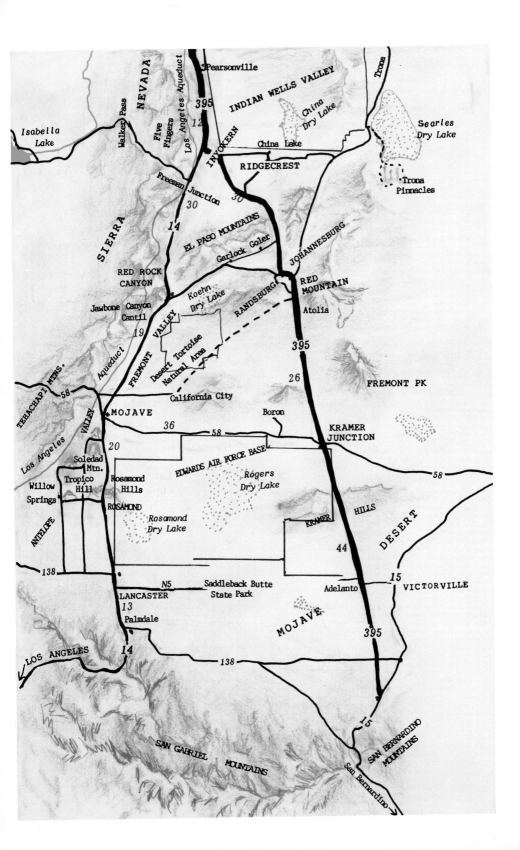

WILDLIFE ADAPTATION

The KANGAROO RAT and ROCK POCKET MOUSE eat dry plants only. Through a special metabolism they can live without water, manufacturing their own body moisture from food they eat.

The JACKRABBIT and DESERT KIT FOX are able to lose their excess body heat through large ears. The COTTONTAIL RABBIT stays cool living in thickets which also protect him from predators. Moisture is obtained from a diet of morning dew on desert grasses and plants as well as from succulent fleshy tissues of cacti stems.

The DESERT TORTOISE has water reservoirs in two storage sacs and a bladder under the hard shell. Feeding on desert grasses and wildflowers in the spring the tortoise receives enough nourishment to last through the hot summer while he stays burrowed under creosote bushes. The shell and scaly skin keeps moisture evaporation to a minimum. He is able to withdraw his head and legs within the shell to keep cool and discourage predators.

RODENTS also live in burrows to keep out of the desert heat and seek refuge from predators. Food is stored in these burrows. Their pale-colored fur helps to reflect the rays of the sun, keeping the small animal cool.

The HORNED LIZARD appears as a prehistoric monster but is actually quite harmless. This reptile is covered with rough, scaly skin and sharp horns to prevent being swallowed by snakes. Ants, insects, flies, and spiders are in his diet. Early prospectors found the 'horny toad' a good pet as he feasted on the spiders and ants found in the rocky shelters of the prospectors.

The COLLARED LIZARD and DESERT IGUANA pant when they become too warm. Some lizards have a black lining under their skin that shields their internal organs from the ultraviolet rays of the sun. When driving through the desert during daytime hours, it is not strange that few animals are seen as they forage in the coolness of the night.

The CHUCKAWALLA is one of the largest lizards and lives in rocky areas. It seeks refuge from predators by lodging itself between boulders. By gulping air, the lungs will become inflated and swell the body so it cannot be dislodged. If, by chance, it is caught from behind, the jointed tail separates from the body. In time a new tail section will grow back to replace the broken portion.

DESERT PLANT
ADAPTATION

SAGEBRUSH, RABBITBRUSH and CREOSOTE BUSHES are the predominant species found along Highway 395. They are tolerant of the winter frost and the alkaline soils that characterize the desert. Sagebrush has slender, three-toothed, silver-green leaves with small greenish-yellow flowers in elongated clusters, and a purplish shaggy bark. The plant has a pleasing pungent aromatic odor similar to the herb sage used in cooking.

The rabbitbrush is a common silvery-green desert shrub. The bright, yellow, distinctive, fragrant flowers produce a white, downy seed in the autumn.

The creosote bush has hard, tough waxy-covered evergreen leaves. The roots branch out extensively to discourage competition for moisture. Through a 'cloning' system they multiply around a central 'stem crown'. As you travel along the highway you will notice that the plants nearest to the road grow larger as they capture water runoff after storms. In higher altitudes where there is more oxygen the bushes can be quite large. A brown oily liquid (creosote) obtained from the plant is used in making wood preservatives such as those used in railroad ties.

The DESERT TRUMPET is a member of the buckwheat family. From a basal cluster of leaves, the main stem swells to contain a sticky liquid which produces nourishment to the plant during the dry season. In the winter the plant appears dead, but by early spring the brown stems become green. The branches of tall hollow stems bear tiny flowers above the swelling.

The true 'belly plant' is the MOJAVE DESERT STAR as it grows very close to the ground. The entire plant nestles the gravel of the desert floor. It is about four inches across, with short stems and a few dark green fuzzy leaves. The dozen or more tiny white fowers with yellow centers present a lovely nosegay. You have to lay down on your stomach to get a good look at them.

Some flowers have only a few scale-like leaves at the base of the stem, such as the MORMON TEA. The leaves are small in size as is the white flower that bears scaly, light brown cones. Dried twigs were steeped in boiling water by the Mormon emigrants to make tea.

The creamy-white, deep-toothed leaf of the DESERT HOLLY reflect the rays of the sun. These plants have been protected by law to save them from being stripped from the desert floor at Christmas.

CACTI has no leaves, but their succulent fleshy stems hold moisture, and their branches have spines. There are many varieties with many shapes and sizes found growing on the desert hillsides, washes and valleys. Some of the most common are the Barrel Cacti, Beavertail, Prickley Pear, and the tiny Pink Viznagita.

The MOJAVE ASTER has hairy leaves and produces a great multitude of seeds that are scattered over the desert floor by winds after the blooming season. Seeds lay dormant, sometimes for years, until the right amount of moisture and weather conditions appear for them to grow.

In the desert lands where life is so fragile, man-made damage in breaking, uprooting, and trampling plants, the scarring of the soil, will take years to recover. In some instances replacement is never accomplished. Evidences of this can be seen in old wagon ruts of the pioneers, old mining roads, and modern motorcycle tracks.

HIGHWAY 395 NORTH

KRAMER JUNCTION, or Four Corners, is the first major interchange beyond I-15. There are cafes and service stations with diesel fuel and propane available. Mexican pottery, brass figurines and other ornamental objects are on sale at one corner.

For a good side trip, about seven miles west on Highway 58 near Boron, the open pit mine of the U.S. Borax and Chemical Corporation invites visitors to come in and see modern mining operations as well as one of the original 20-mule team wagons at the Visitor Center. The glorious days of the romanticized 20-mule team hauling borax ore over the rough desert roads and passes are now legend. With the many uses of borax in our modern world, it is a major business today. It is ironic that when the mule teams laboriously hauled tons of borate out of Death Valley across the bleak desert to Mojave, just a few miles south of the old route was one of the richest deposits of borax imaginable, undiscovered until much later.

On the west side of the road out of Kramer are solar panels capturing the sun's rays for power.

Continuing north up the Highway, FREMONT PEAK (4584') rises out of Golden Valley about seven miles to the right. It was named for the famous American General and explorer John C. Fremont. Although he never was near this peak, in the early days it was a landmark for travelers as it stood alone out on the desert floor. The road gradually climbs up through the slate-gray sagebrush paralleling the old Santa Fe railroad grade. In the springtime a carpet of wildflowers covers the desert floor.

20-Mule Team

20

Billy Wilson at Atolia Mine   *Clark Family Photo*

About 25 miles above Kramer is ATOLIA. The sign for the town has been carried away. Many beige mounds of old tailings on the right identify where the bustling activity in the early 1900's took place. It was the largest tungsten mine in the world in operation at that time. Tungsten (scheelite from quartz monzonite) is a gray-white, heavy, high melting point metallic element. It is used in electrical products, in the making of tools, and as a steel alloy. During World War I, over 4000 people worked and lived near Atolia when tungsten was in great demand for the making of armaments. The mine produced tungsten worth $65 million.

Atolia Mine   *MAC*

MAC

In 1895 gold was discovered in the Rand Mountains, in 1905 tungsten was discovered in Atolia, and in 1918 silver was discovered in RED MOUNTAIN. With all the excitement and concentration of gold interests in the numerous mines within the Rand Mining District, prospectors were blinded to the other minerals that could also have produced riches for them. Two gold miners, Jack Nosser and Hamp Williams, when resting in their search for clay samples, by chance found a chunk of ore that they assayed out to be high grade silver. Their friend, John Kelly financed the Kelly Mine which was one of the richest silver mines at Red Mountain. Other settlements around the fabulous Kelly Mine were Inn City and Hampton. Over $27 million was produced before the price of silver dropped and the mine was closed.

To the left as you enter the town of Red Mountain some old mine structures can be seen from the road. A paved road leading west near the old Kelly Mine is the back road to Randsburg. Just before reaching Randsburg on this road are the tailings and old buildings of Butte Mine.

As the gold mining in Randsburg all but petered out, and the tungsten mining in Atolia was on the want, this rich silver Kelly Mine brought new life back to the mining district. Red Mountain became a wide open, wild town with saloons, hotels, and madams running houses and dance halls. A few of the girls married, but most didn't stay too long in one place as the conditions were rough and money always seemed greener somewhere else. Even though it was Prohibition time, liquor flowed endlessly day and night. A fire some years ago wiped out much of the old town but a few buildings, like the Silver Dollar Cafe are sentinels of the by-gone spirited times.

Just north of Red Mountain, around a curve on the right, the Trona Road leads north over the Summit Range. It joins Highway 178, and will take you through Trona, the Panamints, Death Valley to the east, and Ridgecrest to the west.

MAC

Geologic Map of Rand District, Kern and San Bernardino Counties. After Hulin, 1925, plate 1, and Troxel and Morton, 1962.

Randsburg from Yellow Aster Mine

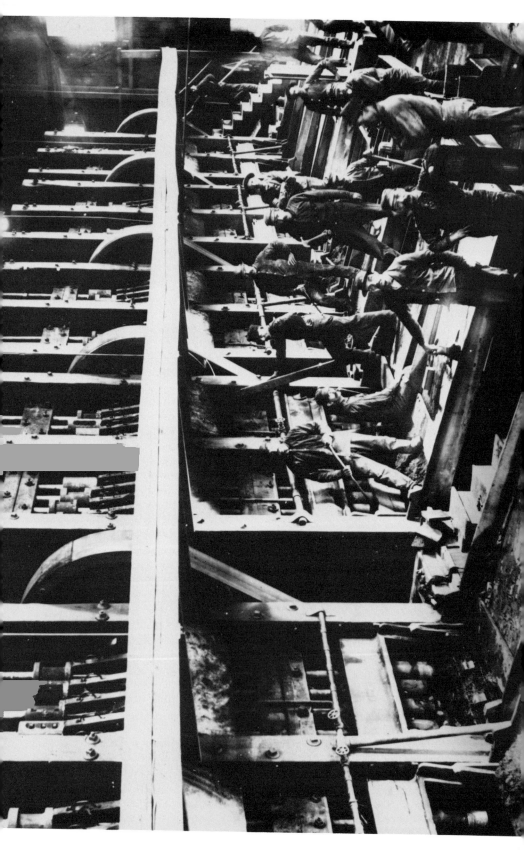

YELLOW ASTER MINE

In 1895 when Charles Burcham, F.M. Mooers and John Singleton found their gold on Rand Mountain, they knew that they had found a 'gold mine', but it is doubtful that they knew just how rich it would be. During the height of operations in the early 1900's there were over 250 men working daily in three shifts. The miners who worked topside with the machinery and stamp mill received $2.50 per day while the miners who worked in the underground tunnels received $3.00 per day. In 1901 the 100-stamp mill was completed, which was one of the largest ever made.

A stamp mill is a belt-driven machine consisting of pestles, moved by water or steam power, for breaking large chunks of raw ore and crushing them to powder for chemical separation of the mineral product. The number 10-stamp mill means 10 pestles were used to pound, grind, crush and mix the ore. At the Yellow Aster Mine there were 10 sets of 10 pestles making up the 100-stamp mill.

The tunnels with many levels — the deepest shaft was over 1200 feet deep — totaled over 11 miles of railroad tracks, with four locomotives and many ore cars transporting the raw, broken ore up to the stamp mills.

The greatest production period of the mine was from 1886 to the middle 1930's. After that time until all gold mines were closed during the World War II, the bonanza days were over. The California Division of Mines and Geology reports that the mine produced some $12 million. After World War II there were no jobs for people to return to, so a few desert-loving citizens inhabited the town. In December of 1969 the mill and all the mine buildings were destroyed by fire set by vandals. Today only the tailing dump on the side of Rand Mountain can be seen.

Yellow Aster Mine

Clark Family Photo

JOHANNESBURG

Unlike many other towns that grew up rapidly when ore was discovered and people flocked into the new mining community, Johannesburg was a planned town. Streets were laid out in an orderly fashion. Here was the railhead and transportation center for the numerous supplies needed for Randsburg, the Rand Mining District, Trona, Ballerat and Skidoo. The Rinaldi and Clark Freight and Stage Line* hauled all the equipment and supplies to the outlying communities.

In 1898 the Santa Fe Railroad spur from Kramer to Johannesburg was completed. Kramer was on the main line of the Santa Fe Railroad from Los Angeles to Las Vegas. Heavy machinery needed for the Yellow Aster Mine in Randsburg, coal for fuel and lumber for housing were hauled up the Golden Valley grade. Ore from the mines that developed was hauled south to the stamp mill at Barstow. The daily afternoon train brought mail, food and household supplies needed for the two communities, and a sense of civilization to the people. After mining operations dwindled, the desert was left to a few remaining citizens and sleeping lizards, old tires strewn among the sage, and echoes of a time gone by. The railroad tracks were torn out in 1933, which marked the end of an exciting era.

The presence of women and children necessitated the building of schools, banks, churches, lodge and community halls, hotels for transients and mine workers, and the opening of many services and businesses. Gamblers, rowdies and dance hall girls had no place in this family-oriented atmosphere. As a matter of fact, unsavory characters were encouraged to leave. Families came by train to live and work in both Johannesburg and Randsburg. There was even a golf course outside of town. Many of the houses standing today were built during the 'glory hole' days. Up on the hill many old timers and miners are buried in the cemetery.

*Billy Clark, one of the partners, was the father of my husband, Lewis Wilbur Clark. For interesting life and times and anecdotes of this period in our history, read HIGH MOUNTAINS & DEEP VALLEYS, The Gold Bonanza Days by Lew and Ginny Clark.

King Soloman Mine, Johannesburg

In 1896, about a year after the Yellow Aster Mine was in full operation at Randsburg the King Soloman Mine at Johannesburg was discovered and produced a good grade of gold ore. In the surrounding hills many smaller mines were producing gold, with such interesting names as Black Nugget, Dutch Cleanser, Minnehaha, Buckboard, Cinderella, St. Elmo, Wedge and Winnie. Through the years scavengers have carried off the rusted tins and bullet-hole pots, old weather-beaten boards, shiny rose quartz with veins that might promise worth, old metal and nails, and bottles. There is little left but some tailings.

Services available at Johannesburg include a post office, Hayden's Frontier Market with fast foods, newspapers and books, gas and tire repair, Howard's Cafe and Service Station, antique and gift shops and a community park for overnight parking behind the Community Hall.

Sketches by Francilu Hansen

Randsburg Barber Shop, March, 1912

Old Photo Courtesy of Mrs. Purington

RANDSBURG

Actually Randsburg and Johannesburg were one large community separated by a low ridge of the Rand Mountain. Many workers of the Yellow Aster lived in 'Joburg' with their families or in boarding hotels. Both towns had telephone and Western Union Service, electricity and facilities of a modern town of that time. The switchboard at Randsburg was a relay point for long distance calls north up to the Inyo-Bishop country and south to 'San Berdo'. Both towns had baseball teams and on Sunday afternoons everyone was at the ball game rooting for their team. Betting was part of the sport so enthusiasm ran high.

Randsburg was strictly a company town. It had a band and orchestra, theatre, and many types of businesses such as dry goods store, laundries, ice house, blacksmith shop, banks, law offices, newspapers and an assay office, along with the saloons and hotels.

One of the most active members of the community and the Yellow Aster Mine was Dr. Rose L. Burcham. Her husband was one of the three original discoverers of the rich gold find on Rand Mountain. She left her flourishing medical practice in San Bernardino to live at the camp and become the fourth owner of the mine. Dr. Rose kept the tent house clean, cooked out-of-doors, did the washing and controlled the finances. When the mine produced enough money Burchams moved into a large house. Dr. Rose continued to be heavily involved with the operation and finances of the mine. She was a smart business woman with superior executive ability and intelligence who could size up a situation or people and weed out frauds. She settled lawsuits over claim boundary disputes and handled many legal matters for the company. She became recognized as the only successful woman mining operator. In 1900 F.M. Mooers died, in 1913 her husband died and in 1914 John Singleton died. She then was the sole surviving member of the Yellow Aster Mine.

Randsburg Today

Today Randsburg is one of the best preserved 'ghost towns' in which people still live and work. Although many of the original buildings were destroyed by fires throughout the years, or collapsed through old age (like the Rinaldi Market building a few years ago) the town has a certain charming authenticity. The people who live there now are 'newcomers' who came after the mining days because they wanted a quiet, low-paced place to live on a modest income.

The museum is open on weekends. Samples of rocks, minerals, and glass are on display along with mining memorabilia of the great 'glory hole' days. Take time to see the stamp mill, and the five-ton steam locomotive from the Yellow Aster Mine out by the side of the building. A shaded picnic table is provided for those wishing to stop, rest, and get a feel for the town. Looking at the buildings, the hills and this unpretentious desert town one wonders what it must have been like to work in the mine not so long ago. Some of the miners and families lived in tents on wooden platforms, even when snow was on the ground.

Today Randsburg has a post office, the General Store and Cafe, a church and many antique shops in the old buildings. At the old Hotel a 'Bed and Breakfast' is planned to give the visitor a feeling of living in the past with modern comforts. The Randsburg Players have performances at the Randsburg Opera House. All tickets are reserved and include a Buffet dinner.

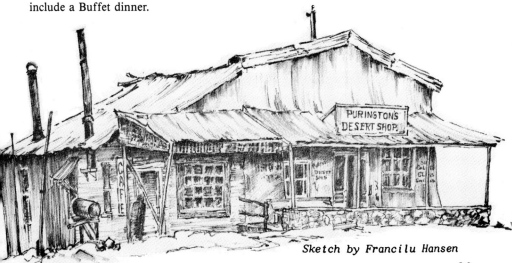

Sketch by Francilu Hansen

Madeline Hall at Wilson Department Store

Randsburg Saloon, March, 1909   Old Photos Courtesy of Mrs. Purington

RANDSBURG NORTH

From Randsburg, Highway 395 leads north and around the El Paso Mountains to reach Ridgecrest and Inyokern. However, before leaving the Mojave Desert area visit Garlock, to the east off the Redrock-Randsburg Road. Still standing are a few old wooden shacks and an old rock building.

GARLOCK

Early cattlemen used the water wells in the area in the early 1880's and called it Cow Wells. It was a stage station and a center for numerous mining camps called El Paso City. In 1893, gold fever was at a high pitch. In all the various little diggings there were more than 2000 miners or prospectors. In 1894 Eugene Garlock brought his eight-stamp mill to the area to process the ore, and the town became known as Garlock. When the Yellow Aster Mine was discovered in 1895 many miners went up to work in the mine, and Garlock processed the ore with his stamp mill. Water was first hauled up the long grade by mule teams from Goler Wells to Randsburg. A pumping station was made by the Yellow Aster and water was pumped up the hill through wooden pipes. When the Yellow Aster had its own stamp mills, they no longer needed the services of Garlock. In a short time the community was reduced to only a few people and the buildings were dismantled and moved up to Johannesburg and Randsburg. In 1909, Garlock became a railroad station stop of the Southern Pacific Railroad, servicing the people of Randsburg and Johannesburg going to Los Angeles via Mojave, as it took less time than via Kramer and the Santa Fe Railroad.

Garlock   MAC

GOLER

Just east of Garlock, the community of Goler had "its day" in 1893 when promising strikes were found up in the canyons of the eastern part of the El Paso Mountains. Prospectors swarmed into the area. John Goler, a member of the Death Valley 49er's Party, came back to the desert many times to search for gold he thought must be in these hills. He was never successful however, but the prospectors were kind enough to name their settlement after this persistent, luckless gold seeker.

Mr. Goler was correct, as there was gold in those hills. At the peak of the rush more than 2000 men were digging in all the canyons hoping for a big strike. Because the strikes were small in these dry-wash camps, and the gold found was very fine with only a few large nuggets, prospectors ventured to other hills to seek their fortune. Only three men did — Burcham, Singleton and Mooers when they stumbled on the Yellow Aster jackpot. A few old sites at the Summit Diggings are now just empty holes in the sage.

EL PASO MOUNTAINS

These mountains are interesting. Both vertical and horizontal geologic action took place here. The Garlock Fault, with its general east-west course terminates the Basin Ranges from the north. Horizontal shifting of the land has been as much as 30 miles. Faulting can be seen on alluvial fans between El Paso Canyons and the Redrock-Randsburg Road between Garlock and Cantil. The steep, loose fans near Goler show recent uplifting fault action across the face of the mountain while nearby are large depressions formed by down-faulting. Erosional forces of wind and water have removed the softer layers beneath the harder, overflow caps. Within the layers are found many evidences of prehistoric non-marine fossils, which include some of the oldest mammal fossils found in California.

In more than 50 square miles of jumbled backcountry, the early prospectors filed scores of claims for copper, coal, gold and galena. There are dozens of old mining trenches, pits, and tailing dumps along with the rusty machinery and empty holes.

VENTURING INTO ANY OF THESE RAVINES AND WASHES RECKLESSLY CAN BE DANGEROUS. BE CAUTIOUS!

Old Mine Diggings

HIGHWAY 395 TO RIDGECREST

Just before the China Lake Blvd. turns off Highway 395 to Ridgecrest, up in the hills to the right are the remnants of the Rademacher Mining District which covered the hill extending above Cerro Coso College. Mines were active from the late 1890's to the early 1900's with no large volume to make the area outstanding. Some of the names of the mines are interesting: Apple Green, Broken Axle, Lost Keys, Prize, Wildcat and Yellow Treasure. With the milling ore averaging one-half ounce or less of gold per ton, it was certainly not a prize or yellow treasure.

City Hall   *Courtesy of Ridgecrest C of C*

RIDGECREST

At the southern end of Indian Wells Valley and the Basin and Range country is the cultural and community center of RIDGECREST. It is one of the largest growing desert communities today. There are beautifully designed malls, banks, churches, a hospital and radio station, museum and community college, newspaper and all the services a visitor would need. The city offers motels, cafes and restaurants, service stations supplying propane and diesel fuel, auto and trailer supply shops. Most of the trailer parks have limited overnight spaces available, but the Desert Empire Fairgrounds have spaces large enough for small RV units.

The town services aero technology plants and the China Lake Naval Weapons Center. The Maturango Museum, now in its lovely new building on East Las Flores Street in midtown Ridgecrest, houses displays and photographs of the upper Mojave Desert, archaeology, etymology, sculptures and the ancient Indian rock drawings of the Coso Range Shoshoni Indians. The Museum offers tours to view the petroglyphs. A special event every year in October is the Chili Cookout.

China Lake was once a settlement for the many Chinese who came to the area to work on the transcontinental railroad. Later they helped in the many mines that were producing ore in the lower Eastern Sierra region, obtaining water for their settlement from Indian Wells. The Chinese dispersed after the mines closed. Today China Lake is the site of the Naval Ordinance Test Station that was established in 1943. Ridgecrest, first known as 'Crumville', became the support community for the base with stores, housing, recreation, and service stations. At the base Mickey Mouse Rockets, Zuni Rockets, the anti-submarine Rat, and the Sidewinder Guided Missile were built.

TRONA PINNACLES

For a day's tour east of Ridgecrest, visit the Trona Pinnacles. About 20 miles from Ridgecrest, off Highway 128, just before the West End Plant on the southwest side of Searles Dry Lake, take the road crossing the railroad tracks. Searles Lake, now a playa, was once a large lake covering some 285 square miles.

The Pinnacles are a rough, porous jasper-agate combination of rock formations left from the Tioga Glacial Stage in prehistoric times. Old timers referred to these unique spires as 'cathedral city'. Deposits of porous lime rock (calcareous tufa) were coated and built up to what is the most impressive example of tufa formation seen in North America. They rise to about 100 feet above the present playa floor.

Readers Note: Because many visitors from Los Angeles use Highway 14 to reach Highway 395 going north, the next section is from north of Los Angeles via Highway 14.

HIGHWAY 14 NORTH TO INYOKERN

From the San Gabriel Mountains in Los Angeles County, Highway 14 crosses the San Andreas Fault just before Palmdale and follows straight through the almost flat alluvial floor of Antelope Valley which is at the western tip of the Mojave Desert triangle. While driving through this valley can you imagine seeing herds of antelope grazing over this desert floor from the Tehachapi Mountains to the west and southwest across the desert as far as the eye can see? At one time there were more than 7,000 antelope grazing among the Joshua trees and sagebrush. It must have been a most awesome sight.

In 1876 when the Southern Pacific Railroad was built to extend from Mojave south to Los Angeles, the grazing land of the antelope was divided in two by the railroad tracks. The antelope were afraid to cross the shiny steel rails over to the larger grazing land. Many starved to death right alongside the tracks. Then in the late 1880's an unusually hard winter storm created such huge snow drifts that the food supply for the animals was buried too deep for them to forage so thousands more starved or froze to death. By the early 1900's miners with families and other settlers who came to service the miners put up fences to keep the antelope out of their settlement and property. The grazing land became smaller and smaller and the remaining herd became smaller and sickly, until they eventually died out. There are no more today.

Palmdale and Lancaster are two modern cities in the Valley, expanding out into the desert more and more each year.

SADDLEBACK BUTTE STATE PARK

East of Lancaster, about twenty miles on N5, E Avenue J is the Antelope Indian Museum, Piute Butte, Saddleback Butte and Joshua Tree State Park. The best time of year to visit and explore this desert area is in late autumn, winter and early spring when temperatures are cool and the animals are not hibernating from the hot sun. The beautifully colored buttes, ragged forest of Joshua trees, and clear smog-free air offer a rewarding time spent there.

Many desert animals and birds — kit fox, desert tortoise, chipmunks, Kangaroo rat, road runner, hawk, cactus thrasher, and desert rattlesnakes — each in its season — can be seen at the Saddleback Buttes State Park. There are lovely camping and picnic grounds for visitors, with cabanas. Take time out to walk among the unique Joshua trees, especially in spring when many wildflowers are in bloom and animals are scurrying about.

The Antelope Valley Indian Museum was initially started by H. Arden Edward, an artist who displayed the Indian material discovered among the surrounding buttes. In 1938, a Mrs. Grace Oliver became interested in this museum and developed it into one of the finest museums anywhere on early and primitive peoples from Alaska to South America. Tucked up against Piute Butte in a lovely desert setting, this collection of basketry, arrowheads, and paintings of Indians is almost unequaled. There is a picnic ground for visitors. A small fee is charged for upkeep. It is open Saturday and Sunday from 11 AM - 3 PM and Tuesday and Thursday. Reservation only.

EDWARDS AIR FORCE BASE

B-2 Bomber   *USAF*

This is the second largest air base in the country. With the dry, clear desert air and the large flat, smooth Rogers and Rosamond Dry Lakes, it is an ideal area for the take-off and landing of fast jet fighter planes. It is also the site of the Space Shuttle's return to earth.

In 1933 the Air Force took over this area and replaced the sports car racing field with aircraft runways to become Muroc Air Force Base, named for two homesteaders. The name was changed to Edwards Air Force Base after Captain Edwards crashed and died while testing the experimental YB49 plane. It is a center for advanced aircraft and missile projects. Chuck Yeager flew out of this base when he broke the sound barrier in the X-1 on October 14, 1947.

At the NASA Ames Dryden Research facility, within the base, new forms of aeronautical designs and techniques are developed and tested. Hour-and-a-half tours through the facility are available every Monday through Friday at 10 AM and 1 PM. It is necessary to phone ahead as the base is closed to the public except by reservation. (805) 258-3446. The security guard will then let you enter. There are no tours on holidays. A film on the history of the research center is included in the tour plus a look at some of the experimental aircraft, and a walk through the hangar. On the premises there is a space and aircraft museum.

ROSAMOND

From Lancaster, Highway 14 descends to the valley trough of the Rosamond Dry Lake, which consists of white patches of saline and alkaline deposits. Water from the surrounding slopes is collected in this valley. The warm, dry air evaporates leaving only the salt and minerals where no plants can survive but the saltbrush, a shrubby plant of the goosefoot family that thrives in dry, alkaline soil. Some years ago a well was drilled through the dry lake bed and the alluvian and deposits were 5000 feet deep.

The present town of Rosamond was originally called Sand Creek. It was a cattle growing and farming community using bunch and other grasses that the dwindling antelope herd grazed on across the desert floor. In 1876 the town name was changed by a Southern Pacific Railroad official when a depot was established there. In the early 1900's with the opening of the Lida Mine by Ezra Hamilton, new activity was brought into the area. When the Los Angeles Aqueduct was being built from the Owens Valley south to Los Angeles the mortgage holder of the town hoped that construction workers would house there, but Rosamond was too far away from the main construction area. In the 1930's when the Tropico Mine was booming again, and the Air Force established the Muroc Air Force Base east of Rosamond then street lights, a water plant and a church were added to the community.

Every March there is a community-sponsored "Gold Panning Days" with a gold panning contest, burro claim-staking races and an old time deep-pit barbeque. Each October on the grounds of Gold Camp below the old Tropico Mine the International Chili Cookoff takes place. Contestants come from each state, regions and foreign countries to vie for the prizes. Many RV units and tents are parked in the surrounding gravelled desert among the creosote bushes. Over 35,000 people attend this gala weekend event each year.

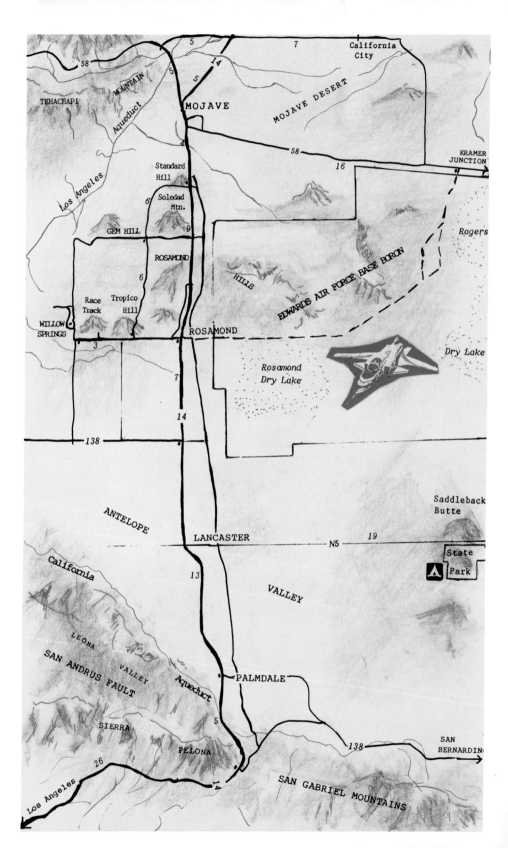

WILLOW SPRINGS

Peaceful Willow Springs, about seven miles west of Rosamond, seems as quiet today as it did to Ezra Hamilton in the early 1900's. The spring, however, is all dried up. By the late 1940's and early 1950's the excessive amount of pumping water from underground wells to irrigate the fields decreased the water table so much that the water supply for the springs was gone. Hamilton enjoyed the dry desert air and the spring so much that when he became rich from his Lida Mine be bought the spring and surrounding land. He designed and built cottages, a hotel, post office, bathhouse, and a public dance hall. He turned the place into a desert health resort. Because Hamilton owned the first car there, he installed a gas pump and had a garage for servicing his automobile.

Earlier travelers enjoyed the springs even before Hamilton came and built his health enterprise. It is recorded that Padre Graces in 1776 stopped to be refreshed on his journeys after just discovering the Tehachapi Pass. He was returning from the San Joaquin Valley en route to the Colorado River to visit the Hopi Indians. The Jayhawker Party out of Death Valley in 1850 stopped at the springs on their way to Los Angeles. John Goler, the unsuccessful prospector who returned to the El Paso Mountains to seek his fortune must have taken a drink here. Later, the Inyo Stage Lines used Willow Springs as a stagecoach stop enroute to Los Angeles. It must have been a great relief for travelers after their dusty, rough trip through the hot desert to find themselves in the cool quiet shade of the trees and to taste the fresh clear water. A hot meal was offered to all the passengers and dormatories were ready for anyone wishing to spend the night.

At the base of Willow Springs Mountain lies the racecourse track for the Willow Springs Toyota Official Pace Car and Truck Raceway.

What is more exciting to Mary and Richard Nelson who have lived at Willow Springs since the 1930's is not Ezra Hamilton, his mine or the Raceway, but Willow Springs being the site of a large Paiute Indian Encampment. As the Hamiltons were laying out the streets for the resort many mortars and pestles were found everywhere. Truck loads were taken out. Beads, arrowheads, baskets and clay bowls were found out on the desert. When the Indians who lived in Owens Valley were led to Fort Tejon, these Paiutes were forced to leave everything and go too. Later some returned to ask if they could once again enjoy a mud bath in Willow Springs. They heated rocks and threw them in the muddy areas below the Springs and wallowed in the warm mud. They would rinse off in the Springs.

37

GOLD MINING IN "DEM DERE HILLS"

Rosamond Blvd., to the left off Highway 14, leads to Rosamond Airport, the old Tropico Mine, the Sportscar Raceway, Willow Springs and into a region of buttes and colorful history.

TROPICO MINE

Back in 1896 Ezra Hamilton came to the Rosamond Hills to get fire clay for a pottery and brick business he had in Los Angeles. On a slack season he started to pan out some clay ore he found and discovered his pot of gold. He named his mine after his wife, Lida. It was the profits of this gold mine that made it possible for him to purchase Willow Springs and make such noteworthy improvements with his health spa. In 1908 he sold the Lida Mine which became known as the Tropico Mine and Hill. It was one of the most lucrative mines in California.

When Hamilton's two sons, Fred and Truman asked their father if they could dig some gold out of the mine — enough to go to the 1904 St. Louis World's Fair, he said all right. The resourceful boys had already picked out their rock of ore and when they showed their father the almost pure gold piece he said, "I didn't mean for you to have THAT much!"

Two brothers, H. Clifford and Cecil Burton who had stock in the Tropico Mining and Milling Company slowly acquired all the stock from other shareholders and became the sole owner. In 1933 the gold mining business here was booming, even as the Yellow Aster Mine was petering out. The boom continued until World War II when all mining ceased. Up to that time the mine had produced some $8 million. After the war came inflation and low gold prices made it unprofitable to do any mining.

THE FIVE BUTTES

The five colorful jagged buttes between Rosamond and Mojave were created by the erosion of the fine sandy rock rich in silicon mineral. The centuries of erosion exposed the hard volcanic plugs and dark lava outcroppings. Between these layers were found veins of gold and silver. The Willow Springs Mountain, Rosamond Hills, Middle Butte, Soledad Mountain and Standard Hill are all rich in various ores from these volcanic and granitic rocks.

MIDDLE BUTTE, where the Cactus Queen Mine was in operation during the 1930's alone produced more than $6 million for the mining of both the gold and silver when all mining in the west was stopped. Before it closed, the Cactus Queen was one of the leading silver mines in California. The gold output from the Middle Butte mines totaled $5 million from the Cactus Queen. Cactus and Burton-Brite-Blank mines.

The Silver Queen Road, north from Tropico Hill, passes through colorful desert hills with interesting outcroppings, some caves in the rocks among the Joshuas. The road leads past Rosamond and Gem Hills to the western side of Soledad Mountains, then around to junction with Highway 14. On the north side of Soledad Mountain the Golden Queen Mine was worked in the early 1930's when the price of gold was sufficient to produce the ore. First called the Silver Queen, for which the road was named, it was later changed to Golden Queen. The mine was sold for a good price, after producing $10 million. Other mines on this hill that were dug in rhyolite — the volcanic rock rich in gold ore — were Elephant, Bobtail, and Excelsior which produced up to World War II. The mines are privately owned and are not open to the public.

Standard Hill, the northernmost and smallest of the buttes became a gold producing mountain in 1894, much earlier than the other mines in the area. George Bowers discovered the claim he named Exposed Treasure which became part of the Standard Group along with Yellow Rover and Desert Queen.

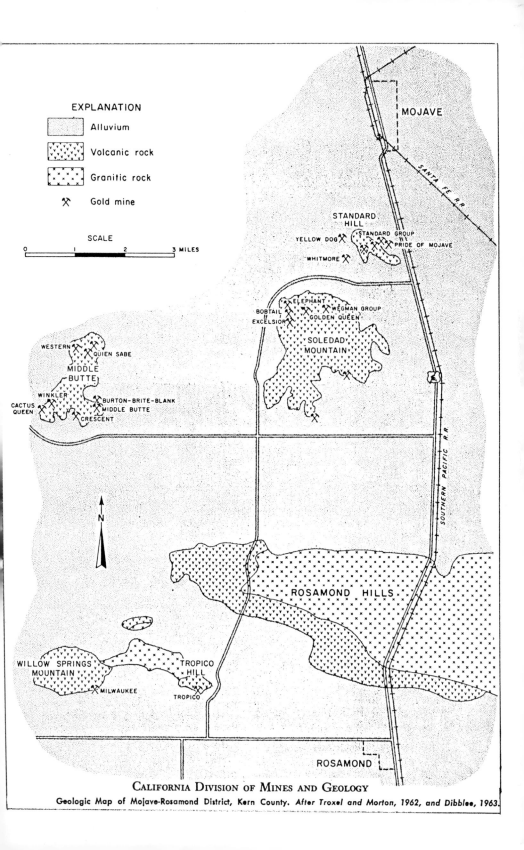

EXPLANATION

Alluvium

Volcanic rock

Granitic rock

⚒ Gold mine

SCALE

0   1   2   3 MILES

MOJAVE

SANTA FE R.R.

STANDARD HILL

YELLOW DOG ⚒   ⚒ STANDARD GROUP
                         PRIDE OF MOJAVE

WHITMORE ⚒

ELEPHANT ⚒   ⚒ WEGMAN GROUP
BOBTAIL &   GOLDEN QUEEN
EXCELSIOR

SOLEDAD
MOUNTAIN

WESTERN ⚒   ⚒ QUIEN SABE

MIDDLE
BUTTE

WINKLER ⚒   ⚒ BURTON-BRITE-BLANK
CACTUS ⚒   MIDDLE BUTTE
QUEEN   ⚒ CRESCENT

SOUTHERN PACIFIC R.R.

N

ROSAMOND HILLS

WILLOW SPRINGS
MOUNTAIN

TROPICO
HILL

⚒ MILWAUKEE

TROPICO

ROSAMOND

CALIFORNIA DIVISION OF MINES AND GEOLOGY

Geologic Map of Mojave-Rosamond District, Kern County. After Troxel and Morton, 1962, and Dibblee, 1963.

MOJAVE

Mojave was, is and always will be a crossroads, the beginning and the end, alive with travelers. It was a crossroads for the many prospectors and miners going in all directions seeking that pot of gold, just over the next hill. For all the men who passed through Mojave, only a small fraction really had a big strike. For many of these men it was the searching not the money or the mining that was important.

It was a logical site for the way station and stagecoach stop for early travelers and settlers as well as miners and prospectors. When the Southern Pacific Railroad connected Owens Valley to Los Angeles, and the Santa Fe connected with Las Vegas, Mojave was the hub of all trails, routes and rails. It was also home base for the 20-Mule Team of the Borax Company that brought the mineral ore over the long, dusty desert trail from Death Valley.

When the aqueduct was built, Mojave was alive with more than 3000 workers coming and going on their various shifts, enjoying the gambling joints, dance halls, saloons, and hotels that lined the single street between the railroad tracks and the desert. It was the focal point of that huge undertaking, which diverted the waters from Owens Valley to Los Angeles.

Today at this crossroad stop, instead of stage and freight teams changing horses, locomotives change rails and cars, trains change freight, and big transports change tires, oil, and refuel. Passing-through-people use the numerous motels, fast food eateries, and gas station. The main street is lined with cars, motorhomes and campers going in all four directions. Each year new places are opened to better serve these people.

Mojave supports an airport, a County Park for picnics and rest stops, a trailer park for overnight accommodations, and the Camelot Golf Course.

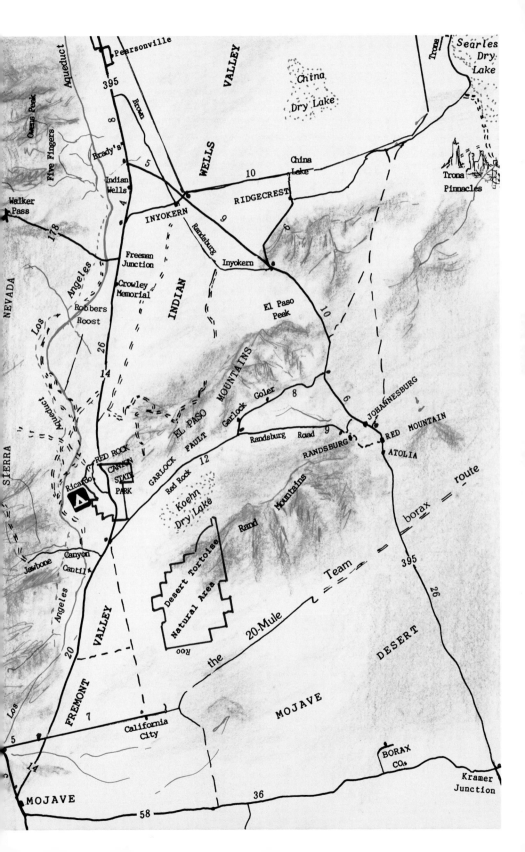

HIGHWAY 14 NORTH

Highway 14 follows northeasterly between the low southern end of the Sierra Nevada and Fremont Valley. Several types of windmills stand like sentinels on the rolling western slopes of Tehachapi Mountains. They supply inexpensive energy as they spin and hum to produce electricity from the strong winds that blow up and over the pass. At the junction with the Randsburg Cutoff-California Blvd., to the east is California City, a development that was never completed, although recently more and more resident homes are being built. From here the 20-Mule Team Parkway follows the old Borax team route and leads east to a junction with Highway 395 near Atolia. On the dirt Randsburg Mojave Road is the Interpretive Center for the Desert Tortoise Natural Area. (temporarily quarantined)

DESERT TORTOISE

The slow moving land turtle with its sleepy eyes was easy prey for people to take home as a pet. It became an endangered species, and the desert tortoise is now protected by a California State Law. It is illegal to collect, damage or have a tortoise in one's possession. Research has shown that this area just north of California City is ideal for a natural reserve area. The tortoise grows to about 15″ in length and can live to be from 50 to 60 years old. In the spring and fall it is quite active. This is when the desert temperatures are moderate and the growth of plants and wildflowers are available for food.

This hoary-looking creature has a water proof hard-scaled shell over which reduces body moisture evaporation from the hot desert sun. The bone shell is the tortoise's 'house' where it can retreat when confronted by danger. Vulnerable head and legs are safe inside. The wrinkly, scaly, armour-like skin keeps the body cool. The hind legs are much stronger than the forefeet.

During the winter the tortoise lives in communal burrows which are built deep in gravelly slopes, but in the summer it rests under bushes or buries itself in the sand to stay out of the sun. With persistant deliberation the tortoise travel around just exploring, basking in a warm sun, eating and sleeping in the shade. They feed on low growing desert flowers and vegetation in the spring. Later in the fall cacti, dry grasses and herbs form their diet. They are related to giant water turtles as well as many other varieties of land tortoises. This species is also found in many other parts of the country.

Just beyond the California City junction on Highway 14 is the Sierra Trails RV Park which has good, shady overnight accommodations with hookups.

Desert Tortoise

JOSHUA TREES

One of the most unique, rugged looking trees of the higher Mojave Desert, common in the Antelope Valley and Tehachepi Mountains, is the Joshua tree, a member of the agave family. They can be seen in elevations from 2000′ to 5000′ along with the creosote bushes and sagebrush in dry mesas and on gravelly slopes. Growing vertically from 15′ to 30′ high, the multiple angular branches create a crown effect. The columnar trunks and branches are a reddish brown to a dull gray color. The shaggy appearance is from the small square plates in the bark. After the first blooming of a growing trunk, reaching from eight to ten feet high, the first branch or branches shoot off at a right angle below the base of the dead flower cluster by splitting the base of a leaf. The branches resemble uplifted arms in their weird, eccentric way.

The stiff leaves are pointed and tapered like bayonets, about six to ten inches long. Animals are unable to feed on the leaves which do not fall off easily, so the tree is protected and can survive for many years. The beautiful white-greenish flower has six petals that are about two feet long and waxen. Surprisingly, the blossom is not sweet but rather musty. Each flower blooms in a cluster from February to April, but not every tree will bloom every year. The cluster yields about 80 pods and each pod contains about 200 seeds that are relished by rodents and larvae. The seeds are round, black and flat, like a watermelon seed. Old tree trunks are easily broken and become homes for birds such as the American kestral, flycatcher and woodpecker.

Highway 14 parallels the Garlock Fault along the base of the Sierra Nevada which borders the Mojave Desert. At Jawbone there is a Texaco gas station, a store that sells motorcycle tires, and the Cantil Post Office. The paved road up Jawbone Canyon ends about four miles west at Hoffman Canyon. A dirt road continues up and around the lower portion of the Sierra Nevada through meadows and timber land to Kelso Valley and the Piute Mountains in the Sierra National Forest. There are many back roads in this area for exploring by jeep or bicycle.

REDROCK-RANDSBURG ROAD follows the Garlock Fault line as it swings eastward along the base of the El Paso Mountains. Cantil was once the station stop of the Southern Pacific. The fertile alfalfa fields are irrigated by underground pools of fresh water seeping down from the surrounding hills. The Koehn Dry Lake is the low point between the Sierra, El Paso Mountains and Rand Mountain. Water from these slopes drains into the basin leaving salty deposits as it evaporates. The dry lake was named for Charlie Koehn, a hard-working German settler. He saved his land from squatters in 1912 before he sold it for $30,000. Today the land is used for farming, that green spot in the open desert landscape.

RED ROCK CANYON STATE PARK   Red Rock Canyon   MAC

Red Rock Canyon cuts through the western section of El Paso Mountains and the uplifted front of the Garlock Fault that stands like a magnificent colorful wall facing the Mojave Desert to the south. The soft bed rocks at the entrance have fossils of saber-tooth tigers, camels, antelopes, deer and rabbits to verify that the region was not always an arid environment. Six to eight million years ago live oaks, pinyon pines and grasses supplied food for the inhabitants.

The imposing fault front reveals stratified rocks of soft picturesque sediments including sand, clay, silt and volcanic debris that lie adjacent to hard dark lava flow formations. The alternate layers of light colored conglomerates, volcanic and granite gravel, bright red and gray sandstone capped by a protective basalt layer provide a window to our geologic past. The physical disintegration and chemical decomposition of the cliff's materials created fluted columns, ridges, alcoves and spires. Geologically, Red Rock Canyon is termed 'badlands' as it is a rough, deeply gullied escarpment that has been eroded and sculptured dramatically by rainfall, drainage on the soft rock and strong winds. The lack of vegetation on the slopes means "bad lands" where nothing can grow.

The "Old People" lived in the Red Rock Canyon and El Paso Mountains area some 20,000 years ago. Petroglyphs have been discovered that are attributed to come from that era. Later came the Kwaiisu Indians, a branch of the Chemehuevi or Mojave Indians. They were a wandering, pastoral poeple similar to the Paiutes who lived to the north. Rock mortars they used to grind seeds and plants were discovered in the canyon. Rock paintings, religious and grave sites were also found in this area.

In the late 1860's when extensive mining activities required large quantities of heavy machinery and tools as well as supplies for workers at the mines, the dry wash through Red Rock Canyon became a scene of almost continuous and vigorous activity. Provisions for Owens Valley, Cerro Gordo, and the Panamint mines passed through here from Bakersfield, Ventura, and Los Angeles. In the canyon there was an overnight way station for the long-line teamsters going north and south. Hay and grain were stockpiled, and water from springs or shallow wells was available. Millions of dollars from the Cerro Gordo were brought out through here by Remi Nadeau and later by his Cerro Gordo Freighting Company. Los Angeles grew from the needs of the towns and business of the mines. San Fernando Valley farmers sold sugar, potatoes, nuts, fruit, and barley to the freighters and miners. The transporting of all these goods was a heroic task for both man and beast. Red Rock was a place of respite sorely needed from the summer heat and winter's ice-laden winds. Stock was rested or replaced, wagon tires reset and tall tales that became legends were exchanged around the sagebrush root campfires.

When prospectors roamed the Red Rock Canyon, as elsewhere in the El Paso Mountains looking for paydirt ore in the late 1890's, one of the well-known figures was Rudolph Hagen. He named a settlement he founded, Ricardo, after his son who died at an early age. After the gold seekers and miners abandoned the canyons Ricardo became a stage stop for travelers going to and from Los Angeles up to Owens Valley. The old settlement today is the site for the Park Headquarters and Ranger Station at the entrance to the Campground.

44

"Apache Land" it was called when the western made in the early years of the movie industry were filmed beneath the colorful cliffs on the eastern side of the Park. Here the large open rest area could accommodate all the movie making paraphenalia. The surrounding desert environment, along with the cliffs, was closer to Los Angeles than Arizona or New Mexico and became an ideal outdoor movie location for westerns. Later, science fiction movies were also made here. "The Ten Commandments", with Moses receiving the stone tablets, was filmed on the cliffs. Moses liberated the Israelites from Egypt here.

The Campground offers a good rest stop for overnight, or for a longer stay to explore the multi-hued columns of rock that look like Victorian petticoats sculptured in stone rising from the desert floor. The area is called White House Cliffs. The air is clear and road sounds are faint, although at night transports can be heard grinding up the long grade. Picnics can be enjoyed at any vacant campsite, or over in the wide open eastern Red Cliffs Preserve. Special Handicap sites, with rest rooms are available.

There are two Natural Preserves that have been established to protect the fragile, magnificent landscape feature where no vehicles are permitted. Signs are placed to designate the areas. On the west side of Highway 14 is Hagen Canyon Natural Preserve that includes the White House Cliffs. Spring and fall are the best time of the year to stay and explore the Park as summer can be extremely hot during the day, though pleasant at night. In winter it is quite cool with bracing winds and freezing temperatures at night. Off-road vehicles are permitted in the campground and on other roads that provide access to Jawbone Canyon and Dove Springs.

Dove Springs, west of Red Rock Canyon State Park is a popular off-road vehicle recreation area that offers a number of dirt roads and trails among rugged hilly terrain. In the fall, the area around Dove Springs is popular for bird watching and hunting.

Coming from the north on Highway 395, Abbot Drive leads down to the Campground. The dirt road from Inyokern to Red Rock Canyon was originally called the Midland Trail. This trail followed along the base of the White-Inyo Mountains on the east side of Owens Valley, and the present route of Highway 395 south to Inyokern. Also, approaching Red Rock Canyon from the north, the uplift of the hills is quite visible. At the crest of the summit, before entering the canyon, there is a grand view of the Mojave Desert to the south.

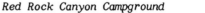

Red Rock Canyon Campground   MAC

EL PASO MOUNTAINS — WEST

A few miles north of Red Rock Canyon, a dirt road leads eastward towards Inyokern and up into the low hills to reach Last Chance Canyon and the interesting 'backyard' of the El Paso Mountains. The road offers breathtaking scenic vistas and in spring, a profusion of wildflowers. But, it is not a road for small cars, campers, or motorhomes. This old road is rough and unmaintained. Some side roads are impassable, so it is best to check before venturing too far off the main dirt road. Roads shown on maps entering El Paso Mountains from the south are steep and frequently blocked with washout debris.

WILLIAM H. SCHMIDT ('Burro Schmidt')

One of the most fascinating, persistent old timers was William H. Schmidt. Every winter from 1906 to 1938 he worked at scooping out a tunnel through the mountain of solid rock. He used a pick, shovel, crowbar, rock hammer, and dynamite. He thought that a tunnel through the middle of the mountain would save hauling copper ore from his claims over the steep, rough country to reach a shipping point. As he dug he loaded the rubble from his daily digging into an ore car that he pushed on a track to his dump at the tunnel opening. As he worked the tunnel he needed more funds so he slowly sold off his mining claims. By the time the tunnel was completed, he had little left to use his tunnel for. He also financed his determined efforts by working during the summer on ranches along the South Fork of the Kern River.

The only means of transportation William Schmidt had to take him to Randsburg for supplies was his team of 'jackasses' or burros. Thus he became known first as "Jackass Schmidt". Although jackass is a common name for burro, people thought that the word burro sounded better so he is now referred to as "Burro Schmidt". It makes worthwhile a rugged trip into the Last Chance Canyon just to visit this monument of one man's perservering endeavor. At the end of his five by seven feet, 2000' long, safe tunnel is a breathtaking panoramic view of the Mojave Desert to the south.

ROBBERS ROOST

The next interesting thing to watch for lies a few miles north and to the west. Robbers Roost is an outcropping that was ideal for bandits and marauders to hang out and hide from the law. They climbed to the top of the rocks and looked out all over the valley to check for any unsuspecting rider, oncoming stagecoaches, and freight teams going to and from the mines. These desperados terrorized the citizens before they were scared off by the law and retreated to Los Angeles.

At one time the mountain behind "The Roost" extended as far out onto the desert floor as the outcropping. Subsequent weathering and erosion washed away the soft rock of the mountain slope leaving this hard rock alone and exposed.

Robbers Roost   MAC

Father Crowley   *Courtesy of East California Museum*

FATHER CROWLEY MEMORIAL PLAQUE

On the side of the road, about three miles north on the highway, is Father Crowley Memorial Plaque. It is near the place where he was killed in an automobile accident in 1940. Father Crowley was known and loved as the Desert Padre who went up and down the valley to encourage the people of Owens Valley to cater to tourists. They had lost hope when their farming water was diverted and sent down to Los Angeles, destroying their livelihood. The Desert Padre knew that the land was beautiful and that visitors would appreciate and enjoy its beauty. The recreational opportunities in the lakes and streams for boating and fishing, the mountain slopes for skiing, and the forest lands for summer resorts could supply revenue for the people, and replace what they had lost with their water.

FREEMAN JUNCTION

First called Coyote Hole, this junction was at one time a lively stage station with travelers passing in three directions. In 1874, Freeman S. Raymond, who had been a member of the Death Valley 49er's Emigrant Party, established a way station. Miners, freighters, and prospectors went from Los Angeles to Cerro Gordo mines. From Bakersfield and the Kern River country travelers crossed the Walker Pass to reach the Owens Valley. The mining in Kern country was active in the 1860's but never was as extensive as the mines in the Mojave and Eastern Sierra. By 1889 a post office was established and the name was changed to Freeman. When Cerro Gordo petered out and not as many travelers frequented the roads, the junction buildings slowly deteriorated and today there is nothing left but a large, colorful sign on the road where Highway 178 meets Highway 14.

THE WALKER PASS (5245′)

The Walker Pass was named for Captain Joseph Reddeford Walker, a Tennessee trapper and Mountain Man. He was the first white man to ride up and over the Pass from Monterey and the San Joaquin Valley in 1834. He climbed the foothills in a southeasterly direction, up the Greenhorn Mountains (probably through Basket Pass), past Keysville to the North and South Forks of the Kern River — near the present day site of Isabella Dam. Then he went up the South Fork and Camelrake Creek, and southeast over the pass down into Freeman Canyon. By entering the Kern River country from the north via the Greenhorn Mountains, he avoided the steep, impassable gorge of the Kern River flowing south into the San Joaquin Valley. His party consisted of 52 men, 315 horses that carried their provisions of flour, beans and Indian corn, plus 47 beef cattle and 30 dogs. According to Walker's clerk, Zenas Leonard, they lost 64 horses, 10 cows and 15 dogs. They quenched their parched throats by drinking the blood of the slaughtered cattle.

In 1843 Walker led the Second Chiles Emigrant Party from Walker Lake through Owens Valley to Walker Pass. They were forced to abandon their heavy over-loaded wagons, which they burned, and packed whatever provisions and belongings they could on their backs and on their livestock to cross the Pass on foot. Later, in 1845, he guided Fremont's Third Expedition which was led by Theodore Talbot across the Pass to reach Sutters Fort (Sacramento), even though it meant riding down the long Owens Valley. This lower, less hazardous pass across the Sierra was safer and easier for the men and horses.

When the transcontinental railroad was being considered, Mr. Walker proposed a route west from Las Vegas, through the desert below the Panamint Mountains and Death Valley. Then, crossing Walker Pass it would follow his route down into the San Joaquin Valley, cutting through the Coastal Range to Gilroy and on to San Jose and San Francisco. This route was seriously considered. However, the final decision resulted in the present Salt Lake City to San Francisco route.

KERN RIVER COUNTRY

The renowned Kern River Country and Isabella Lake have been established as one of the finest recreational areas of the Sierra. The name Kern is for Edward Kern, the artist-cartographer who traveled with John Fremont on his Third Expedition. The many forks of the Kern River spread out into Sequoia National Park, Sequoia National Forest and Bureau of Land Management lands with tumbling trout-filled streams that meander through magnificent forests and grassy foothills. Hunting and fishing are both popular and rewarding. There are many dirt roads and trails for the sportsmen to follow. Isabella Lake is a boating paradise with marinas, water skiing and bass fishing. The Pacific Crest Trail passes through this country leading north to the Golden Trout Wilderness Area and beyond.

About two miles north on Highway 14, Highway 178 leads eastward down the alluvial fan to Inyokern and Ridgecrest. Inyokern, a true crossroad community, has service stations, a cafe and the Inyokern Airport that provides Ridgecrest and China Lake with private and commercial aviation operations including scheduled air lines and glider soaring.

HOMESTEAD AND INDIAN WELLS
When the Shoshoni Indians went from their Sierra summer camps eastward to their winter camps in the Panamint Valley, they stopped at Homestead and Indian Wells. It was an oasis for the Jayhawkers who crossed the desert en route to Los Angeles from Death Valley in 1849. It was a refreshing and restful spot in their long journey across the desert. It provided the first water they had seen since leaving the Argus Range. Later, Indian Wells became a major watering place for the pioneers, and when gold was discovered in the Coso Range it became the ideal stage station for dusty, thirsty, weary miners, freighters, and people going up and down the desert road. When the aqueduct was built, waters that fed the wells slowly dried up.

INYOKERN
Highway 395 passes between Ridgecrest and Inyokern where the Indian Wells Valley-Inyokern Airport is situated. At Inyokern are service stations, a few cafes, bar, antique shops and a store.

This "Southern Crossroads to the High Sierra" near the junction of Highways 395 and 14, was a supply camp during the construction of the Los Angeles Aqueduct known as Siding 16. The crossroads had serviced many travelers and workers for the mines in the Eastern Sierra region and had been a railhead for the Mojave-Los Angeles spur of the Southern Pacific Railroad. In 1913 the name was changed to Magnolia when the first post office was built. The name Inyokern came later.

In the early 1940's the Ordinance Test Station was established on the site of the present airport before the Navy transfered all operations to China Lake to become the Navel Weapons Center. Each year in October there is an airshow held at the airport.

At one time there were high expectations of developing the Indian Wells Valley as a great agricultural center, with settlers coming in to farm the open lands. It never materialized as a great center, but today there are over 2000 acres producing such varied crops as alfalfa, pistachio, almond and fruits.

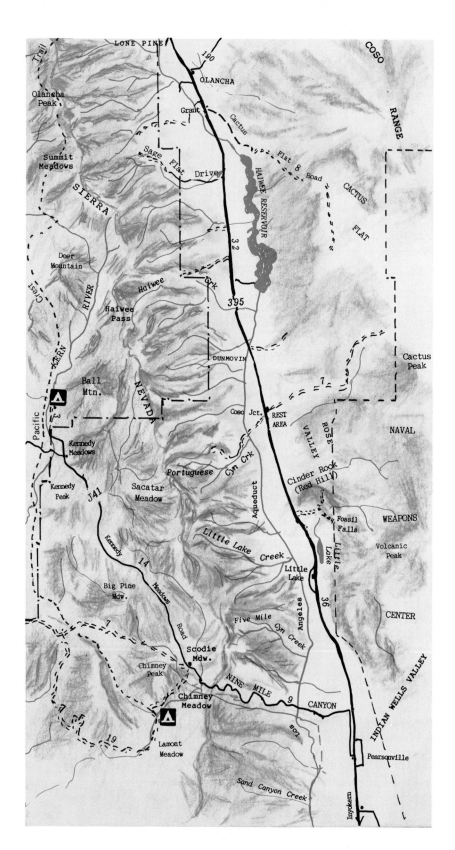

PEARSONVILLE (2470')
Lucy Pearson

As the highway divides into four lanes, the road to the right leads to Pearsonville where a lady named Lucy Pearson oversees the 'Hubcap Capital of the World'. If you need to replace a hubcap on your car or truck, it is quite likely that Lucy will have it in her large, unbelievable selection.

Lucy and her husband, Ted, along with their two children, went up to Cartago in 1959 from the San Fernando Valley to look at some property. They camped out, sleeping on the ground. They heard about some land available north of Inyokern and came down to look at it. Eighty acres with beautiful mountains to the west, under clear autumn skies, sublime quiet desert lands, and soft hazy distant valley views quickened their hearts and they decided to stay.

The Pearsons started a wrecking yard and auto towing business. The first building was only a 12'x12' shed. No electricity was available so they used kerosene lamps. For the first few years the nearest water supply was 13 miles south at Inyokern. Fifty-five gallon oil drums were cleaned, placed in the back of their car and carried their water up the road. Because well drillers needed cash-as-you-go, and money was slow in coming, it took about a year to drill the 400' well.

An old wood stove was used to heat water for fuel, cleaning, cooking and warmth. Everyone collected sagebrush roots for fuel. Groceries were purchased at Ridgecrest. The two children went to school in Olancha and Lone Pine via a school bus. They had the distinction of traveling 58 miles each way, making it the longest ride for a school bus in California in 1963. The bus picked them up at 6:30 in the morning and brought them home at 5 PM.

However, there was lots of tourist traffic and business was good. Lucy started collecting hub caps and slowly built up the immense collection she has today. The family sold various belts and other auto parts as well. The original buildings, erected during the beginning years, were torn down when the present four-lane highway was constructed through their property.

Today Pearsonville consists of a gas station and mini mart along with the auto parts and hub caps. The mini mart sells white, brown, blue-green bottles of all shapes and sizes Lucy has found in the desert, old tins and dishes collected from old mines, books on the area as well as knicknacks, snacks and food.

NINE MILE CANYON TO KENNEDY MEADOWS

Highway 141 up Nine Mile Canyon leads to the west off Highway 395 to many camping, hiking, biking, and fishing areas. The road winds up and up steeply to reach the 6500' summit before passing through some lovely flowered and grassy meadows where herds of cattle graze in the summer. This is the last trans-Sierra vehicular route south of the Tioga Pass Road, and the closest road to reach the Domeland Wilderness Area from the east side. After Nine Mile Canyon Road reaches the Black Rock Forest Service Station the road ascends through white pines and red firs to Sherman Pass (9170'). This mountain road then twists and turns, descending into the main Kern River country, Kernville and Isabella Lake.

Kennedy Meadows, named for Andrew L. Kennedy who first leased this meadow land for cattle grazing in 1886, has a Forest Service Station, store and pack station. The Pacific Crest Trail passes through this Sequoia National Forest where well-placed campgrounds allow easy access to the trail as well as many jeep and bike roads.

Proceeding north on Highway 395, the road leaves Indian Wells Valley and passes through an interesting volcanic gorge. The gorge was carved out by the ancient Owens River that went from Owens Basin to the north, flowing into the China Basin, then southward to Indian Wells Valley. The tremendous violent volcanic activity that took place years ago can be seen along the road through this volcanic field, with lava flow formations, red cinder blowouts, and ancient black ridges of lava blisters on this west side of the Coso Range.

LITTLE LAKE

The Little Lake Lodge sits on the rocky knoll on the left side of the road. It has been a commercial resort for the past hundred years. This rustic 21-room hotel, with its rock front, is an Historical Landmark. It has been renovated to include a cafe specializing in Basque food, a bar, Trading Post and gas station.

Little Lake, just beyond, is a spring-fed lake once called Little Owens Lake. It is a haven for many migratory water birds such as the Pintail Mallard and other species of geese and ducks. In the winter whistling swans might be seen even though their usual habitat is in the San Joaquin Valley. The bulrushes, sedges and grasses that grow by the lake offer abundant feed for these birds. The lake is privately owned, lock-gated and stocked with fish. For thousands of years this watering place has been used by man. The early 'Pinto' people were known to have resided here as, later, did the Paiutes and Shoshoni Indians. Travelers to and from the numerous Coso Range and Owens Valley mines and mining facilities stopped at the lake to be refreshed after their long and dusty stagecoach or freight team journeys.

The unique black wall on the eastern shore of the lake is a volcanic material that shrunk as it cooled and broke away, creating vertical columns just as it did at Devils Postpile in the Middle Fork of the San Joaquin River Valley west of Mammoth Lakes. The Shoshoni Indians called the columned cliffs "The Rattlesnake". The old volcanic flow around Little Lake presents an unusual contrast to the forested granite hills to the west and the sagebrush-covered Mojave Desert to the south. A few miles north visit Fossil Falls to see the force and shape of Mother Nature.

MAC

FOSSIL FALLS

Take the eastward road at the south base of Red Hill and follow the road for about a half mile. Turn south and drive to the cul-de-sac to park. A well-traveled trail leads southeast about a mile to the top of the hill. Various types of lava and volcanic rocks can be seen along the way. The red cinders were spewed from the cinder cone of Red Hill, and a pumice specimen of light gray solidified foam is easy to pick up as it weighs so little. It is possible to go down the deep gorge of the former falls although it is slippery. Care should be taken as you work your way to the bottom.

Thousands of years ago the Owens River overflowed and the force of the water carved and polished unusual shapes in the lava bed. The pot holes were made as the swirling water ground the rocks around and around.

RED HILL (3952') (Cinder Rock)

At one time Red Hill was wanted by companies for the clean, dark red volcanic cinders that made attractive building blocks. Efforts were made by citizens to save the hill. The cone was created by a series of volcanic explosions that built it up to its present size. There is a scoria mine at the base of the dome. Scoria, a porous, light weight rock, is used for insulation, landscaping and roofing.

On each side of the highway there are lava blisters that resulted when gases under the top crust of the lava flow pushed up the crust and broke it apart, leaving bulges that hardened and cooled. Volcanic Peak (5352') to the east of Little Lake was the source of the lava flows and blisters that formed the land in Little Lake Basin.

As Highway 395 circles around the base of Cinder Rock and descends into the valley, shadows from the clouds above passing from the Sierra block slowly and silently move eastward over the desert mesa toward the Coso Ridge.

COSO JUNCTION REST AREA

With shade trees, picnic tables, RV dump, clear sparkling water and modern facilities this rest area in Rose Valley is a much-visited oasis especially during summer days when temperatures are high and the long road through the desert stretches ahead. REACT, out of Ridgecrest, offers free coffee and punch for travelers on long holiday weekends. In the springtime many flowers, some rather unique, can be seen in this Rose Valley area. In recent years a mini mart, cafe, and gas station, with towing and RV repair has been added. The Junction Tavern, where pool and TV games can be played, serves beer and wine.

The road eastward up the wash leads to the pumice mines of the Coso Mountains. At one time Coso Hot Springs was a popular spa, but the Naval Weapons Center fenced it off and restricted the area for Naval Ordinance Test Station purposes, just northwest of Sugarloaf Mountains.

HAIWEE RESERVOIR

The Haiwee Reservoir has two parts — North and South — and is one of the largest collecting basins of the Los Angeles Water System. There are three such reservoirs along the Los Angeles Aqueduct. Before the dams were built this area was a large, beautiful, grassy meadow called Hayway Meadow that supported many thousands of goats. Haiwee is an Indian name for dove *(haiwai).* When the Indians lived here, this area was a habitat for many wild pigeons. Watch out for cattle, as they sometimes sleep on the warm road at night.

At one time a road over the Haiwee Pass was considered. It would have been west of the highway, and cross over the Kern River Plateau to meet roads going eastward from Porterville. Until such a road is built the only access into the back country in this section of the Sierra is by hiking or pack train.

OWENS VALLEY

OLANCHA

"Yawlanche" was the Shoshoni name for Olancha. There has been a settlement here since 1860, distinguished by the beautiful, tall cottonwood trees along the highway. The trees were transplanted from Cottonwood Creek, several miles to the north, when the settlement was first established. They make a cool resting place on a hot summer's day. The lovely green fields beyond are an unexpected lushness after the desert environment to the south. A convenience store, cafe, and service station with propane are located just before the road to Death Valley that branches off to the east (Highway 190).

As with so many places along Highway 395, Olancha was also a way station for early travelers. One of the old adobe buildings still stands. A mill was built here in 1861 for M.H. Farley's mine up in the Coso Mountains. In the 1870's there were large corrals to hold and feed animals for the numerous freight teams that carried supplies and ore to and from the Cerro Gordo mines.

Olancha Peak (12,123 '), to the west, is the southernmost peak exceeding 12,000 feet in the Sierra Nevada and can be seen from the road. A trail leads up Olancha Creek to cross the crest just south of Olancha Peak, and leads to Hessian, Monache, Beck and Brown Meadows along the Kern River.

OWENS LAKE

Today only soft ores are mined in the now virtually dry alkaline sink called Owens Lake. The material had been accumulating and building up from run-offs emptying into the lake for centuries. The brine under the crust, the sodium carbonate salt that crystallized at the bottom of the lake, and other soda solutions have produced over a million tons of sediment. The redness of the evaporation ponds seen on the lake bed was created by brine shrimp living on the bacteria and protozoa in the lake. It was a salty, shallow lake before the water was diverted by the Los Angeles Aqueduct. Centuries of evaporation had shrunk the lake from its original size. It was measured in 1891 and found to be 15 miles long, 9 miles wide and 50 feet deep. Ancient shore lines and remnants of ancient beaches can be seen on the north end. John Fremont named the lake for Richard Owens, a member of his Third Expedition to the west. Mr. Owens never traveled through Owens Valley or saw the lake that was named for him.

When the wind blows, great white clouds of alkaline dust and sand swirls over the land. In the days of freighting this smarting dust made the trip from Lone Pine to Swansea and Keeler extremely uncomfortable.

Highway 395 climbs over a ridge to 4000' through creosote scrub and sagebrush. In the spring this section is alive with desert blossoms.

Just before reaching GRANT, you'll find the Rustic Motel and Wagon RV Camp to the west. The community was named for John Grant who built the Ranch Motel in 1948. *Aqueduct near Long Pine   Courtesy of East California Museum*

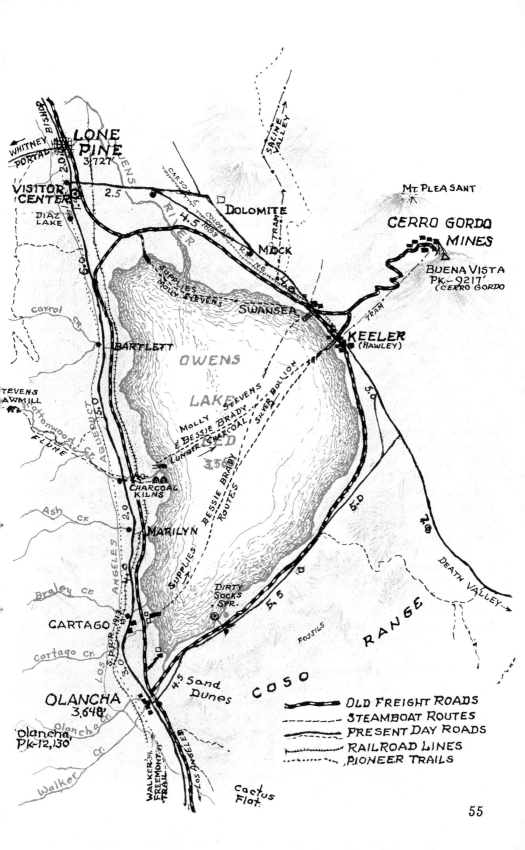

WHITNEY PORTAL RD →
LONE PINE 3,727'
395
VISITOR CENTER
DIAZ LAKE
Carroll Cr.
2.5
OWENS RIVER
CARSON & COLORADO R.R. N.G. 1883
DOLOMITE
4.5
MACK
SALINE VALLEY →
TRAM
Mt. PLEASANT
CERRO GORDO MINES
BUENA VISTA Pk.–9,217' (CERRO GORDO)
SUPPLIES
MOLLY STEVENS
SWANSEA
TRAM
KEELER (HAWLEY)
STEVENS SAWMILL
COTTONWOOD Cr. FLUME
BARTLETT
AQUEDUCT 1.5
OWENS
LAKE [BED] 3,560'
MOLLY STEVENS & BESSIE BRADY Lumber CHARCOAL
SILVER BULLION
BESSIE BRADY ROUTES
CHARCOAL KILNS
Ash Cr.
2.0
MARILYN
SUPPLIES
LOS ANGELES
5.0
5.0
2.0
DEATH VALLEY
Braley Cr.
S.P.R.R. 1913
DIRTY SOCKS SPR.
5.5
FOSSILS
COSO RANGE
CARTAGO
Cartago Cr.
2.0
4.5 Sand Dunes
OLANCHA 3,648'
Olancha Pk–12,130'
Olancha Cr.
Walker Cr.
WALKER & FREMONT '45 TRAIL
LOS ANGELES
Cactus Flat

━∿━∿━ OLD FREIGHT ROADS
– – – – STEAMBOAT ROUTES
═══════ PRESENT DAY ROADS
—┼—┼— RAILROAD LINES
·········· PIONEER TRAILS

55

AROUND OWENS LAKE

Explore the historical and natural wonders around Owens Lake. Starting at Olancha, 4.5 miles east will bring you to DIRTY SOCKS MINERAL HOT SPRINGS, located at the southeast end of Owens Lake bed. A dirt road leads to the large cement-lined pool of warm, saline water that was constructed some years ago as a resort endeavor that never materialized. A deep well was drilled in the early 1900's and it had been hoped that the place would become a profitable health spa. The odor of 'dirty socks' is probably from sulphurous minerals brought to the surface by the artesian fed waters.

Magnificent views from the Hot Springs include the Sierra Nevada, the Coso Range and the Inyo Mountains, with the lake in the foreground. The soft sandy ground can be hazardous, so stay on the firm packed road. If the road is "undistinguishable" walk down, parking on the side so as not to get stuck in the muck.

FOSSIL BEDS

In the Coso Range prospectors found some hardrock ores and precious metals to increase their wealth. However, in 1930 a scientific bonanza was discovered. Many fossil beds were uncovered in the hills across the road from Dirty Socks Mineral Hot Springs. There are several widely separated fossil areas of large peccary, short-jawed mastodons, tiny meadow mice, and horses that grazed the grasslands of the ancient Coso hills. According to paleontologists these creatures were here as recently as one million years ago. A short trip into the fossil areas can be made by jeep or bike, followed by hiking for a good, hard, three miles. The adventure should be taken by experienced desert cross-country hikers only.

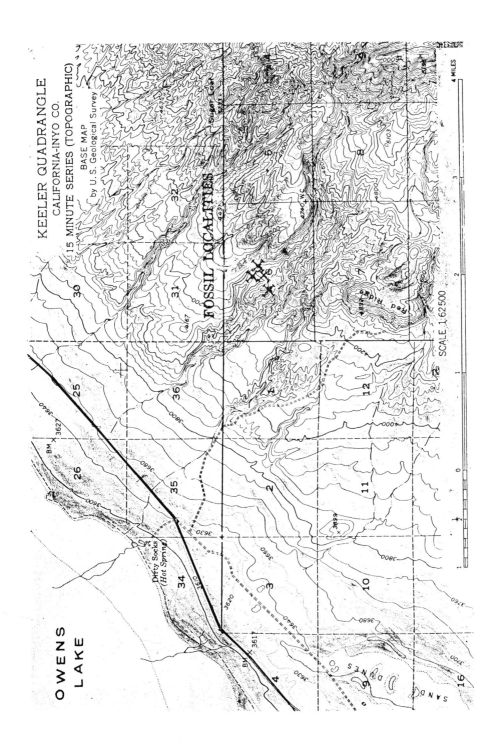

KEELER QUADRANGLE
CALIFORNIA-INYO CO.
15 MINUTE SERIES (TOPOGRAPHIC)

BASE MAP
by U. S. Geological Survey

FOSSIL LOCALITIES

OWENS LAKE

SCALE 1:62500

4 MILES

Red Ridge

Dirty Socks
(Hot Spring)

SAND DUNES CO.

57

About 10.5 miles past the Hot Springs, Highway 190 junctions with Highway 136 to Death Valley. To the left the road leads to Keeler and Swansea.

Keeler still has the old Carson & Colorado Railroad depot that was the end of the line. Today it is a small community where people live and work. A Mr. Julius M. Keeler was manager of a marble quarry nearby, and in 1879 brought new life to the Cerro Gordo mines. In 1882 the settlement was named for him. Part of the old tramway up to Cerro Gordo is all that is left from the great mining activity. Some $15 million worth of ore was produced from Cerro Gordo with no other California group of mines matching that for silver, lead and zinc.

At Swansea there is a plaque commemorating the Owens Lake Silver Lead Furnace as an Historical Landmark. In 1874 an avalanche, resulting from a cloudburst, buried most of the once busy port of Swansea and the smelters were filled with mud. All of the wooden buildings up on the slope above Owens Lake have collapsed and have been decimated by scavengers and the desert.

CARTAGO

The unpretentious community of Cartago does not reflect the immense activity that once made it an important and busy port. The ore from Cerro Gordo mines was carried across saline Owens Lake by the *Bessie Brady*, an 85-foot steamboat that resembled a barge. The Owens Lake Steam Navigation Company was formed and the steamboat hauled its first load of silver bullion out of Swansea and crossed the lake. It saved the freight teams over 50 miles and a four or five days trip around the southern end of the lake to reach Cartago — initially Daneri's Landing. Owens Lake, at that time, was over 100 square miles and at its deepest point was over 50 feet.

The production at the mines was such that almost a million dollars in bullion were stacked up at Swansea and Cartago landings awaiting shipment to Los Angeles. And the lumber, charcoal, machinery, grain, food and liquor for the mines were waiting to be shipped back across the waters. At the Cartago landing teamsters, swampers, and blacksmiths worked almost around the clock to keep the precious freight moving. As many as 80 long-line freight outfits were on the road at one time. In Los Angeles it became an almost unnoticed hourly event for a team to rumble through town delivering another load of silver ingots to the wharf where ships were waiting to sail them to San Francisco for refining. The freighting business, hauling ore into Los Angeles for export from the many mines, and all of the provisions and equipment needed at the mines, helped Los Angeles to grow into a rapidly expanding metropolis.

The *Molly Stevens,* second steamboat to haul cargo across the lake, transported fuel, lumber, and charcoal for the smelters. But in 1877 the Stevens Cottonwood flume burned, along with 64,000 feet of cut lumber, and the silver business went into decline. The second phase of Cerro Gordo came in 1879 when Julius Keeler brought in new money and life. He repaired the Stevens Cottonwood flume, and got the *Molly Stevens* to steam across the lake again. But he thought the boat too inefficient, so he unbeached the *Bessie Brady*, which was at Ferguson's Landing, south of Lone Pine, renovated the hull and put the big propeller and engine from the *Molly Stevens* into the *Bessie Brady* in 1882. Unfortunately, it only made a few trips before it caught fire and was destroyed. Steamboats became a thing of the past. Some years later the three-foot 300 pound propeller of the *Molly Stevens* was found in the dry Owens lakebed.

Bessie Brady

There are two pack stations that offer trips into the Cottonwood Lakes and the Golden Trout Wilderness Area: Cottonwood Pack Station out of Horseshoe Meadows and Mt. Whitney Pack Station out of Whitney Portal.

CHARCOAL KILNS

When the pinyon pines and junipers on the slopes of the Inyo Mountains around Cerro Gordo were completely stripped it became necessary to locate other sources of lumber for shacks, wood for fuel, and charcoal for the smelters. Colonel Sherman Stevens then built a sawmill up Cottonwood Creek, and a flume that extended from the mill down Cottonwood Creek to the Owens Lake loading platforms. The logs were cut to a special length and thickness, put into the adobe brick kiln from the rear door near the top, slowly burned down to charcoal and removed through the large door in front. During the passing years these beehive shaped kilns have deteriorated and some time ago they were sprayed with a preservative so they could be saved with no further erosion of their adobe walls. However, the holes at the top are fragile and are being eroded by weather.

On the left side of the highway there is a road part way up Cottonwood Creek to a trail that leads up to Horseshoe Meadow and the Cottonwood Lakes. The main route into this high country to Horseshoe Meadows and the Cottonwood Lakes is out of Lone Pine.

Charcoal Kilns   MAC

COTTONWOOD LAKES — HORSESHOE MEADOWS

This southern entry into the backcountry begins at an 8000' elevation in a beautiful forest setting with sparkling streams, lakes and great fishing. Trails lead over the Sierra Crest with two routes to choose from. Both trails are excellent, with a series of switchbacks along the cirque walls, passing marmots sunning themselves along the way. The Pacific Crest Trail leads from here to Crabtree Meadows, and into some of the finest backcountry of Sequoia National Park.

From Horseshoe Meadows the trail passes through dense forest cover and flowered meadows into a delicate alpine environment. The trail continues over Mulkey Pass into the famous Golden Trout Wilderness Area.

GOLDEN TROUT WILDERNESS AREA

The magnificent Kern River and its tributaries have long been recognized for great hunting and fishing. Its high country streams and lakes are the home of the unique Golden Trout, which is California's state fish, native to these southern Sierra waters.

With its brilliant color of gold and scarlet, able to survive cold winters and high elevations, the Golden Trout is an excellent and popular sport fish. The California Fish and Game preserves some of the Cottonwood Lakes for hatcheries. Each spring the eggs are transported by mules down the mountain to hatcheries where they grow and then are planted in other Sierra lakes.

Mt. Whitney   *Cliff Dennell*

The Lukken Canyon Trailer Park, south of Lone Pine, offers overnight accommodations as well as boat and RV parking.

DIAZ LAKE

The Diaz brothers, Eleuterio and Rafael owned a cattle ranch that later became a lake created by the 1872 earthquake. This sparkling little natural lake, with the massive Sierra escarpment in the background, offers swimming, water skiing, and fishing for rainbow and brown trout, catfish and bass. At times, in the hot summer months it can get a little 'buggy'. Some 200 spaces accommodate trailers, motorhomes, campers or tenters. There are flush toilets, stoves, and tables under shade trees. This lovely camping area, with a playground and restaurant, is open all year and is a good place to spend a few days exploring the beauties around Lone Pine.

MT. WHITNEY GOLF CLUB is a public golf course, 9-hole, par 36, 3215 yards, located to the west, just before Highway 136 to Death Valley junctions on the east. The club has a Snack Bar and Golf Shop with electric and hand carts available. Club sets and driving range facilities are for rent.

The EASTERN SIERRA INTERAGENCY VISITOR CENTER is at the junction of Highways 395 and 136. It is a joint project of Inyo County, City of Los Angeles, the State of California and U.S. Government agencies. Extensive information on the geology, history, and ecology of the mountains, desert and Owens Valley is available through photographs, displays and exhibits. A large selection of maps and books pertaining to the entire Eastern Sierra region is for sale. The personnel are extremely helpful and knowledgeable about the area and are eager to answer questions and give guidance if needed. There is ample parking; rest rooms with handicap facilities and picnic tables with an exquisite view of Mt. Whitney seen through the trees. This Visitor Center is powered by solar energy.

Just beyond the intersection is the LONE PINE MUNICIPAL AIRPORT that has one N-S 2500′ lighted runway and one NW-SE 2535′ unlighted runway at 3700′. Flights are offered over the Sierra Crest, or Owens Valley and desert regions. Each year sailplane soaring contests are held here with glider planes from all over the world. Storage is available for private planes.

The Pheasant Club for hunting meets at the airport. In the autumn hunting is very popular in Owens Valley and is permitted in many riverside, marsh and mountain areas. Seasons are open for grouse, dove, quail, pheasant, water fowl, rabbits, tule elk and deer. For the specific dates of openings, periods, areas, seasons and bag limits consult California Fish and Game.

The MT. WHITNEY RANGER STATION is on the right as you enter town. Wilderness Permits and other Forest Service information on quotas, trail, road and weather conditions can be obtained. The address is 690 S. Main St., Lone Pine, Calif. 93545. (619) 876-4660. A RV sanitary dump station is here also, on Inyo Street.

There are four campgrounds in the Lone Pine-Mt. Whitney area, two near town, one up the Whitney Road and one at Whitney Portal. Check the campground chart at the back of the book for specifics.

LONE PINE (3733')

Lone Pine is the second largest community in the Owens Valley region and the commercial center for southern Owens Valley and eastern desert country. For more than a hundred years the town has been the gateway to the southern Sierra and the desert mining districts to the east. With the recreational offerings of fishing, hiking, backpacking, and camping in the mountains, rock hounding and ghost town exploring in the desert mountains, it is as much a center now as it was when occupied by the miners, prospectors, promoters, and ranchers of yesterday.

Two brothers, Bart and Alney McGee were the first white men to settle here and built their cabin up on Lone Pine Creek in 1861. The lone Jeffrey pine, that the town and creek were named for, was swept away many years ago in a storm. A few years later, in 1865, when the Cerro Gordo mines were first opened, many families and miners came from various parts of the world to work and build homes, commercial enterprises, and to supply the growing population. It became quite a mixture of nationalities, many from Mexico.

Farmers raised large quantities of hay for the stock used by the long-line teams of Remi Nadeau and other freighters during the mining boom. Tons of fruit from the orchards and vegetables from the truck farms supplemented the regular diet of bacon, beans, sheep and beef for miners at Cerro Gordo, Darwin, Candelaria and Montgomery. Water from the east Sierra slopes was abundant in those days when the valley flourished and hundreds of small farm homesteads were scattered throughout the area. Thousands of sheep were driven through the valley from the upper Kern River country on their way to the Mono Lake area and the Bodie Hills for summer grazing. Most of the sheep drives went via trails along the base of the White-Inyo Mountains, east of Owens River.

In 1904 Los Angeles began using the water of Owens River for its needs. By 1907 the first portion of the aqueduct was completed. A decade later the valley still produced corn, wheat, potatoes, alfalfa, and grapes. Then, in 1921 when Los Angeles was expanding rapidly, due partly from all of the mining activity in this part of the country, it became necessary to acquire more water rights. Farms were bought up by Los Angeles interests. Water was pumped into the aqueduct and farms faded from the once fertile valley. With the disappearance of the mining towns, and the water supply, the people of the valley no longer were supported by ranching and farming. The green of their product today is in recreation money spent by the millions of year-round visitors who travel up and down the highway, as foreseen by Father Crowley.

Besides the motels, stores, service stations, gift shops, restaurant and cafes, there is a community swimming pool located next to the high school, one block east of the highway. No fee is charged for the use of the lighted tennis courts. The Southern Inyo Hospital has 24-hour Emergency Room Service. There are nine churches of various religious faiths to welcome the visitor. Lone Pine County Park, at the north end of town has picnic tables, swings, slides, water, rest rooms and a gazebo for community activities and entertainments.

The largest earthquake in California's recorded history, registering 8.3 on the Richter scale, shook Lone Pine on March 26, 1872 at 2:30 in the morning. Lone Pine suffered the most damage as the majority of buildings were just blocks of dried mud piled on top of each other and plastered with more mud. The walls crumbled and tumbled over the sleeping occupants. The mass grave site of 16 of the 27 victims is up on a slope at the north end of town. West of Lone Pine the earthquake produced a "scarp" 20 feet in depth.

Fishermen note: the California Fish and Game stock Whitney Creek during summer, but not Tuttle Creek.

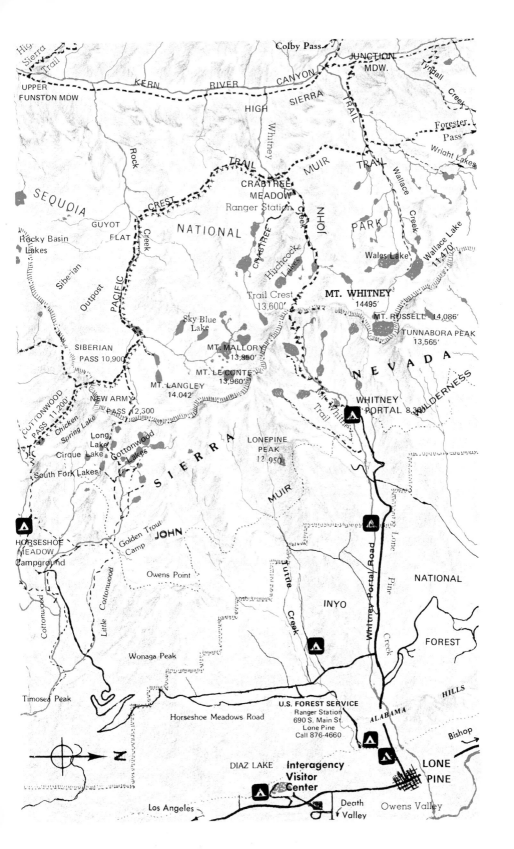

MOUNT WHITNEY (14,495')

The Whitney group of summits over 14,000', along with the Sierra Crest, is the climax of a vast region of mountain peaks, glacial-carved canyons, and a multitude of skyline lakes and tumbling streams where the scenery is matched by the quality of its fishing and hunting. Well-built trails lead into eastern entries that explore the country of the John Muir-Pacific Crest Trail.

A good oiled road leads up to Whitney Portal. It is a worthwhile trip in itself just for the excellent views eastward across the high desert lands of Owens Valley and the Alabama Hills, and to see the east face of Mt. Whitney with its pinnacles, buttresses and surrounding peaks close up through the pine and fir forest. There is a store with basic supplies, showers, a cafe and pack station.

The Mt. Whitney Trail between Whitney Portal and the summit, built and maintained by the U.S. Forest Service, is much traveled. It traverses the John Muir Wilderness Area and Wilderness Permits must be secured before entering it. The upper section of the trail is through open, barren country with little vegetation. Late in the season no water is available past Wotans Throne. The path ascends the face of the greatest escarpment on a well-graded, seemingly endless series of switchbacks to Trail Crest, junctioning with the John Muir Trail leading to the summit.

The view from the crest is outstanding. To the east is the sweep of the Owens River basin lying more than 10,000' below. Beyond, the desert basins of the Mojave and Death Valley country and the White-Inyo Mountain Range. To the west lies the Kern River Gorge and the Kaweah peaks. Along the Muir Crest can be seen six peaks whose summits exceed 14,000'.

From Trail Crest the trail ascends the talus slope, then along a knife-edge ridge passing "windows" from which can be seen magnificent views. On the eastern lip of Mt. Whitney summit is a small, two-room stone hut built by the Smithsonian Institute some years ago as a shelter for scientists who stayed there making observations.

WHAT IT IS LIKE ON TOP

It is simple tremendous! To the north and west the view is a continuous landscape of barren rock pushed up from deep in the earth in the ancient past, and now shaped into deep river valleys, glacial cirques, and ragged ranges which extend off into the blue mist of the horizon.

The summit itself is about one and a half acres and is comparatively flat. The almost table-like top is littered with huge granite boulders and slabs which have a distinct type of weathering called nivation — the result of prolonged action by frost. Little if any effect of erosion by water can be seen because nearly all precipitation falls in the form of dry snow rather than rain. Prevailing winds keep it swept clear of deep drifts. What snow does remain disappears mostly through evaporation rather than by melting and stream-type runoff.

Top of Mt. Whitney   Bob Weir

THE NAMING OF MT. WHITNEY

Clarence King, a member of the California State Geological Survey was a flamboyant mountaineer geologist who wanted to be the first person on record to climb the highest peak in the United States. In 1864 he and a companion had to turn back from two attempts due to inclement weather, errors in judging the escarpment of the eastern wall of the peak, and lack of food to continue. He did reach the top of Mt. Tyndall (14,018 ') near Shepherd Pass. In 1871, with a Frenchman, Paul Pinson, he tried again. In his book "Mountaineering in the Sierra Nevada", he described how treacherous and difficult this second venture was. Storm clouds hung low over the Sierra range but a break in the clouds revealed Mt. Tyndall to the north so he thought he succeeded in reaching Mt. Whitney. Excitedly he scratched his name on a coin and planted it under a rock, declaring this peak, 'Mt. Whitney' for his director, Josiah D. Whitney. He told the nation through lectures, media and magazine articles about his great and self-satisfying feat.

The Owens Valley and especially the Lone Pine people were not impressed with these "outsiders" coming in and nosing around naming their mountains and streams, especailly without consulting them, and when they learned how much these government men were making, they were doubly unimpressed. In fact, the mountain had been there and anybody could go up if they wanted to, so why all this fuss and nonsense about this great expedition? In July 1873 Mr. Belshew of Cerro Gordo and Mr. William Goodyear, a state mineralogist, decided to check out the peak that Mr. King was so excited about climbing and naming. They braced themselves for a demanding undertaking from the written accounts. They were dismayed to find that they could ride their mules right up to the top. Then they realized it was Mt. Langley (14,042 '), southwest of Mt. Whitney. The people in Owens Valley were hilarously jubilant. Mr. King was naturally upset on two counts. He had not been the first man to climb the highest peak, and it was a very embarrassing and humiliating situation for him.

Three fishermen, John Lucas, Charles Begole and Albert Johnson worked their way up the escarpment to the top of the higher middle peak and later casually related how they had left a piece of paper in a tin can on the flat-topped granite peak to prove it. They called it Fishermen's Peak. Clarence King was stunned. So in the afternoon of September 1873, a month later, he set out to reach the elusive summit of Mt. Whitney (14,495 ') and found the paper. Another party claimed to have been the first, but later evidence showed they went up after the fishermen.

Mr. King thought the name "Fishermen's Peak" was most undignified for the highest peak in the United States and wanted it named for his boss, Mr. Whitney. After many hours of deliberation and media footage with the three men, King, and the Owens Valley people, the name went from "Fishermen's Peak," to "Dome of the Continent," to "Dome of Inyo" to the final name "Mt. Whitney," as Clarence King had always wanted.

Through the great efforts of the Geological Survey team, including such men as Messrs. King, Whitney, Brewer, Gardner and Cotter, the most difficult task of measuring and exploring the Sierra Nevada was an heroic and remarkable accomplishment. Clarence King was successful in finding Paleozoic fossils in the Inyo Mountains and Owens Valley that proved the last link he needed for his geological theory of the basin region.

THE BASIN AND RANGE COUNTRY   MAC

It is hard to believe looking over the land of this southwestern corner of the great desert that at one time it was filled with inland seas and fresh water lakes. The interconnecting depressions between the ranges were, during the Ice Age, filled to great depths with these lakes. Then as the glaciers receded, the lowest places became the collection basins for the salts, nitrates, and borates in depths of more than a thousand feet. Upon these minerals were washed the muds and rocky debris from neighboring mountains. The most westerly of the ranges, now called the Sierra Nevada, continued to rise until its summits far exceeded its present 14,000 + ' elevation. In general, the Basin and Range country could be characterized as a place where the tearing down forces of nature, such as earthquakes, down-faulting, weather erosion and landslides has been countered by the down-faulting of the basins and the uplifting of its ranges.

As eons passed, with the Sierra Nevada rising higher and higher, the needed moisture to sustain the inland seas and lush vegetation was ultimately stopped. The sea-moistened air and westerly winds from the Pacific Ocean were unable to extend past the Sierra barrier. By the time the winds and clouds carrying the moisture reach the crest, most of the moisture is gone. Thus, in this vast arid region, the annual precipitation in the low valleys and basins averages less than three-to-four inches. In some areas it is less than a half-inch of rainfall which, in the warm to hot dry air, promptly evaporates. Any moisture that does fall on higher slopes and ridges creates many streams and freshets that soon disappear on their downward course. Environmental regions change drastically between the lower basin floors that support creosote, sagebrush and cacti, and the upper mountain areas that receive more moisture, where one finds juniper and pinyon, Jeffrey, limber, and bristlecone pines.

The White-Inyo Range is a single massive and gigantic fault block that is 110 miles long, with an average elevation about 10,000 '. Exceptions are the depressed connecting area of Westgard Pass (7276 ') and White Mountain Peak (14,242 '). The White Mountains contain a dozen peaks well above 11,000 ' elevation while the Inyo Mountains include only a half dozen peaks over 11,000 ' elevation. The rocks are intensely folded and broken by severe earth movements. The southern end of the range is covered with a thick mass of basaltic lava flow with the faulting and erosion prominently visible. The Coso Range and Inyo Mountains are rich in the minerals and ore that have lured prospectors to unearth its treasure, leaving these ranges riddled with old mine sites, shafts, tunnels and tailings. In the southern part of the Inyo Mountains there has been found some 1800 feet of fossil-bearing marine shale and limestone of the Triassic Age. The Sierra Nevada, however, is a mass of granitic rock sculptured by alpine glaciation.

With the White-Inyo Range on the east reaching over 11,000 ' in elevation and the massive block of the Sierra Nevada to the west and the long narrow basin of Owens Valley sandwiched in between, it is a most awesome landscape. The Owens Valley is 100 miles long and ranges from two to eight miles wide. At Lone Pine the elevation is 3700 ' with the Sierra crest at 13,000 ' to 14,000 '. The floor of the valley at Owens Lake is 3000 ' elevation and at the northern end it rises to 8000 '.

Earth movements, both vertical and horizontal are more pronounced along the east front fault line of the Sierra Nevada. The most violent was the earthquake in 1872 when all but two of the buildings in Lone Pine were leveled, killing 27 people. In the space of a few minutes the entire mountain range rose vertically over 12 feet in relation to the valley floor, and horizontally some 20 feet. The fault scarp can be seen on the alluvial apron to the west at the base of the range.

DIMENSIONS OF THE SIERRA

The over-all Sierra block is some 400 miles long and varies from 35 to 80 miles wide covering an area of more than 20,000 square miles. Most of it is between 3000' to 10,000' elevation and supports environmental areas ranging from desert to alpine. It is a single massive block so tilted that it slopes gently to the west from 14,000' along its crest to less than 100' in the San Joaquin Valley. Its east face presents a bold, aggressive frontal escarpment rising an abrupt 10,000' above the Owens Valley. Its total dimensions make it higher, wider, and more spectacular than any other mountain range in the United States.

Twice the length of the Rocky Mountains, it stands 4000' higher above its adjacent valleys than the Rockies do above the Great Plains. Pioneers found this formidable barrier a final challenge on their westward trek. Today visitors can enjoy a top of the world experience crossing the Sierra at Tioga Pass to Yosemite National Park at 9941' elevation, with 12-13,000' peaks surrounding them.

Upon the face of this vast block lies a series of lesser ranges lying in a general northwest to south-east pattern. Most of these would present a bulk of adequate dimension to warrant considerable attention if put into settings by themselves. In the south the Great Western Divide separates the Kern-Kaweah Basins. The 12,000' crest is often mistaken by visitors at Giant Forest to be the main crest of the Sierra Nevada, which lies 14 miles farther east and is 2500 feet higher. The Le Conte-White Divide and Kaiser Ridge separates the Kings and San Joaquin Rivers. In the heart of Yosemite lies the 25-mile-long Cathedral-Ritter Range that includes a score of named and unnamed peaks above 10,000'. All of these minor ranges stand a good 2500 to 4000 feet above their surrounding valley floors. Along the main Sierra Nevada range are found 285 peaks over 12,000', 140 over 13,000' and 11 above 14,000'.

More than a dozen master streams carry the waters of this giant, westward-tilted monolith down into the Central Valley. North are the Feather, Yuba, Mokelume, and Stanislaus Rivers. In Yosemite the Tuolumne and Merced Rivers pass through the outstanding valleys. The waters of the San Joaquin carry the melting snows from the main basin and tributaries covering almost a thousand miles. South out of Kings Canyon and Sequoia National Parks are the Kings, Kaweah and Kern Rivers.

The deepest of the Sierra canyons lie in the heart of the Kings Canyon-Sequoia country. Here the roaring, tumbling streams are enclosed in great granite basins some 5000' to 700' below their surrounding peaks. Into the deepest canyons tumbling cascades and free-falling waters from hanging valleys add their beauty to the wild array.

Following each summer's cloudbursts and thunderstorms the flooded streams carry coarse rock and gravel from the canyons and ravines down the steep slope onto the alluvial apron. This apron is composed of large and small alluvial fans of the eroded materials that wear down the mountain and increase the size of the fans as they spread out. The alluvial apron separates the Sierra Nevada from the Alabama Hills. On the eastern side of Owens Valley the size of the fans are smaller and separate from each other.   MAC

ALABAMA HILLS RECREATIONAL AREA

These picturesque, well photographed hills are on a fault-bound block and stand isolated on the Owens Valley floor. They seem to lose their significance and prominence by the height and size of their neighbor to the west. Some of the rocks are known to be 100 million years old and have remnants of rocks found on the upper part of Mt. Whitney and the White Mountains. Some geologists contend that the Alabama Hills are a fragment of the landscape separated from the uplift of the Sierra block and from the bedrock under Owens Valley by faulting and disruptions. These hills, named for a Civil War Confederate gunboat, have been molded by the volcanic action of eons and more recent earthquakes and have been eroded by fierce winds, glaciers, snow, rain and sand blasting winds.

The hills with their dramatic High Sierra backdrop present an impressive gateway to the Mt. Whitney region. These weathered-carved, colorful, rounded granite formations have been the scene of spellbinding movie scenes of the Old West. In the 1920's Tom Mix, The Lone Ranger and Gene Autry were all riding proud in their saddles, avenging the bad guys and protecting the innocent. Sheriffs have tracked the outlaws with posses through these intriguing canyons. Sections of other classic movies were filmed here — "How the West Was Won," "Springfield Rifle," and "Gunga Din." Good roads lead to excellent photographic and picnic sites. For a good loop trip through the hills, follow the signs for Alabama Hills Scenic Route and Movie Road.

Before the settlers came, these hills were the winter camp of many Paiutes. The fissures and outcroppings of the weathered hills protected them somewhat from the winter storms and cold winds. During the war between the settlers and Indians, one of the last battles was fought here.

On May 24, 1969 some 30,000 acres were dedicated by the Bureau of Land Management to be called the Alabama Hills Recreation Area. Plans are still being made for their protection as well as for the best usage of this historical, photogenic, and scenic ancient part of Owens Valley.

Safeway Store in Lone Pine   Courtesy of East California Museum

THE LONE PINE MINT

Charles H. Aaron, an Englishman who had enough of the sailor's life on the high seas, arrived in California in 1853 and became interested in placer and river gold mining. For years he mined and wrote weekly reports for the "San Francisco Mining and Scientific Press". In 1863 he began studying assaying and metallurgy, especially with regard to the reaction of chemicals that would aid in the amalgamation of silver ores.

In 1867 he invented the 'Aaron Process' for treating silver ore without roasting. He improved his process when working up in Benton, north of Bishop. The great silver find at Cerro Gordo with some 700 silver mines in a square mile radius intrigued him. He moved to Long Pine, away from the lawless tent city in Cerro Gordo, preferring more creature comforts than the rough camp could provide. At first he was involved with the smelting process at the mines as there was difficulty working with such rich ore. When coins were needed he used his knowledge of metallurgy and opened his shop in Lone Pine.

Aarron bought silver that had been through the furnaces at Cerro Gordo, combined it with gold from the Coso mining region, and melted them down. When the metals were pure, he poured them into cold water to become granulated. This material was carefully weighed and divided into small piles — some weighing $86/100$ of an ounce, and some weighing $172/100$ or nearly two ounces. Thus divided, the metal was placed in separate crucibles used for melting substances requiring high heat, and remelted. The boiling metal was then poured into an iron mold. After the liquid cooled and became solid, the new coin was taken out. The $1 coin was ⅛th of an inch thick with rounded edges and somewhat convex, stamped '86' on one side and 'C.A.' under the '$1' on the other. The $2 coin was ¼ " diameter with '172' and 'C.H.A.' under '$2' stamped on it. He made $5, $2, and $1. When the demand for coins slackened he discontinued their manufacture. If found today they would be of great value.

MANZANAR

The name 'Manzanar' provokes memories of the emotional state of the country after Pearl Harbor. Japanese Americans were interned here at the Japanese Relocation Camp. The plaque on the stone guardhouse, still standing, with the oriental-shaped pagoda roof reads:

"In the early part of World War II, 110,000 persons of Japanese ancestry were interned in relocation centers by executive order #9066, issued February 19, 1942. Manzanar, the first of ten such concentration camps, was bounded by barbed wire and guard towers, confining 10,000 persons, the majority being American citizens. May this injustice and humiliation suffered here as a result of hysteria, racism, and economic exploitation never emerge again."

The Japanese farmers created a 22-mile cement-lined irrigation system in some 400 acres of their farm area. There were three dozen varieties of vegetables grown in 1943 with 25 tons of dehydrated vegetables. Fifty-four tons were pickled and 386 tons were stored for the winter. The Japanese bought them at about 26¢ to 34¢ for each person daily.

Beside the stone entrance, the large wooden building that was the auditorium and high school gym during the encampment, houses the Inyo County Equipment Maintenance Station. Some of the old cement foundations are resting among the sagebrush and straggly old trees that are still in the old orchard. Within the fenced area alfalfa is now grown.

Manzanar, from the Spanish word "manazanar", meaning apple orchard, was originally a productive farm community with a school, blacksmith shop, lumber yard, general store and a large packing plant for the exportation of the fruits grown and harvested. From 1910 to 1932 the apple and pear orchards supported an important contribution to the economy of Owens Valley. The warm sun and dry air yielded lush, sweet fruit, some of the finest in the state of California. When the Los Angeles Aqueduct took over the land and the water rights, the orchard dried up and was abandoned. The last harvest was in 1932 and the Mayor of Los Angeles distributed the fruit to the poor.

Manaznar Fruit Packing Plant   Courtesy of East California Museum

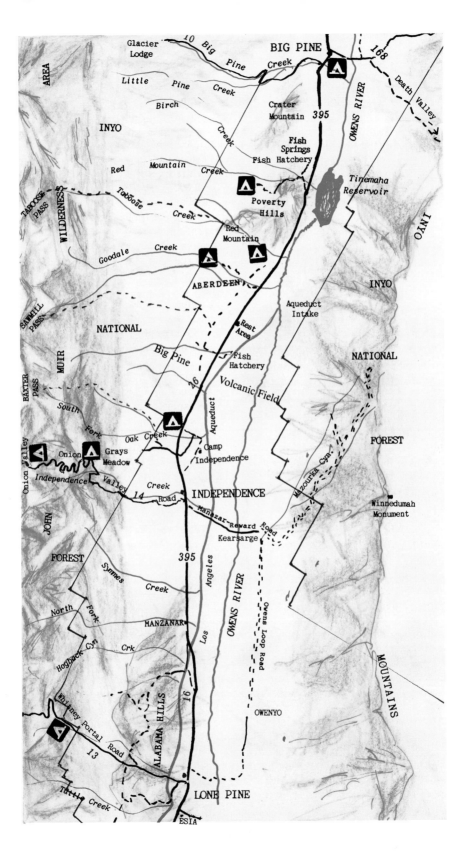

To the right, the Manzanar-Reward Road crosses the Owens River and leads into the Inyo Mountains and the old airport that was used by the U.S. Army during the Japanese encampment. For an impressive sweep of the Sierra escarpment and a different loop trip visit to old ghost town sites and mining activity in the southern Inyo Mountains, a dirt road south follows the old railbed of the narrow gauge Carson and Colorado Railroad to Owenyo. This station was the connecting terminal for the Southern Pacific standard gauge railroad coming north from Mojave to Lone Pine, and the narrow gauge line going from Keeler to Mound House up near Carson City, Nevada. It is now, unfortunately, only the site of what was once an active railroad stop and farm community with many workers. Originally the town was established by the William Penn Colonial Association with some 42 miles of canals and over 13,000 acres of fertile farm lands. The founding Quakers from the eastern seaboard were unaccustomed to such farming conditions and soon sold their homesteads to Los Angeles interests.

For an extended loop trip to Lone Pine via Hwys. 136 and 395, go south to see Dolomite Hills at the base of Inyo Mountains. Dolomite is a marble or limestone rich in magnesium carbonate that is used for decorative purposes.

On the western front of Inyo Mountains gold was discovered in 1878 and the mill was in operation until World War I. The Reward Mine or the Brown Monster group of mines provided the largest source of gold in the area. Later, during the depression years, and during the late 1930's and 1940's the Reward mines were active again when the price of gold was high enough to make it feasible to dig it out of the ground. There were moderate amounts of lead, silver, and copper as well as gold taken from these canyons.

Mt. Whitney Station   *Courtesy of East California Museum*

When Charlotte Barnes lived with her family at Mt. Whitney Station in the 1920's, there was never any lack for amusement. She and her sister would ride the three-wheel hand cart down the tracks to Owens Lake and skate on the dry lake bed. They would jump over the large cracks in the earth. Buster, their red Irish setter, would jump along with them.

On weekends no trains ran so the girls would get up on the freight cars, jump from car to car and run along the tops. The cattle cars had rods to separate the cattle, which they used for acrobatic stunts.

The local school was a rail car on the siding in Owenyo. Desks were installed for the children, who were mostly Mexican. Their fathers worked for the railroad. In the morning the train from Keeler would pick up the girls and take them to school. They were the only passengers. If they all sat on one side of the coach, the conductor would say, "spread out, you'll tip the car over." For a Sunday drive, the family would take the gasoline section car that ran on the tracks down to Keeler and back.

Even though they lived in the only habitable structure in primitive style, with no electricity, indoor plumbing, only a kerosene stove for cooking, and water brought in a tank once a week, mother and girls would be clean with freshly starched dresses and ready for dinner when her Father came home from work.

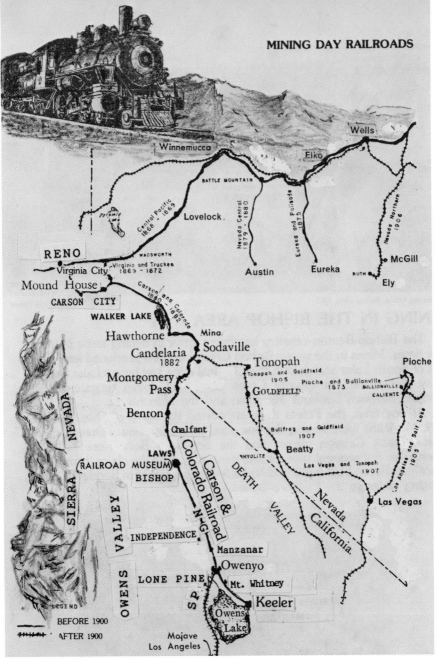

MINING DAY RAILROADS

Wells

Winnemucca

Elko

BATTLE MOUNTAIN

Central Pacific 1868 - 1869

Lovelock

Nevada Central 1879 - 1880

Eureka and Palisade 1875

Nevada Northern 1906

RENO

WADSWORTH

Virginia City

Virginia and Truckee 1869 - 1872

Austin

Eureka

McGill

RUTH

Ely

Mound House

CARSON CITY

Carson and Colorado 1880 - 1882

WALKER LAKE

Mina

Hawthorne

Sodaville

Tonopah

Pioche

Candelaria 1882

Tonopah and Goldfield 1905

Pioche and Bullionville 1873

BULLIONVILLE

Montgomery Pass

GOLDFIELD

CALIENTE

Benton

Bullfrog and Goldfield 1907

Los Angeles and Salt Lake 1905

Chalfant

Beatty

LAWS

(RAILROAD MUSEUM)

RHYOLITE

Las Vegas and Tonopah 1907

BISHOP

Carson & Colorado Railroad N-G

DEATH

NEVADA

SIERRA

INDEPENDENCE

VALLEY

Nevada California

OWENS VALLEY

Manzanar

Owenyo

LONE PINE

Mt. Whitney

S P

Keeler

LEGEND

BEFORE 1900

Owens Lake

AFTER 1900

Mojave
Los Angeles

Las Vegas

Engine 22 - most powerful and biggest engine - broke rails when cold
Courtesy of East California Museum

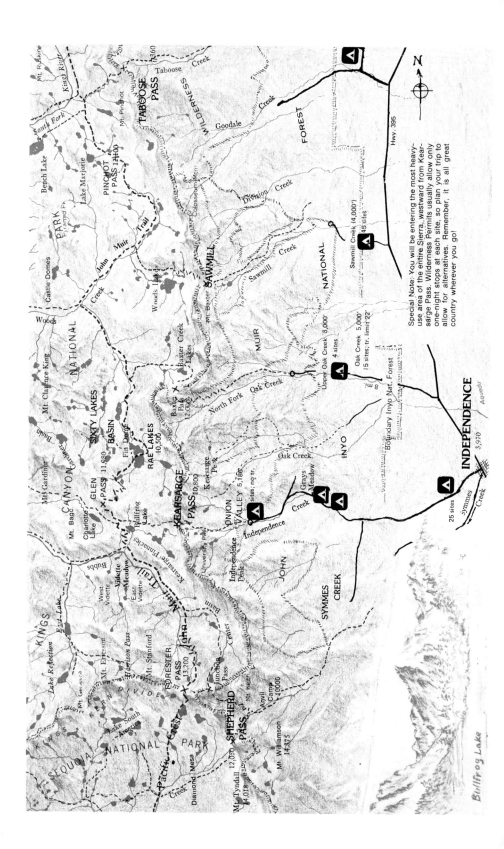

N

Taboose Creek
Mt. Ruskin
Kings River
Taboose
7360
South Fork
TABOOSE PASS
Mt. Pinchot
Goodale
Creek
FOREST

Special Note: You will be entering the most heavy-
use area of the entire Sierra, westward from Kearsarge Pass. Wilderness Permits usually allow only
one-night stops at each site, so plan your trip to
allow for alternatives. Remember, it is all great
country wherever you go!

Hwy. 395

Bench Lake
Lake Marjorie
PINCHOT PASS 12400
Pyramyd Pk.

PARK

Division Creek

Castle Domes
John Muir Trail
Woods Lake
Creek

SAWMILL

Sawmill
Creek
Sawmill Creek (4,000')
45 sites

NATIONAL

Woods
Mt. Clarence King
Creek

Mt. Baxter
MUIR

NATIONAL

Baxter Creek
Lakes

Upper Oak Creek 6,000'
4 sites

Oak Creek 5,000'
15 sites; tr. limit 22'

Mt. Gardiner
Basin
SIXTY LAKES

North Fork
Oak Creek

Boundary Inyo Nat. Forest

8 mi.

INDEPENDENCE

CANYON
Mt. Bago
GLEN PASS 11,980
BASIN
RAE LAKES 10,500
Fin Dome

Oak Creek

INYO

3,970
Aquedu

NATIONAL

Charlotte Lake
Bullfrog Lake
KEARSARGE PASS 10,800
Kearsarge Peak

ONION VALLEY 5,180
4 sites; no tr.

Grays Meadow
Creek

25 sites
Symmes Creek

West Vidette
East Vidette
Bubbs
Muir Trail
Kearsarge Pinnacles

University Pass
Independence
Independence Peak

JOHN

KINGS

Lake Reflection
East Lake
Mt. Ericsson
Center Basin
SYMMES CREEK

Lake Genevra
Harrison Pass
Mt. Stanford
John Muir Trail
Junction Pass

D   I   V   I   D   E
FORESTER PASS 13,200

Lake South America

Mt. Keith
Anvil Camp 10000

KERN

Shepherd Creek
SHEPHERD PASS 12,050
Mt. Tyndall 14,018

PACIFIC CREST TRAIL

Diamond Mesa
Mt. Williamson 14,375

SEQUOIA NATIONAL PARK

Bollfrog Lake

INDEPENDENCE (3925')

Independence Day Parade   MAC

There are several historical homes and buildings in the Inyo County Seat of Independence, which is the third largest town in Owens Valley. Inyo County was established in 1866. The word 'Inyo' is Indian for "dwelling place of a great spirit". The name of the town — originally Putnam's, after one Charles Putnam — was changed to Independence from the name of Camp Independence, that was three miles to the north. It was the first township laid out in named streets with 50'x130' lots, six blocks long and six blocks wide.

The present impressive Inyo County Courthouse in the center of town was built in 1921. The first courthouse was shattered in the 1872 earthquake. The second one built to replace it was destroyed in the July 30th, 1886 fire that swept through the central portion of town. It was then rebuilt in 1887 and that building was used until 1921 when it became too small for the needs of the growing county. The Inyo County Free Library is now housed in the present Courthouse. The library has an extensive and excellent selection of materials on desert life and of Owens Valley history.

In the center of town on Highway 395, near the Courthouse, is the Commander's House. Originally it was on the base of Camp Independence. This eastern-farmhouse-type structure was built in 1872 to replace the camp's adobe building that was demolished by the earthquake. The building is open to the public Friday thru Tuesday from 10 AM to 4 PM. The Camp Independence Hospital Building (not open to the public) also had to be rebuilt after the earthquake. These two structures are all that remain of Camp Independence dwellings. All of the other buildings at the camp were auctioned off and dismantled when the camp was abandoned in 1877, after the Indians were dispersed. The Commander's House and Hospital were then moved into town. The Museum Association completely refurbished the Commander's House in the style of the 1870's.

Mary Austin's house (also not open to the public) is one of historical value as she was the author of "Land of Little Rain". On Market Street is the oldest house in Independence, built in 1865 and known as the Edwards House. It has also been called the Shepherd House and Irwin House.

DEHY COMMUNITY PARK with restrooms, picnic tables and water is at the north end of town. One of the locomotives — Engine 18 of the old Carson & Colorado Railroad — is in the park. This little engine hauled heavy ore from Keeler up the long valley to Benton, then puffed up over the Montgomery Pass to reach Mina and Mound House. Passengers and freight were also carried up and down the line.

The COUNTY CAMPGROUND is located north out of town.

Every Fourth of July there is a colorful home town parade with outhouse races and a bazaar of homemade crafts items, oil paintings, jellies and pies. On late afternoons there is a barbeque and later, when dark, the annual fireworks display. What better place is there to spend Independence Day but in Independence?

EASTERN CALIFORNIA MUSEUM   Little Pine Village   MAC

This museum, a few blocks west of the highway should be a "must" on any visit to Owens Valley, for its historical indoor displays and outdoor exhibits. Inside are old documents, photographs of many historical events, maps, Paiute baskets and arrowheads, guns and uniforms from the camp days, rocks, buttons, dolls, old stoves, and office equipment. One of the most prized relics of the past is the old-fashioned standing music box that uses round metal notched discs. This Regina Rosewood Music Box was made in 1890, bought by the Jack Gunn family from Sherman Clay in San Francisco. A run-through of the 1837 song, *When Robins Come to Town*, is possible by asking the attendant. Books on many subjects pertaining to the eastern Sierra country — anthropology, history, geology, up-to-date information on trails and roads can be purchased here.

Outdoors on the grounds are old metal and iron farming equipment, large old buckets and pipes, wagons from mining days and "The Little Pine Village", a street of old buildings and houses each with interesting artifacts. Pets and smoking are not allowed in either the indoor or outdoor museums. Picnic tables are provided under shade trees. The museum is open Sunday, Monday, Thursday and Friday from 12 noon to 4 PM, and on Saturdays from 10 AM to 4 PM.

Third Courthouse   Courtesy of East California Museum

WINNEDUMAH PAIUTE MONUMENT (8369')

There are various legends concerning the granite monolith that stands about 60 feet high and some 40 feet in diameter at its base, up in the Inyo Mountains east of Independence. The tale goes that Winnedumah, a medicine man and brother of Tinemaha, for whom the reservoir, creek, road and Mt. Tinemaha (12,561') were named, was turned into stone high on the crest of the Inyo Mountains so he would be able to watch over his people, the Paiutes. He went up the mountain to find his brother who had been slain in battle. At the top of the mountain he prayed to Taupee, the God of the Paiutes, for the deliverance of his people.

To see the monument, stand outside of the Eastern California Museum, on the steps. Look towards the Courthouse's flagpole, then straight up to the top of Inyo Mountains where a small thumb-like boulder or protrusion can be seen on the horizon. That is the Winnedumah Paiute Monument.

EAST OF INDEPENDENCE

Just after the aqueduct crossing, traveling east of Independence, the fault scarp from the 1872 earthquake can be seen as the road dips down about 15 feet. After crossing the Owens River the site of the old railroad station stop at Kearsarge is beside the old Carson & Colorado Railroad bed. Only a few scattered bricks are left. It might seem lonely now, but in the late 1800's and early 1900's it was a bustling area with trains coming and going up and down the Owens Valley from the mining and farming activities carrying produce from the fruit orchards.

Up in Mazourka Canyon the dry placer method of mining was used to secure gold between 1894 and 1906. Then, during the depression years, the mine tailings were worked again. A few of the old diggings still can be seen. One of the most productive was the Blue Bell Mine. A journey up the canyon can be made by jeep or four-wheeler. Check the map to see the various routes that can be taken. In springtime the wildflowers are most outstanding, with the snow-capped Sierra Crest against the western sky. There is no water up this canyon, so be sure to take enough for this strenuous uphill climb. One of the most unusual aspects of Mazourka Canyon is that it runs parallel with the Owens River — north and south — and not east and west as do most other canyons in the Sierra or White Inyo Mountains.

ROAD TO ONION VALLEY — 14 miles   MAC

In summer the road ascends through a beautiful wildflower garden with rosy pink fireweed, yellow and orange corn and tiger lilies, dainty pink mountain hemp and blue monkshood on either side of the road. The great crest of the Sierra is ahead, with Mt. Williamson (14,375'), the second highest peak in the Sierra Nevada, to the left. After entering the John Muir Wilderness Area the road switchbacks up Independence Creek Canyon leading to the lovely Onion Valley. Two campgrounds are along the road up the alluvial apron — Lower Gray Meadow and Upper Gray Meadow Campground, open from March to October. The sites are nice, some with trees for wind protection. Although rather small, they do have a spectacular view of Owens Valley and across to the White Mountains. From the Upper Gray Meadow Campground there is a trail leading up to Kearsarge Peak.

At Onion Valley there is a campground with tables, stoves, piped water, open from June to September. Solar toilets have been placed at these high altitude campgrounds up Independence Creek Canyon. Onion Valley has backcountry parking and a Ranger Station, open from July to September.

The ride up to Onion Valley makes a good side trip with the Sierra crest and canyons ahead. It's especially beautiful in the evening when looking back over Owens Valley and Independence and watching the sunset's glow diminish as it creeps up the White-Inyo Mountains.

KEARSARGE MINE

Gold quartz was found on the shoulder of Kearsarge Peak in 1864 by Thomas Hill, a woodcutter. Estimates on the potential wealth was very high so investment money flourished. The mine even had a 10-stamp mill to process the ore. However, it never developed as a paying operation because the value of the ore was not as high as initially assayed. Both gold and silver were mined. The Silver Spout Mine (11,500') was on the south side just below the summit while the Red Montis Mine (12,000') was on the north side of the eastern shoulder of the peak. Many difficulties beset the mining operations including an avalanche that killed many people and destroyed most of the buildings. The remaining people moved down to the present site of Kearsarge. It is believed that the ore was never fully extracted from these high altitude, frozen shafts.

Little remains today among the rocks and sagebrush along the trail that leads up to the mines but parts of the old stone buildings might still be standing.

CALIFORNIA BIGHORN SHEEP

The California Bighorn Sheep Zoological Area includes the high eastern Sierra between Tunnabora Peak near Mt. Whitney to Mt. Perkins, north of Sawmill Pass. Once very common in the high mountains and desert plateaus of the west, the bighorn sheep are now quite rare. Depletion of herds was partly due to kills for meat by miners and early settlers. Another larger factor, however, was the take-over by domestic flocks of sheep from Europe that introduced diseases to the bighorn and over-grazed their food supply. Small remnants of herds are now found along the high eastern front of the Sierra, especially in this Zoological Area. The sheep's preference for alpine plant food and their shy tendencies to seek privacy have somewhat stabilized their existence. Travel restrictions and peoples' concern are needed to preserve the seclusion of these high wilderness dwellers.

SHEPHERDS PASS

Backpacking up to Shepherds Pass (12,018 ') involves a long, hot, rough trail similar to all the eastern Sierra entries into Kings Canyon country. It goes through a high desert area of pinyon pines and sagebrush at the lower elevations, then switchbacks up steeply to a ridge between Symnes and Shepherd Creeks. Water is scarce until you reach the upper level. Anvil Camp (10,000 ') is a good place for an overnight stop. Symnes Creek Campground has been closed permanently since the fire of 1985 that destroyed the camp. Once over the crest, it is downhill all the way along Tyndall Creek and into the U-shaped Upper Kern River Canyon with its beautiful Milestone Lake and South America Lake Basins.

KEARSARGE PASS

The most popular, as well as easiest, entry into the southern Kings Canyon country is via the Kearsarge Pass (11,823 '). But, because it is so popular and easy, reservations for the Wilderness Permit should be made early as the quotas fill up fast. There are limitations on camping as well as on trail travel in this area. Exploring this most beautiful section of the Sierra and the John Muir-Pacific Crest Trail country in the late spring, early or late summer, or early fall should find it somewhat less congested than in top season. There are other alternative routes, not as desirable, but at least providing a way to get over the Sierra Crest into the backcountry.

The Kearsarge Pass route into the spectacular Rae Lakes and Sixty Lakes Basin follows the old Paiute Indian trail. It is a moderate, four-mile climb from Onion Valley roadend to the pass, then an easy descent to Bullfrog Lake and the junction with the John Muir-Pacific Crest Trail. There is no camping at Bullfrog Lake but check for available overnight camping at Kearsarge Lakes. No wood fires are allowed in these areas. The remote sky blue lakes, sparkling streams, granite walls and the sublime alpine atmosphere does make for an experience to remember.

The alternate routes are via Shepherd and Forester Passes, Baxter Pass (12,051 ') and Sawmill Pass (11,347 '). They are truly secondary routes as they are not too well developed or maintained, and all involves long, arduous ascents. Rigid trail regulations apply through the narrow corridor of the California Bighorn Zoological Area. The trail from the roadend at the North Fork of Oak Creek, ascending to Baxter Pass, is a steep dry climb. But travelling through Jeffrey pine groves and other shaded cover along the creek make this trail more pleasurable than the exposed long, steep and rough climb up to Sawmill Pass.   *Kearsarge Pass*   *Rocky Rockwell*

CAMP INDEPENDENCE

Site of Camp Independence   MAC

Schabbel Lane, about three miles above Independence, is the road to Camp Independence. A historical marker indicates the site where a few badly eroded caves can be seen. In the ravine is where the soldiers had to dig out caves to live in. A little farther down Schabbel Lane is the Soldiers' Cemetery where a few white monuments still stand. Most of the soldiers were buried where they fell in the war with the Indians, and those who were buried here during the campaign days were removed and shipped to the Presidio in San Francisco. The soldiers buried here now were veterans who lived in the area, having remained when the camp was abandoned.

THE INDIAN CAMPAIGN

The Paiutes were a friendly people. Few incidents of friction occurred between them and the white settlers who invaded their land before 1860. However, in the winter of 1861 a cowhand shot a starving Indian who was stealing a cow grazing in his pinyon pines hunting area. The Indians retaliated by killing a white settler and the war was on. By May the Indians, being more numerous than the settlers, controlled the valley. Miners prospecting the hills, and the settlers and cattlemen were terrified and pleaded with the U.S. Army for help.

In March 1862 a small volunteer detachment under Lt. Colonel George S. Evans came into the valley and rescued a group of settlers who were beseiged at Putnam's Fort and Trading Post, which is now Independence. Charles Putnam built a stone house that was considered somewhat of a fort for the neighboring white men. From Putnam's, Evans went north to Bishop Creek where the Indians were well established in strong, natural positions. Evans did not have sufficient equipment or provisions for a large campaign against the well fortified natives, so he returned to Los Angeles. In June of the same year he returned with a larger, well-equipped force of some 200 men from the Second Cavalry, California Volunteers. They had 42 wagons that carried a two-months supply. Initially Evans had planned to set up a base at Pine Creek (near Big Pine), but found that Putnam's stone house had been burned and everything had been carried away leaving only a blackened shell.

The swollen Owens River and streams from the melting Sierra snows made it impossible to get the wagons and provisions farther north than Oak Creek, about three miles north of Independence. Since the detachment had reached the banks of the stream and did not attempt to cross on July 4th, Evans decided to name the base "Camp Independence".

It was a difficult fight against the Indians. They were crafty, diligent fighters who were protecting their homeland with knowledge about the terrain that was foreign to the soldiers. It was particularly tough on the soldiers, who did not have time to build housing and had to live in caves dug in the walls of the large ravine. In the fall the camp was able to devote time to constructing adobe buildings on the north side of the creek where the topography offered more favorable protection from ambush by the Indians. Snow came early in the fall of 1862 and it was to be one of the bitterest winters in years. A supply train from Los Angeles managed to arrive in time to save the men who were really suffering.

In May 1863, the Paiutes' "Chief George" asked for a truce. Nine hundred Indians wearily walked into camp under a white flag and acknowledged defeat. They were then rounded up and taken by force to be escorted from Owens Valley to San Sebastian, near Fort Tejon. Peace seemed to come to the valley. Many more settlers came in and mining activities increased. The post was abandoned since the Army felt the war was over despite the fact that some of the Indians did not like the restricted life of the reservation and returned to their homes in Owens Valley.

The Indians became restless when many more people moved into their homeland. They murdered Mary McQuire and her son, Johnny at Haiwee Meadows where there was a small way station, which the Indians burned. The settlers at Lone Pine repaid the Paiutes by massacring some 40 men, women and children and destroying their meager winter food supply. The Army then sent in three companies of infantry and one of cavalry to show their force. With the Army garrison in the valley the remaining Indians were compelled to subdue and give up the struggle. Finally the post was closed on July 9, 1877.

MAC

MT. WHITNEY FISH HATCHERY

The road to the west at Schabbel Lane leads to Mt. Whitney Fish hatchery, which no longer produces and grows fish. The whirling disease was found in the fish a few years ago. However, the grounds are open daily from 8 AM to 5 PM where there are walks around the lovely building and rather large pond. Ducks are willing to take the food that is provided and some large king size breeding trout lazily swim about in this beautiful setting.

Farther up on the road is the NORTH OAK CREEK CAMPGROUND with tent and small RV spaces, open all year. From here the trail takes off up along the North Fork of Oak Creek to Baxter Pass (12,051 '). No fish are stocked along this creek.

FORT INDEPENDENCE CAMPGROUND

Just past the Fish Hatchery Road, to the west, is the RV Campground, situated on the Mesa in the Indian Reservation. There are electrical and water hookups, dump station, tables, stoves and flush toilets. It is open all year.

BIG PINE VOLCANIC FIELD

The cinder cones and blackish basaltic lava flows seen on both sides of the highway are part of the Big Pine Volcanic Field. Basaltic lava is about 50% silica, which freezes at a lower temperature, is less explosive than rhyolite, and is rarely used for glass. Older rocks like rhyolite, an acidic volcanic rock that is the lava form of granite, cool faster to produce glass. Some rhyolite and lippllus, a glassy fragment thrown out in a volcanic eruption, can be found among the basaltic debris in this field. The road crosses the lava field at Taboose Creek.

SAWMILL CREEK ROAD

The road to the west leads to Tinnemaha Road and Division Creek Powerhouse, which generates electricity from the waters of Division Creek. From there the Sawmill Pass Trail crosses the alluvial apron, ascending along Sawmill Creek and Lake to reach the Sawmill Pass (11,347'). From the Pass the trail leads to beautiful Woods Lake and the John Muir-Pacific Crest Trail country.

There are over ten volcanic cones in various sizes across Owens Valley from the Sierra base to the Inyo Mountains. Some are over 100,000 years old while others are as recent as 10,000 years ago. Most of them are on the alluvial apron projected from the Sierra or from the lower bedrock slopes of the Inyo Range. The basaltic rocks in the flows are extremely rough, hard-burned slags. The Little Lakes Lava Field and the Big Pine Volcanic Flow are not the same as the Mammoth-Mono Volcanic Field to the north, which is a rhyolite and rhyodacitic granite base.

ROADSIDE REST AREA

Within the black rock lava fields, the Rest Area has picnic tables under shade trees, modern restrooms and facilities for handicapped, phone and an RV dump station. The next rest area north is 78 miles between Mammoth and June Lakes.

ABERDEEN

Aberdeen Resort, on Goodale Creek, was named for a station stop on the Carson & Colorado Railroad. There must have been a Scotsman in charge who initially named the station stop, as Aberdeen was named for the city of northeast Scotland. The resort is now a mobile home park.

The station site is about a mile north and east on Taboose Creek Road. This was the initial starting point of the Los Angeles Aqueduct and is the intake point of the Owens River to the water system. When the river was cut off at Aberdeen the waters from all the marshes, sloughs, and river that fed the springs were cut out. The old springs, along with the vegetation and habitat have all disappeared.

BICYCLE TRIPS   MAC

There are several possible bicycle trips east of Owens River starting at Black Rock Fish Hatchery going north to the Aberdeen Station Road, returning south via Tinnemaha and Sawmill Creek Roads. From Aberdeen bicycle trips can be made along Tinnemaha Road to Poverty Hills, south down to Sawmill Creek, over to Black Rock Fish Hatchery, returning along the Fish Hatchery Spring Road, just east of Highway 395. There are dirt roads to explore up Goodale, Taboose, Red Mountain and Fuller Creeks. Spring and autumn would be the best time to bike in this open high desert environment.

NAMES OF CREEKS

Many creeks flowing eastward from the Sierra were named for pioneer families who settled in this part of Owens Valley: Shepherd, Symnes, Goodale, Clancy, and Thibault. Taboose comes from the Indian word for an edible ground nut they found along Division Creek, while Tinemaha is for the Paiute leader and brother of Winnedumah.

TABOOSE CREEK ROAD

From the roadend of Taboose Creek Road, a trail goes up the long, hot, dry approach to Taboose Pass (11,366') and enters the upper basin of the South Fork of the Kings River. Once you've mastered the ascent, the view is most rewarding. Spread out below in Owens Valley is the rugged black Big Pine Volcanic Field with the massive White-Inyo Mountains on the other side. To the west you look into the upper basin of the South Fork of the Kings River with a view down the rugged, rocky, impassable Muro Blanco Canyon. Mt. Ruskin (12,920') stands out to the right with Striped Mountain (13,160') to the south. It is magnificent.

GOODALE CREEK CAMPGROUND and
TABOOSE CREEK CAMPGROUND

These two high desert campgrounds have spaces for tent and RV units, some with young cottonwoods growing for future shade. There is no potable water. Campfire permits are required. Goodale is open from May to October and Taboose is open all year. Both creeks are stocked with trout for good fishing.

The view south over the Owens Valley and up the fans to the Sierra peaks is outstanding. Very early on a summer morning when cool mountain breezes gently caress the land, suddenly a pink glow touches the tips of the western crest. Slowly and silently the dawn's blush creeps down the entire western slope and fan, welcoming another day. By the time the sun's full rays reach the valley floor, the heat of the day begins.

RED MOUNTAIN

Red Mountain (5188 '), to the west, was formed by an explosion of red cinders from fissures at Goodale Mountain. The cone is about 600 feet high above the alluvial apron. The red fragments of lava cinders are angular with some chunks over six inches in diameter. The mountain has been so eroded by weathering through the years, as well as being partly buried by alluvial materials, that a perfect symmetrical cone has been created. For a closer look at the beautiful cone, take the road to Fish Springs and circle south around Poverty Hills to the campground on Tinemaha Creek.

TINEMAH CREEK CAMPGROUND is open all year, with well water and pit toilets. It makes an excellent camp in the early spring or fall when the weather is moderate. It is on the southwest side of Poverty Hills. For a good view of the Big Pine Volcanic Field, Tinemaha Reservoir and Red Mountain, take a walk up to the top of Poverty Hills near the Microwave Relay Towers.

POVERTY HILLS

Poverty Hills was named for the prospectors who were unsuccessful in their attempts to find paydirt near Fish Springs in the 1860's. Their slim pickings led to poverty. Strangely enough, these hills were not formed by volcanic action like the land around them but rather by isolated uplifts, resulting in fault-bound blocks made up of ancient granite and marble bedrock.

On the east side of the highway, another large cinder cone with many small ones clustered around was formed from a vent in the fault along the base of the Inyo Mountains.

TINEMAHA RESERVOIR, actually part of the Owens River, is a large collecting basin and part of the Los Angeles Aqueduct System.

TULE ELK VIEWPOINT

About three miles north of Taboose Creek is the turnoff road to a reserve that maintains a refuge for the tule elk that are now found here and in Colusa County, north of San Francisco. They are also known as dwarf or California elk *(Cervus Nonnodes)*. They are a deerlike animal, with a large almost-white rump patch. The male is larger than the female, with great spreading antlers which are shed every year. The female has no antlers. Both sexes are much smaller and paler in color than the Wapiti or Rocky Mountain elk. This species is not a high mountain animal but likes lower, warmer elevations and climates. Signs along the highway show where some elk may be seen.

Before 1860 the tule elk lived in marshes and plains in both the San Joaquin and Sacramento Valleys in great numbers. Hunters gradually killed off many and farmers damaged their feeding ground with cultivated lands so the elk were almost extinct. Today they exist in a wild state in places such as this elk reserve in sheltered Owens Valley. Early morning and late afternoon are the most likely times for seeing them when they are feeding. During the hot midday hours they tend to rest in the shade or lay in the tall grasses.

At FISH SPRINGS, when water was available for farming, the Red Mountain Ranch produced beautiful apples, peaches and grapes. The farmers at that time enjoyed sufficient water, a long hot growing season with excellent soil and very few bugs. The biggest handicap was transporting their produce to market. During the active mining days, the crops were consumed locally or within freighting distances, such as up to Cerro Gordo, Aurora and Virginia City. The Carson & Colorado Railroad transported the produce, although longer hauls as far away as Los Angeles made the transportation cost expensive. Eventually it became unprofitable for the farmers to continue.

BIG PINE COUNTRY
Middle Glacier   *Rocky Rockwell*

The outstanding features of Big Pine country are the glaciers. The Palisade Glacier (14,242´) is the largest in the Sierra with an area covering some three-fourths of a square mile. It was first ascended by J.N. LeConte in 1903. The Middle Palisade Glacier at the head of the South Fork of Big Pine Creek is smaller, but just as jagged and impressive with its thin serrated ridge. F.P. Farquhar and A.F. Hall were the first to climb this glacier in 1921. Split Mountain (14,058´) which was once referred to as South Palisade was first climbed in 1887 by a party led by Frank Saulque. The Palisade Crest (13,520´) is a grand example of its name. With capped pinnacles it has small glaciers below that melt into the South Fork of the Big Pine Creek. This crest was first climbed by John and Ruth Mendenhall in 1954.

Typical of the Sierra glaciers that lie close up against shaded north walls of the Sierra escarpment, these are the most southerly glaciers in the United States. The large mass of snow and ice that was formed on these north walls, where the rate of snowfall constantly exceeds the rate at which the snow melts, moves slowly down the mountain slope until it melts or breaks away at the glacier's tongue. At one time, during the Ice Age, the glaciers extended down Big Pine Creek to First Bridge Campground (5100´). The glaciers are still active, moving in one season perhaps as much as 40 feet. The milky green waters of the First, Second and Third Lakes below Palisade Glacier are evidence of their action, grinding granite boulders into fine "glacier flour". In these basins lie magnificent, gentle wilderness in all its natural beauty.

There are seven main lakes in the Big Pine Lake Basin, with First Lake being only three miles from roadend, reached by a moderate climb. It is about seven and a half miles from roadend to Palisade Glacier with very strenuous hiking, especially beyond the lake basin. Plan at least two days to make a round trip visit to the glacier.

The waters of Big Pine Creek have two distinct run-offs, the first with the spring thaw of snows swelling the streams, then again when the heat of summer melts the tongue of the glacier. Fishing in both the streams and lakes in Big Pine Lakes Basin and up the South Fork is extremely good for eastern brooks, rainbow trout, and some golden. There are campgrounds and backcountry parking at the roadend.

No trails or mountain passes lead from Big Pine Creek across the glaciers into Kings Canyon National Park. The only trail to the John Muir-Pacific Crest Trail is via Bishop Creek. From the roadend the trail heads north, follows around Baker Lake, goes over the ridge to Green Lake, and down to South Lake where it picks up the trail leading over Bishop Pass (12,000´) to Dusy Basin and Creek, junctioning with the famous trail.

BIG PINE (3985')

The group of large pine trees that Big Pine was named for in the 1860's are no longer standing. In 1864 a sawmill built near the First Bridge Campground on Big Pine Creek served the mines and towns in the Owens Valley. Lumber was hauled by hand-built wagons pulled by teams of oxen. The large wheels had iron rims with wooden spokes, large enough to carry the weight of the cargo. During the late 1860's it was a common sight to see lumber being hauled down the Owens Valley all the way to Cerro Gordo, or up to Aurora, Nevada, or over the White-Inyo Westgard Pass to White Mountain City.

Big Pine, the fourth largest city in Owens Valley, is the entrance to three special, varied tours: to view glaciers along the eastern escarpment of the Sierra, to see the oldest living trees, and to take a circle trip around the White Mountains.

There are services for the visitor — groceries, gas, cafes, and motels. Just north of town, past the Highway 168, is Klondike Lake, a recent summer swimming, sailboating and water skiing lake which is open to the public.

Glacier Lodge
Barbara Gray

BIG PINE CREEK

GLACIER LODGE, open all year, has groceries, ice, fishing supplies and firewood in the store. There are rooms in the Lodge and cabins for rent. There is a restaurant, and showers for a small fee. The trout pond is regularly stocked. In winter the Lodge is closed Tuesdays and Wednesdays.

GLACIER PACK TRAIN offers horseback rides up to the glaciers, trips up Big Pine Creek and to Baker Lake. Longer excursions into the backcountry can be made via Sawmill or Taboose Passes going into the Kings Canyon National Park. The Stewarts at the pack station recommend two days to view the glacier, camping overnight near Fifth Lake, since there is a two-mile hike up to the glacier after leaving the horses.

BIG PINE TRAILER PARK on Glacier Lodge Road also is open all year. There are camping and trailer hookups, rentals, RV tank disposal, propane, firewood and showers. The trout pond is regularly stocked and there is a swimming pool.

Campgrounds are situated along the Glacier Lodge Road. Check the campground chart at the back of the book for specifics.

At the north end of Big Pine on Highway 395, near the junction with Highway 168 where a large sequoia tree stands, is BIG PINE TRIANGLE CAMPGROUND. It is open from mid-April through November.

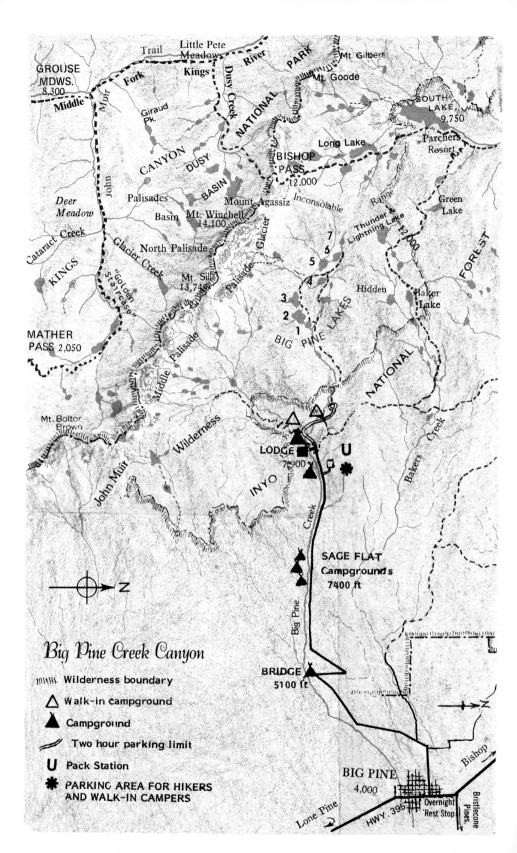

Big Pine Creek Canyon

Wilderness boundary

△ Walk-in campground

▲ Campground

Two hour parking limit

U Pack Station

✳ PARKING AREA FOR HIKERS
AND WALK-IN CAMPERS

Big Pine, 1914   *Courtesy of East California Museum*

CAL TECH'S RADIO OBSERVATORY

Off to the east at the base of the White Mountains are three large discs of the Owens Valley Observatory. There are two 90-foot radio "ears" and "eyes", and one 130' dish antennae. These discs, placed on an 1800' railroad track, have been able through radio waves to receive signals from outer space providing knowledge of the universe. Built in 1960 by the California Institute of Technology, funded by the Office of Naval Research, the discs travel on tracks to pick up from many angles the out-in-space radio waves. Owens Valley was selected as an ideal site for such a project since it lies between two mountain ranges and there is no interference from man-made radio or television waves. Authorized personal only are allowed on the site. These powerful telescopes have discovered stars that are over six billion light years away. The science of radio astronomy is fairly new, and involves the study of radio wave lengths emanating from other planets and galaxies.

North of Big Pine is a sign "Grand Army of the Republic, Highway 395", named for the men who fought so long ago for the North in the Civil War. The slavery issue was important to the settlers even out in California, and county boundaries were determined by the varying community factions.

KEOUGHS HOT SPRINGS

Three artesian springs feed the beautiful swimming pool at Keoughs Hot Springs. The continuous flowing water gushes out over one million gallons per day at 127 °F. and is cooled to 90 °F. for the pool. The overflow runs down the alluvial fan in Hot Ditch and eventually mixes with Freeman Creek flowing into the Owens River. Keough was the name of a pioneer family who homesteaded and lived in this area for many years. The Mobile Home Park at the Hot Springs do have spaces for overnighters with complete hookups. There is no public telephone.

Keoughs Hot Springs is a membership swimming club costing $50 for 20 tickets to be used by adults only. It is open all year from 7 AM to 10 PM, but closed on Mondays and Thursdays. Monday is cleaning day when the pool is empty and looks like a giant bathtub. There is no unpleasant sulphurous odor from the artesian wells as there is down at Dirty Socks Hot Springs. Dick Denniss, the owner says, "this is the most body-loving water and finest swimming pool in the entire state of California."

THE ANCIENT BRISTLECONE PINE FOREST

It seems that the perversity of the Bristlecone Pines in growing where conditions are the most difficult must, in some way, contribute to their ability to survive. These conditions have aided them to escape man's destructive intrusion into their environs. Their lifespan on the rugged crests is much longer than of those that grow in more sheltered places where soil and precipitation have been more ample. In the dolomite (limestone) soil of the White Mountains' higher elevations are found the oldest trees, up in Patriarch Grove. It seems a most fitting phenomenon that earth's oldest living things cling to life with far reaching roots to gather their strength from soils made up from fossil beds of ancient sea life.

In contrast to the massive giant sequoias located on the western Sierra slopes, or to the towering coast redwoods, the bristlecone seldom reach more than 25 to 30 feet tall. Many of these develop great matts of limbs that hug the ground so that winter snows pile up around them, sheltering them from the ice-laden Sierran winds.

To see the Patriarch Grove (11,000'), the northernmost group, the total mileage is 35, one way. This is a remote area with no services, so be well supplied with water, gas, spare tire, jacket, lunch, camera and film. The only campground is at Grandview (8500') about ten miles past the entrance. The Pinyon Picnic Area (8000') is a little over three miles. At the Sierra Overlook (9000') there is an absolutely tremendous view of the grand Sierra expanse extending from Mt. Whitney at the south to Mt. Dana in Yosemite National Park to the north. Owens Valley lies peacefully below, while to the east lies Deep Springs Valley with Death Valley peaks on the horizon. Displays indicate some of the more important Sierra peaks and geological features.

The Schulman Grove (10,000') is a general activity center with radio contact to Owens Valley Forest Service Station, picnic tables, restrooms, Visitor Information Center and parking. Two easy, self-guided walks enable visitors to explore the area on their own. The twisted and beautifully formed trunks of these old trees (the oldest is 4600 years) especially delight the artist and photographer. Limber pines are also seen in this area and can be distinguished from the bristlecone by the short tufts at the ends of their branches. Bristlecone needles run back along the branch.

North of Schulman Grove the road is dirt, narrow and sometimes only one-way (the traffic is usually light), but safe if driven with care. The last three miles is rather exhilerating as the steep climb up through the burly bristlecones in open forest is rough. But enjoy the exploratory-type adventure. Heavy or long RV's should never attempt this part. In some places the road traverses high, open sagebrush-covered country where, in season, wildflowers, birds, small animals and deer are frequently seen. There is a large parking and picnic area at the end of the road on this cold, windy, rugged mountainside. It is only a short, easy walk to "The Patriarch", the world's largest bristlecone pine tree.

The magnificent Patriarch is about 1500 years old. Its trunk is a composite of several units resulting in a circumference of 36'-8". The setting is truly a photographers paradise. Standing alone with no obstructions, beauty is found in the minute lines of the old, eroded, weatherbeaten trunks in extreme closeups or of twisted, gnarled limbs silhouetted against great piles of cumulus clouds in a deep blue sky of summer. Views from here are extensive with misty blue valleys below and layers of blue turning to gray in the far distant mountains.

Because these pines are intolerant to shade and never form dense stands, they are scattered on slopes where the snow melts early and evaporation is rapid. Fortunately fires seldom destroy them as there is little or no underbrush to feed a fire.

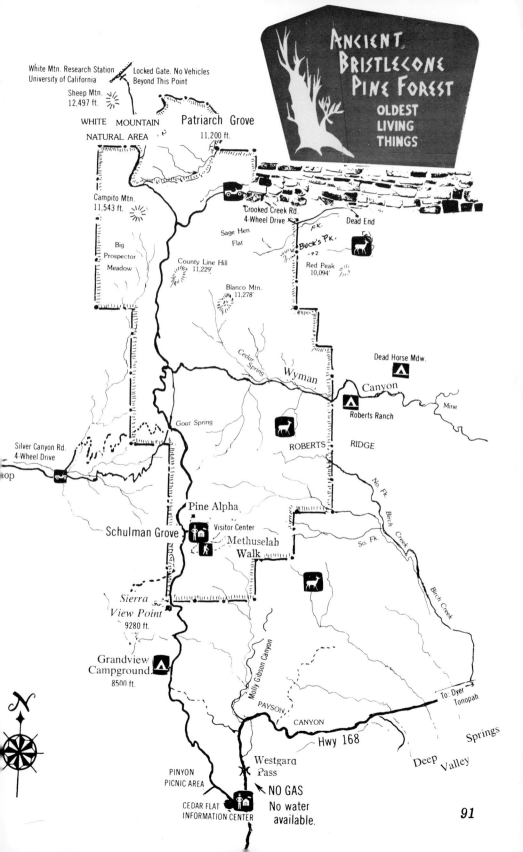

ANCIENT BRISTLECONE PINE FOREST
OLDEST LIVING THINGS

White Mtn. Research Station
University of California

Locked Gate. No Vehicles
Beyond This Point

Sheep Mtn.
12,497 ft.

WHITE MOUNTAIN
NATURAL AREA

Patriarch Grove
11,200 ft.

Campito Mtn.
11,543 ft.

Crooked Creek Rd.
4-Wheel Drive

Dead End

Sage Hen
Flat

FK.
BUCK'S PK.

Big
Prospector
Meadow

County Line Hill
11,229'

Red Peak
10,094'

Blanco Mtn.
11,278'

Cedar Spring

Wyman

Dead Horse Mdw.

Canyon

Mine

Goat Spring

Roberts Ranch

ROBERTS   RIDGE

Silver Canyon Rd.
4-Wheel Drive

No. Fk. Birch Creek

op

Pine Alpha

So. Fk.

Schulman Grove

Visitor Center

Methuselah
Walk

Birch Creek

Sierra
View Point
9280 ft.

Grandview
Campground.
8500 ft.

Molly Gibson Canyon

To: Dyer
Tonopah

PAYSON

CANYON

Springs

Hwy 168

Deep Valley

PINYON
PICNIC AREA

Westgard
Pass

NO GAS
No water
available.

CEDAR FLAT
INFORMATION CENTER

N

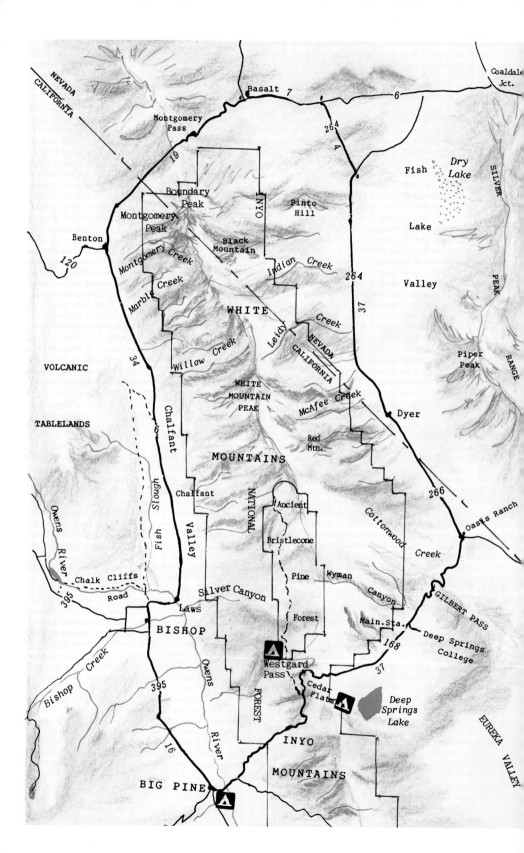

Bristlecone Pine
Rocky Rockwell

WHITE MOUNTAIN CIRCLE TRIP

For an interesting spring or fall auto tour, take the 160-mile trip around the White Mountains. The scenery is varied with both desert and mountain views and good roads. It takes about a half-day, depending on how much time is spent picnicking or sightseeing. In the spring wildflowers abound along the route and give an added measure to the excursion.

After crossing the Owens River on Highway 168 out of Big Pine, and passing the paved road to the California Technical Radio Telescopes, a road leading to Death Valley turns off to the right. The climb up through knobby hills covered with sage, rabbitbrush and trumpet vine leads to the old toll station at Tollhouse Springs. Miners were charged 25¢ for a rider with horse, and $1.00 for a wagon with two animals, to use this road. When the old rough road proved inadequate for the increased mining activity, this toll road through the pass was built to service the Deep Springs Mining District.

Upon entering the winding, narrow ascent through the pinyon forest, look for the greenish lichen caressing the dark metamorphic rock. These rocks are older than the granite of the Sierra by some hundred million years. The canyon was carved out by rushing streams, breaking the bedrock and exposing the tilted layers on either side.

At 7000' is Cedar Flat Plateau where the Cedar Flat Group Campground is situated among the pinyon and juniper trees. In mining days junipers were called cedars. Just beyond is the junction and entrance road to the Bristlecone Pine Forest. Westgard Pass (7271') was named for L. Westgaard who envisioned a transcontinental highway through here. It is no transcontinental highway. However, it is a most pleasurable drive through varied scenic wonders, not the least of which is a view of the Palisade Glacier to the west. This depression in the White-Inyo Range provided an easy crossing for Indians, prospectors and miners between the Owens Valley and Deep Springs Valley.

Just past the summit the road enters a roller-coaster type descent through narrow, dark basaltic lava protrusions on either side of the winding road through Payson Canyon. After the 6000' sign there is a spectacular valley view of the basin beyond and Deep Springs Lake to the right. The varying greenish blue or reddish colors edged by the white salts of the spring-fed lake stands out in the dried sagebrush country surrounding it. Brine shrimp feeding in the lake produce the reddish tone. Potash was once mined here. The long, straight road across the valley meets the Deep Springs College road and the settlement at the Deep Springs Maintenance Station. To the left, at the settlement, is a dirt road leading to the site of White Mountain City, up Wyman Canyon, where much mining activity took place years ago.

L.Dean Clark

The climb to the Gilbert Summit (6374 ') offers interesting views of the Sierra to the west, with sage, desert mallow and bunch grass covering the desert mountains, and volcanic hills to the right adding contrast. The road rapidly descends for another roller-coaster ride through the narrow canyon — a desert slalom — before straightening out to meet Highway 266. Through the canyon 25 MPH speed is recommended in order to stay on the right side of the road. A big truck or bus could be hidden just around the next corner. (The junction is 37 miles from Big Pine.)

The long Fish Lake Valley presents an oasis effect with sprawling alfalfa ranches and cattle munching bunch grass between the sagebrush. On the left is a fault scarp at the base of the lofty White Mountains, interrupting the gradual slope of the alluvial fan. To the right is colorful Silver Peak Range and Piper Peak (9500 ').

In Dyers, at the Esmeralda, is a general store, saloon, deli, laundromat and Chevron gas. Outside are old iron wagons with wooden spokes from mining days. The Boonies is a restaurant and saloon. The Post Office is on the left, going north. Here are beautiful views of the east face of the White Mountains with dramatic contours, canyons and peaks. After passing a historical marker, the Fish Lake Valley Park and Community Center, on Blue Bird Road, there are picnic tables, a ball field, corral and playground. It is an ideal stop for a picnic with valley and mountain views.

Near the Tonopah/Bishop junction the beautiful multicolored volcanic hills are in front and basaltic lava flow materials from Black Mountain are on the left. The road to Highwy 6 is an easy, gradual climb with lofty Boundary Peak (13,140 ') changing its contour as you circle from the east, to north, then west of it. The California-Nevada boundary line passes through it. The mountain and desert vistas along here are outstanding. (The junction at Highway 6 is about 78 miles from Big Pine.)

To the left of the junction is a mine of large white, chalky material. Along here, as well as in Fish Lake Valley, bull signs are posted for open range. Basalt had been a water tank stop for the Carson & Colorado Railroad. The old tank is no longer standing. Montgomery Pass (7162 ') in the pinyon-juniper forest has a hotel, casino, cafe, bar and phone.

Descending the long alluvial fan the vegetation is now sage — covered desert with cholla cacti scattered throughout and good views of the Sierra. The old grade of the Carson & Colorado Railroad can be seen on the alluvial fan slope. Five miles past the California border is the Agricultural stop (5461 ').

At Benton is Smalley's Market with cafe and groceries; a restaurant, gas, and a library at the school. The great Montgomery Peak (13,441 ') towers above the town. The pale gray, almost white peak, especially in the afternoon sun, was the reason this range was called White Mountains. There is the Sand and Sage RV Park at the junction, with Highway 120 going east to Benton Hot Springs and Highway 395.

From Benton to Bishop the road gradually slopes along the alluvial fan following the old railroad grade through ranch lands eastward of the Blind Springs Hills. Old mines and mining roads leading up foothill slopes and deep canyons can be seen. White Mountain Peak (14,246') is not white but is dark brown with reddish streaks overlooking Chalfant Valley.

In 1863 prospectors searched the Blind Spring Hill and found gold and silver lodes rich in ore. The Diane mine was shipping out five silver bars a month by 1875, each weighing 94 lbs. at 94% purity. Some of the other mines were called Cornucopia, which was one of the largest producers, Comanche, Kerrick and Modoc. From 1863 to 1881 production was recorded at $4,353,967. With the Carson & Colorado Railroad at Benton so near at hand, shipping ore out of the valley was no problem.

During the 1860's and 1870's gold was mined from placer deposits found in the streams located in the canyons on the west flank of the White Mountains. Principal mines were the Sacramento and Twenty Grand. Later the lode deposits with gold-quartz veins in the granite rocks were discovered.

The Mercantile at Chalfant Valley offers grocery products, meat, deli, liquor, feed and a cafe featuring fried chicken and homemade chili. From Chalfant Valley to Laws many ranches are on either side of the road. Laws was the station stop for the Bishop area on the Carson & Colorado Railroad. The station, engine, buildings and Museum is a must to visit.

For a complete circle trip follow Highway 395 south of Bishop to Big Pine.

L. Dean Clark

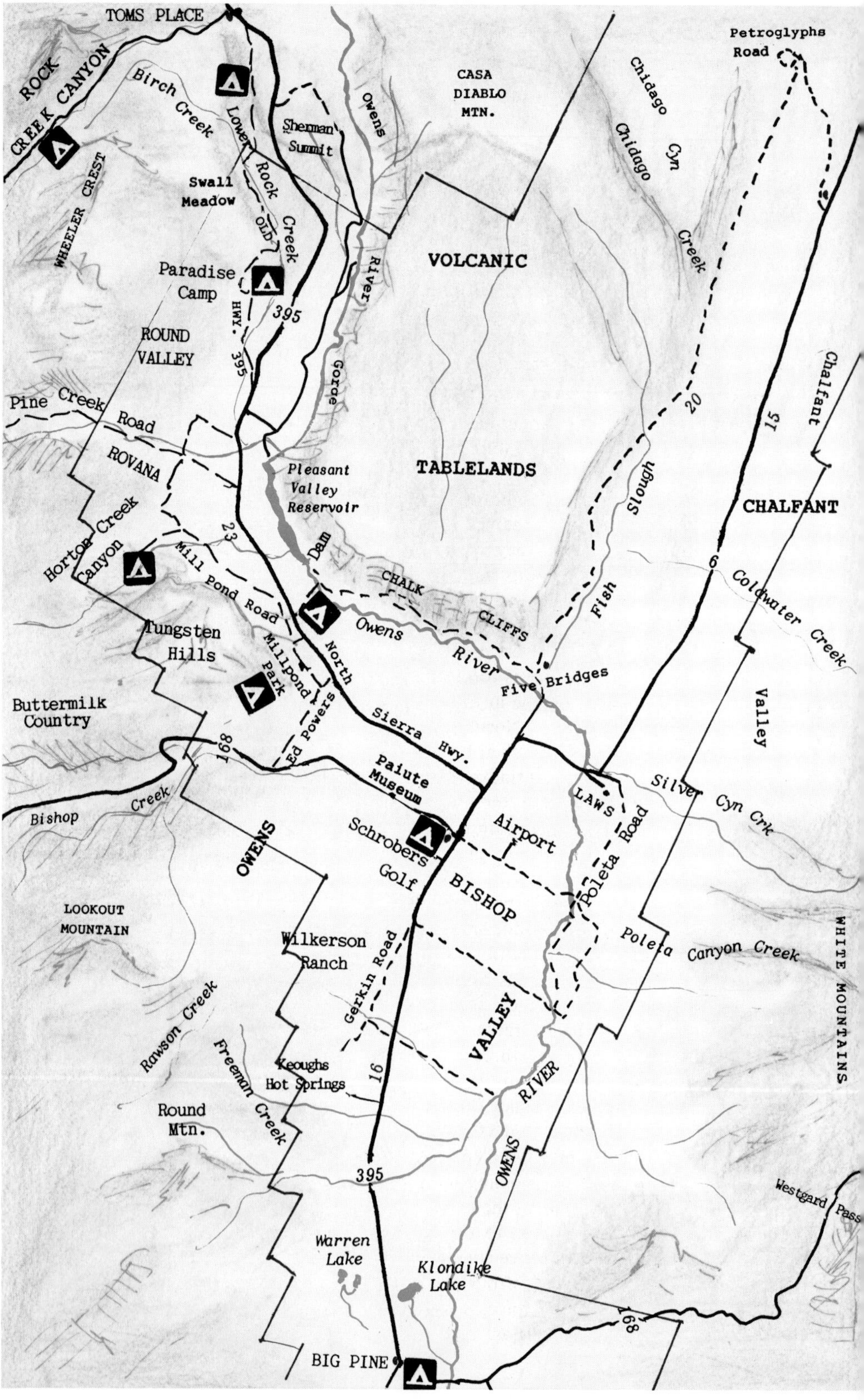
TOMS PLACE
ROCK CREEK CANYON
Birch Creek
Lower Rock Creek
Sherman Summit
Owens
CASA DIABLO MTN.
Petroglyphs Road
Chidago
Chidago Cyn
Chidago Creek
Swall Meadow
WHEELER CREST
OLD HWY. 395
Paradise Camp
395
River
VOLCANIC
ROUND VALLEY
Gorge
Pine Creek Road
ROVANA
Pleasant Valley Reservoir
TABLELANDS
20
Slough
Chalfant
15
CHALFANT
Horton Creek Canyon
23
Mill Pond Road
Dam
CHALK CLIFFS
Fish
6
Coldwater Creek
Tungsten Hills
Millpond Park
North
Owens River
Five Bridges
Valley
Buttermilk Country
Ed Powers
Sierra Hwy.
168
Paiute Museum
Bishop Creek
LAWS
Silver Cyn Crk
Poleta Road
Airport
Schrobers Golf
OWENS
BISHOP
LOOKOUT MOUNTAIN
Wilkerson Ranch
Gerkin Road
Poleta Canyon Creek
WHITE MOUNTAINS
Rawson Creek
VALLEY
RIVER
Freeman Creek
Keoughs Hot Springs
16
Round Mtn.
OWENS
395
Westgard Pass
Warren Lake
Klondike Lake
168
BIG PINE

BISHOP (4140')
Courtesy of Mammoth Lakes Pack Outfit

When Samuel Addison Bishop, his wife Frances, and cattlemen entered the Bishop Creek country from Fort Tejon in August of 1861, driving a herd of some 600 cattle and 50 horses up the valley floor, they looked at the mountains on either side of the lush meadows and knew they had found paradise. Sweet plentiful waters and the tall green grass along the marshes and creeks were just right for cattle grazing. Tall pines under the blue summer skies, magnificent peaks tipped with spots of snow to the west and colorful desert hills to the east, were just right for a place to be called home. They built two small log and whip-sawed cabins and named it "San Frances Ranch". However, troubled times lay ahead. That peaceful valley they had found so enjoyable was soon blaring with bugle horns, pistol and gun shots as the Indian war started. It was no longer the paradise that had so impressed the Bishops.

By 1864 the town of Bishop Creek was laid out some three miles to the north of the ranch. The Civil War and the slavery question was also disquieting to the settlers, along with their own war. Ranch life was too inactive for such an industrious person as Mr. Bishop, so they left. Settlers came in to homestead. Prospectors and miners appeared when gold was discovered up the North Fork, lead and silver were found east of South lake, and tungsten up Coyote Creek at Lookout Mountain. The town grew. By the time the Carson & Colorado Railroad tracks were laid along the valley floor in 1893 parallel-ing the eastern White-Inyo range, there were business services to amply supply the increasing population. The mining camps provided the impetus to settle in the valley, either to work in the mines or to produce livestock and crops for the miners at the camps.

Today Bishop is the only incorporated city in Inyo County and is the pivotal center for the surrounding area. Mr. Bishop was correct in his analysis of this grassland valley. It is a paradise — a vacation paradise with a true western flavor. The fishing, hunting, camping, hiking, golfing, horseback riding, touring, and just looking at the mountains makes it an ideal place. It is the most accessible passageway to the great Middle Fork of the Kings River and has some gorgeous lake basins that are easy to reach.

Bishop is a friendly town with three annual western-type events: the Mule Days held during the Memorial Day weekend; Tri-County Fair held around the middle of July, and the Rodeo held during the Labor Day weekend. Bishop Park, in town, has a heated swimming pool open in the summer for all ages. There is a wading pool for the very young, horseshoe courts, playground equipment, picnic tables, piped water, barbeques and shaded green grass. The welcoming sounds are provided by the quack-quacking of numerous ducks that swim along the creek. The Bishop Chamber of Commerce and Visitor Center is housed adjacent to the creek at 690 North Main Street. The Inyo National Forest Supervisor's Office is at 871 North Main Street. The White Mountain District Ranger's Office is 798 North Main Street. The Department of Fish and Game for fishing and hunting information is at 407 West Line Street. The Post Office is at 595 West Line St. The airport is off East Line Street.

Just past the beautiful 18-hole Bishop Golf Club (public) and Station KBOV is Brown's Schober Lane Campground and Museum. Shaded with trees and lovely green grass, the 150 tent and RV sites (some pull-throughs) are large and inviting, with electricity and water available. Clean restrooms and showers are locked for safety. There is a Mini Mart with beer, ice, snacks, firewood, souvenirs and books. Golf lessons are offered. The free picnic area with tables, stoves and playground is under shade, and if you didn't bring your own, try the Snack Bar for hot dogs, sausage, ice cream and popcorn. While picnicking stroll along the boardwalk of the Museum buildings — Valley View Hotel, Palace, old jail, service station, blacksmith shop, and see the little train cart and old wagons.

Alpha Air services the Bishop, Mammoth and June Lakes area out of Los Angeles, Burbank, San Diego, San Jose and Oakland...the only instrument approach in the valley. The runway and airport was a military base until 1943, Squadron 66 still is at the airport as an offshoot of the military. It is a search and rescue unit for locating any downed pilots. Each year two seminars are held for out-of-area pilots who are unfamiliar with mountain, canyon and desert flying. They need to be safe when trying to locate others.

At one time there were quite a few gliders but the weather has changed. The 'sierra wave' that was so helpful for glidering has not occurred lately. The air is good, however, for hang gliders, the sport that has become popular. They jump off the White Mountains in the Bishop area and off Kennedy Meadows down in Lone Pine. Each year there are international meets out of Lone Pine for endurance, distance, and working various courses. At the airport there are two different outfits to maintain planes, one for the frame and body of the plane, and the other for the power unit. No one helps with electronics. Charter flights are available for business or scenery-viewing.

Bishop is the home of Erick Schat's Bakery with the well-known Original Sheepherder Bread.® The beginning of the bread's tradition goes back to Robert Schoch who owned the Vienna Bakery in the early 1900's. He used a special blend of flour, pure well water and other local ingredients pleasing to a sheepherder. The bread became so popular that the recipe was copyrighted in 1938. The copyright was purchased by Erik Schat in 1962 who carries on the tradition. With his talent as a Dutch baker, he has added Honi Squaw Bread and other specialities.

On West Line Street the Paiute-Shoshone Indian Cultural Center presents exhibitions of their basketry and weaving, displays of food, implements and customs to maintain the heritage of the past. After peace came the Paiutes lived and worked in the valley, held their Pine Nut Festivals and became active members of the community. The men worked on the ranches and for the railroad. Indian women and girls were employed by the women of the ranches and by town people to do garden work, laundry and cleaning. Some families, working together, became quite good friends.

Museum hours vary with the season. During the summer it is open from Monday to Sunday, 10 AM to 4 PM. Information and books are available at the museum concerning the life of the Indians and the neighboring area.

For a half-day drive out of Bishop, take East Line Street past the Airport, and cross the Owens River on the Poleta-Laws Road, where large irrigation ditches (part of the McNally Canal) can be seen. Views across the valley, and beyond Bishop and Bishop Creek Canyon to the Sierra Crest, makes this scenic trip along the base of the White Mountains even more enjoyable. The circle trip continues north to Laws, then west on Highway 6, returning to the center of town.

Another trip in Bishop Country is up Chalfant Valley, named for Mr. W.A. Chalfant, founding publisher and editor of the *Inyo Register*, who became one of the best authorities on the region. The beautiful White Mountains to the east, with many ranches along the valley road, follows the old route of the Carson & Colorado Railroad. For an interesting loop trip, turn right on Red Rock Canyon Road to the Volcanic Tableland country with its many fault scarps. The road south passes Fish Slough, follows it through the southern end via Chalk Bluff and Five Bridges and returns to Bishop. Petroglyphs can be seen at various sites along the edge of the Tableland where Paiutes long ago left their drawings.

Several RV parks are within the city limits of Bishop: Highlands RV Park and J-Diamond Mobile Ranch. Check the RV Park and campground chart in the back of the book for specifics. The Coach & Camper Service sells complete RV parts.

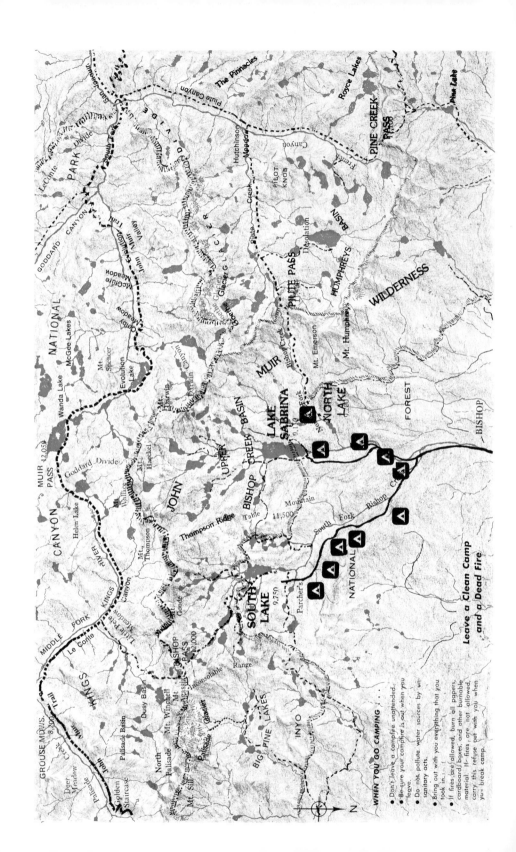

**Leave a Clean Camp
and a Dead Fire**

WHEN YOU GO CAMPING . . .

- Don't leave a campfire unattended.
- Be sure your campfire is out when you leave.
- Do not pollute water sources by unsanitary acts.
- Bring out with you everything that you took in . . .
- If fires are/allowed, burn all papers, cardboard/boxes, and other burnable material. If fires are not allowed, carry this refuse out with you when you break camp.

BISHOP CREEK CANYON   MAC

This is without a doubt one of the most magnificent, most accessible canyons in all of the Sierra Nevada, for fishermen, photographers, hunters, and nature lovers who just want to sit near sparkling waters, walk through a meadow of wildflowers or hike along an alpine lake with pine trees reflected on the water. Almost half ot the 200 lakes and streams in this largest of the eastern Sierra basins, and the canyon of Bishop Creek, can be reached from the road or road ends in a few hours. From West Line Street the road leads west up the alluvial fan before entering the canyon.

Buttermilk Road going off to the right about five miles up the fan, goes to the Tungsten Hills mines, a residential area, and grazing lands for a dairy company known as Buttermilk Country. In the late 1890's teamsters would stop there for the rich, delicious buttermilk from mountain-grass-fed cows. The Tungsten Mines were operating at peak production starting around 1916 when high prices for the mineral during World War I encouraged extensive mining. When the price dropped after the war the mine was closed. There has been little activity since.

From the Buttermilk Country roadend, past the McGee Creek crossing, a trail leads into the John Muir Wilderness Area. It follows along the upper end of Horton Creek to the beautiful Horton Lakes Basin, below Basin Mountain (13,240') and Four Gables (12,691').

The road is a long, steep climb before reaching the top at Lake Sabrina, or to South Lake. Watch the gauge so as not to overhead your engine, especially on a hot summer afternoon. The narrow dirt road up to North Lake and the North Fork lakes and basin, and up to the South Fork backcountry parking area beyond South Lake, are steep with no turnaround spots. Large RV motor homes or towing vehicles are not recommended on these two roads.

The North Fork, heading up Piute Pass (11,423') in the John Muir Wilderness Area, has trails leading to Lamarck and Wonder Lakes, Loch Levan, Emerson and Piute Lakes most of which are above 10,000' and feature rainbow, Eastern brook and brown trout.

The Middle Fork with the grand basin of lakes below the Sierra Crest lies at the foot of the cirque topped by Mt. Thompson (13,494'), Mt. Wallace (13,377'), Mt. Hoeckel (13,435') and Mt. Darwin (13,494'). Trails heading west of Lake Sabrina reach the high alpine lake country between the Thompson Ridge and Sierra Crest, with elevations ranging from Blue Lake at 10,400' to Echo Lake at 11,650'.

The South Fork country between Thompson Ridge and the Inconsolable Range tops off at Bishop Pass (11,972'). The many lakes have rainbow, golden and Eastern brook trout. Fish are stocked by the California Fish and Game in some 83 of the Bishop Creek lakes and many miles of streams between them.

Lake Sabrina   MAC

Camping facilities vary from sites on a high desert hill at Four Jeffreys, to rustic sites along a bustling stream at Sabrina, or walk-in camps for hikers or for those who enjoy being away from the road in a natural mountain environment such as North Lake. Habegger's Resort on South Creek has trailer spaces, trailer rentals, propane, firewood, showers, laundry, public telephone, cafe, gift shop and fishing supplies. Parchers Resort has a restaurant, public telephone with cabin and boat rentals. At Bishop Creek Lodge there are telephones, restaurant, cabin rentals, groceries, gasoline and fishing supplies.

At Lake Sabrina on the Middle Fork, a cafe overlooks the lake to watch the fishermen and boaters. You'll also find gasoline for boats, boat rentals, public telephone, fishing supplies and sundries for sale. Cardinal Village, just past Aspendell on the lower North Fork is a lovely mountain resort. Here one can enjoy the beauties of Bishop Creek country while fishing and relaxing in the warm summer sun, or brisk autumn air, amid the ever-fluttering aspens. Cabins are for rent; some of them from the days of the Cardinal Mine are interestingly named. The cabin called "Drunken Sailor" was once the schoolhouse up at the mine village. The lodge serves cocktails and meals. The store carries supplies for campers and fishermen and books on the area.

Schober Pack Station is located at North Fork. It features pack trips into the many fishing lakes around the Bishop Creek Basin, over Piute pass to Humphrey's Basin, or along the rugged Piute Creek country below the Glacier Divide. Deer hunting trips in the fall can be arranged.

There are several types of backcountry trips available:

DAY TRIP: Hire a horse, leave early and return before dark. Guides can be hired.

SPOT TRIP: Packers will take a party to a campsite of the party's choice in the backcountry, leave party there for a specified time, and return to take the party out. Cost is determined by the distance packed in and the number of horses needed for gear and food.

EXTENDED TRIP: Packer and stock remain with the party, staying at one camp and making side trips for fishing, hunting, or sightseeing along the trail. The party furnishes all the food and camping gear.

ALL EXPENSE TRIP: Packer supplies the guide, stock, food and equipment except sleeping and personal gear.

The electric power potential in wildly tumbling Bishop Creek, rushing down some 5500 feet in just 14 miles, was first recognized by Loren Curtis and Charles Hobbs who had come from Nevada in 1904 seeking wealth in silver. They found that the water might be a means for more profit than the precious metal. With financial backing from Denver, the California Electric Power Company was born.

It was a monstrous undertaking at best, with extremely difficult working conditions at 10,000 feet elevation across rugged, rocky mountain slopes in harsh winter weather. The hot dry desert heat in the summer was just as uncomfortable for the workers. Tons of heavy equipment were brought in by the Carson & Colorado Railroad, then 42-mule teams hauled the machinery up the long steep canyon. Redwood was used for the flowline as well as for the dam facings. They knew concrete would not hold up in the freezing winter temperatures. Sections of the flowline can be seen from the road.

When the first hydroelectric power plant and the man-made reservoir (Lake Sabrina) was completed, a power line was strung over the White Mountains via Montgomery Pass to service the Tonopah and Goldfield mines and communities. At that time it was the longest transmission line in the world. As the mining industry petered out, new areas were sought to use this great supply of power. Bakersfield and Redding needed electricity, so a 236-mile power line went over the mountains to those communities. Now lines go to all the communities in the Owens Valley as well.

Four powerhouses along Bishop Creek are producing electricity via all of the lines, using the same water four times. Then, the well-used waters flow down into the Owens River and out along the Aqueduct to Los Angeles.

BISHOP PASS COUNTRY (11,972')

Glaciation formed the beautiful Bishop Creek Canyon, leaving such visible evidences as cirques, knife-edged ridges, lake basins, U-shaped valleys and lateral moraines that can be seen along the road. With most of the region above timberline, the rock formations are so exposed that geologists can study them conveniently and determine the glacial history and development of the entire Sierra bloc. These ragged peaks with steep chutes and loose talus slopes, diagonal ledges and summit pinnacles, entice the climbing mountaineer with many challenges ranging through all classes.

It is only seven miles from the backcountry parking area at South Lake up to Bishop Pass, with a moderate climb passing Long Lake (10,700'), Saddlerock Lake (11,100') and Bishop Lake (11,200'). It is surrounded by the towering wall of the Inconsolable Range and peaks along the Sierra Crest. In a sub-alpine setting of aspen glens, with wildflower meadows, it passes first lodgepole then whitebark pines, and finally reaches above timberline. The last switchbacks through boulders up to the Pass is steep. But the views are breathtaking from the abrupt intimate face of the crest between the Palisades and Mt. Darwin. To the west lies the tremendous trough of the LeConte Canyon and the rugged Black Divide. Southwest are the Dusy Basin, Little Pete Meadows and the John Muir-Pacific Crest Trail along the grand Middle Fork of the Kings River.

Bishop Pass   Jim Wilson

Wilshire-Bishop Milling Co.,1912   Courtesy of East California Museum

CARDINAL MINE

Mr. Gaylord Wilshire of Los Angeles founded the Wilshire-Bishop Creek Mine in the early 1900's, producing gold on a large scale. His mine was the principal source of gold in the Bishop area. Four different ore chutes were developed, varying in size from 20 feet to 300 feet in length and from 6 feet to 16 feet in width. The ore was mined from a 600-foot shaft, the first 100 foot being vertical with the remaining 500 feet inclined. The total number of feet of shafts developed in the mine was over 4000 feet. Two sinking pumps and a three-inch centrifugal pump handled the water from the 300 foot level where a 350 gpm triplex pump boosted water up to the surface.

Production up to November 1937 by the Cardinal Gold Mining Company was $1,570,000. By 1938, however, operations had ceased. Over 100 men were employed with about 100 cabins that housed the miners, workers and their families. The village consisted of a store, post office and schoolhouse. Eleven of the old cabins still exist and are used at the Cardinal Village as vacation lodgings.

Weather and time have erased all major buildings and machinery at the mine, although old foundations of the original structures can be seen. Pieces of old iron and wood are scattered amid the rocks and rubble in the canyon, and the talus of remains are on the hillside. The shafts are closed and boarded up for safety. There is still gold and tungsten in the mine, but no operations are planned in the near future.

An extensive irrigation system was developed by the resourceful Paiutes living along Bishop and Pine Creeks. Their almost six square miles of irrigated lands were called *pitana patu*. No soil was prepared, seeding done, or land cultivated. The women would just gather the harvest of wild plants that gave seeds and bulbs from the watered lands. There were ten different irrigation sites from Pine Creek south to Independence.

ROCKING CHAIR RANCH

RANCH LANDS
L.Dean Clark

The first cattle drive over the Walker Pass from Visalia was made in 1859, en route to the mining camps in Nevada. Since that time livestock and ranching has played an important part in the economy of the valley. Drovers noticed the good grazing possibilities and stayed to homestead and raise the cattle here, eliminating the long drive over the mountains.

Sheep were introduced along with the cattle to supply food for the miners. By 1862 there were over 2500 sheep, and just ten years later over 200,000 head of livestock grazed on the land. In 1912 some 80,000 head of sheep were in the valley, with over 2000 carloads shipped out via the Carson & Colorado Railroad. Tons of wool were exported to Los Angeles.

Sufficient water, good soil and hot summers provided the necessary ingredients for growing thousands of acres of alfalfa to feed the increasing number of livestock. Now cattle and sheep are driven to higher elevations during the summer months and are rounded up and brought back to the valley for the winter.

As all ranchers know, horses have an important role to play. Before machinery became available, draft horses did all the ranch work of plowing and harvesting. A special breed of horse has been developed in this area that are acclimated to the weather and physical conditions of the valley. Breeding stock from these horses are highly regarded. Good sturdy mules are raised here and are used for the many pack trains that go into the backcountry for pleasure or as work animals along the trail. Mules, being sure-footed, can withstand the rough, rocky trails more consistently than horses.

Ranches at Round Valley who did not sell out to Los Angeles have been able to maintain their large spreads, making the country a lush farmland. Many ranches are up in Chalfant Valley as well. Each year during Mule Days, the local Tri-County Fair or Rodeo cowboys show off their ranching skills to the public.

Some ranches lease land from the City of Los Angeles to grow alfalfa for their livestock while other ranches never sold out and receive their water from artesian wells, making lush green areas stand out in the brown desert landscape. Creeks leading down to the Owens River edged with willows and shrubs also enhance the beauty along the road.

105

LAWS

MAC

To capture the spirit and the romance of the narrow gauge railroads — a touch of yesterday — visit Laws, about six miles northeast of Bishop on Highway 6. The museum features depot, Engine #9 (a 10-wheel Baldwin), cars, equipment, farm wagons, mining memoriabilia and many interesting restored buildings. There is a Wells Fargo office with Indian, mining and milling artifacts, a country store with supplies, and a doctor's office with antique instruments, to name a few things. Laws is open from 10 A.M. to 4 P.M. during the busy summer season, and on weekends during the winter.

After the tracks were pulled up, the Southern Pacific gave the buildings, remaining cars, and Engine #9 to Inyo County and the City of Bishop in the form of a gift deed. Laws was turned into an outdoor and indoor museum. It opened officially on April 1, 1966. Children can climb all over the cars and into the cab to ring the bell, making believe they are the engineer bringing a load of gold or silver into the station.

The depot was built in 1883 and is in good condition today. It was constructed with a large attic where the workers slept. Fires in a large pot-bellied stove were kept burning to keep the building warm. Lumber for the building was hauled by freight team down the hill from Mammoth Lakes. The town of Laws, first called Bishop Creek, had two boarding houses, a blacksmith shop, grocery store, school, pool hall and a post office.

In the Museum are many old photographs, posters, and a gift shop with books on railroading, museums and topics pertaining to the area.

Stamp Mill

at Laws

L. Dean Clark

106

DESERT RAILS

As the activity of the mines increased, faster transportation was needed than the freight teams could provide. Iron rails were laid out along the desert floor from Mojave north around the El Paso Mountains, up along Owens Lake, and into Lone Pine. With this branch of the Southern Pacific Railroad, a southern transcontinental railway service was available to the Owens Valley people.

When the Central Pacific Railroad met the Union Pacific in mid-May 1869, a northern transcontinental route was established. To connect the Owens Valley with this northern route, the Virginia & Truckee Railroad established the Carson & Colorado Narrow Gauge Railroad in 1883 to service the many mines in both Nevada and California. Starting at Mound House, ten miles east of Carson City, the line ran eastward to Churchill, south along Walker Lake to Tonopah Junction, over the Montgomery Pass to Benton, Laws and down to Keeler. Now both the highest point in the country — Mt. Whitney — and the lowest point — Death Valley — were within reach by rail to the rest of the United States.

The trains passed through beautiful rangeland and orchards below the snow-capped Sierra and White-Inyo peaks, past cottonwoods and poplars, marshlands and over streams. It was an isolated run with the little train puffing along the desert floor on the long straight rails over the sagebrush fans. Whistles blew at crossings and black smoke trailed behind the engine and cars of the "Slim Princess", an affectionate name given the line. The tracks were laid on the eastern side of the Owens River because the train would be closer to the mines and less disturbance to farmers who were not anxious to have their hayfields and farms broken up by the rails.

Livestock, wool, alfalfa, honey, potatoes, fruits and poultry were shipped in abundance to the north and south. Both San Francisco and Los Angeles were now able to enjoy these Owens Valley commodities. Some of the many ores carried out of the valley included talc, soda compounds, pumice, clay, soapstone, lead ore and silver. The changeover from narrow gauge to standard occurred at Owenyo in the south, and Mound House in the north. Loading docks of the two different gauge railways were placed side by side so that freight could be shifted from one car to the other. A special A-frame railroad car was used for bulk shipments. The narrow gauge track was elevated on a ramp above the standard gauge and boxes were lowered into the cars.

The railroad men were friendly and casual in their duties. They were known to stop their trains to go swimming in Walker Lake or, in the fall, to go hunting. Rides were given people walking along the tracks and all Indians rode free on top of the freight cars. It must have been a colorful sight to see them sitting there. Indians sold fish they caught to the passengers. Some Indians were employed by the railroad companies to lay track, as sectionhands, and to help at the various stations.

During the 1920's passengers from Owens Valley could take the train, travel south to Owenyo, have a lunch stop before boarding the Southern Pacific to ride overnight in the sleeper or coach to Los Angeles. Passengers could change at Mojave to the Atcheson, Topeka and Sante Fe for east-bound trains to Chicago, or west-bound to Bakersfield.

About the time the mines ceased to be profitable and the miners left with their families, the farmers' water supply was diverted to Los Angeles by the Aqueduct. The Southern Pacific bought up the Carson & Colorado and they operated the Keeler Branch from 1924 to 1957. It was the last operating narrow gauge railway west of the Rocky Mountains. The last train out of Keeler went down the tracks in 1957 to become a memory of days in a glorious past.

NORTH OF BISHOP   MAC

A few miles past the business section of North Sierra Highway (Highway 395) is BROWN'S MILLPOND CAMPGROUND, off Sawmill Road. It is a most impressive and beautifully well-kept family recreation center with tall shade trees and lovely green lawn and shrubs. Many summer sporting activities are available: two softball parks, swimming, tennis court and horseshoe pits. It has a clean area for camping and picnicking in a pleasant atmosphere, with cabanas, tables, barbeques, water and electrical hookups, restrooms and showers for single units or for groups. Telephones and a concession stand are there for the visitor's convenience.

Almost across the highway to the right is PLEASANT VALLEY COUNTY PARK, along the cottonwood and willowed banks of the Owens River at the base of the Volcanic Tablelands. Fire pits and tables are scattered in an agreeable, non-structured way with river fishing right at the campsite. Across the bridge over the Owens River is Chalk Bluff Road, leading eastward along the river and back to Bishop.

VOLCANIC TABLELANDS, the northern boundary of Owens Valley, present a colorful white, beige and tawny backdrop to the Owens River at the base of the bluff. Upstream, north of Pleasant Valley Reservoir, the Owens River cuts a gorge through the cooled, layered volcanic ash material called tuff. Eruptions from vents south of Mono Lake first deposited a layer of white pumice over the gravelled earth. Later a 200-foot layer of fine beige volcanic rock material covered the pumice. That was capped by a 500-foot layer of tawny colored rock materials. To get a closer look at the bluff a loop trip can be made via the North Sierra Highway and the Chalk Bluff Road.

The volcanic ash of minute rock fragments is gray in color when initially compressed as a comglomerate, but when exposed to the air pastel hues appear. When the River cut through the Tablelands, the color of the stratified gorge and frontal cliff was changed from gray to the soft beige, white and tawny shades seen. Since the rock is comparatively soft it can be cut into slabs, polished and mortared to the sides of buildings. These slabs become crusty and hard, protecting the surface from weathering. Many of the famous buildings of Rome were made of tuff from eruptions in Italy, as were buildings made in the Mother Lode country of California.

OWENS VALLEY WILD TROUT AREA is just beyond the Pleasant Valley County Park, along the Pleasant Valley Spawning Channel of the Owens River. This channel is a small artificial stream with spawning gravel and controlled flows. Brown trout migrating upstream in the fall are directed into the channel. Females select a nest site in the gravel, create a depression to hold their eggs and, after fertilization by the male fish is over, the eggs are covered with the gravel. Eggs hatch during the winter and young trout commence life in the river in the spring. The channel and the river near the channel are closed to fishing to protect the spawners.

On Mill Creek Road off North Sierra Highway 395 you'll find Round Valley Inn, a mini mart, gas, diesel fuel and a telephone.

Wild
Trout
Area
MAC

Look west to view the beautiful ranch lands of ROUND VALLEY nestled against the mountains, and to see how Owens Valley must have appeared in ranching days when water was plentiful enough to support orchards, cattle ranches with irrigation ditches bordered by willows and cottonwoods. Round Valley is surrounded by the brown Tungsten Hills to the south, Basin Mountain (13,240'), Mt. Tom (13,652') and the impressive Wheeler Crest to the west and northwest. The Volcanic Tablelands are to the northeast and east. Like Poverty and Alabama Hills south of Owens Valley, Tungsten Hills are isolated uplifts of fault-bound granite. Old mining road switchbacks can be seen on the slopes of Tungsten Hills.

HORTON CREEK CAMPGROUND on South Round Valley Road has large rustic sites with tables, stoves and young trees growing among the sage and rabbitbrush. The road ascends the lower base slope of Mt. Tom along Horton Creek. Views to the east from the campground sites are breathtaking. No water is available but there is fishing along the creek.

ROVENA is a residential area for the workers at the Union Carbide Nuclear Company's Pine Creek Mine, a major producer of tungsten. Copper, gold, silver, molybdenite and scheelite are also processed at the plant.

At the north end of Round Valley, Little Rock Creek Road ascends along the creek to PARADISE LODGE & RV PARK at 5000' elevation, featuring quiet, off-the-highway, shaded and open RV sites. A restaurant and cabins are situated among the trees along a creek stocked with trout.

PINE CREEK   *MAC*

The road up Pine Creek Canyon passes between two long moraines and leads west up to the mine, parking, Pine Creek Pack Station (7580'), and backcountry entry points. The mine road beyond is private, ascending the north side of the canyon to reach open pit mines at 11,000' elevation between Broken Finger Peak and Mt. Morgan (13,738'). Large RV units are not encouraged to go up the steep no-nonsense road to the limited parking area near the mill and pack station. "Moraine" is a French word meaning 'rocky rubble' and that is what you see driving through this narrow canyon between the two lateral moraines left by the glaciers.

PINE CREEK PACK STATION offers all types of pack trips and trail rides with old western style horse groups and deer hunting parties in the fall.

From the backcountry parking area a three-mile trail goes steeply up to Gable Lakes (10,400'-10,800'). Pine Creek Pass (11,000') is seven miles from the roadend. The colorful black, white and deep red rocks in this dramatically gouged-out canyon form precipitous slopes that make hiking into the high backcountry an adventure. Ancient glaciers carved the walls and left behind the U-shaped valley typical of the Kings River basin of Kings Canyon National Park.

Once over the pass, Eastern brook and golden trout are found in the many lakes of French Creek Canyon and up Piute Creek to Humphrey's Basin. This high, wind-swept barren basin with lakes ranging from Honeymoon lake (10,440') to Humphreys (12,000') lies against the Glacier Divide. The lakes are separated by rolling granite slopes and are famous for catches of golden trout.

By ascending westward past Honeymoon Lake you'll reach the upper basin called Granite Park, a truly magnificent, high, glacial-carved amphitheater. One climbs up and over Italy Pass (12,300') to enter the Hilgard Creek and Bear Lakes Country. The trail borders mile long Lake Italy (11,154') shimmering in barren splendor joining the scenic John Muir-Pacific Crest Trail. The Bear Creek drainage is a designated golden trout area with excellent fishing near and above timberline in some of the most dramatic surroundings of the Sierra.

From the mine road a trail leads west to Morgan Lakes and Pass (10,800'), then descends north into Little Lake Valley and Rock Creek Canyon.

MONO COUNTRY
MAC

The word Mono comes from the Indian word 'monacha' or 'fly people'. These Indians resided on the eastern Sierran slopes and along Mono Lake. They subsisted partly on the pupae of flies blown across the lake. It is appropriate that the County, Lake, Pass, Craters, Basin and Monoville be named for these people who lived here for so long.

James L.C. Sherwin came to Round Valley from Kentucky and built a wagon road up to the northern slope of the valley, along Lower Rock Creek, to service his sawmill. Later, when news of the gold strike up in Mammoth enticed many up the big hill, Sherwin built an extension up and over the grade. He charged a fee, instigating the Sherwin Toll Road. Now called the Lower Rock Creek Road, it was part of the old Highway 395 or 'El Camino Sierra' before the well-graded four-lane road was built. A small campground is near the top of the ridge past Sherwin Summit (6427 ') and Birch Creek.

Sherwin sold his toll road in 1892 for $125.00. When Mono County developed the free roads, the old toll roads were bought and included in the system.

Highway 395 climbs up to Sherwin Summit (7000 '), passes into Mono County and undergoes an environmental change with pinyon and Jeffrey pines, and a land strewn with volcanic ash debris known as Bishop Tuff. The mountains are much closer and canyons become more accessible, with roads and trails to many fishing lakes and streams. The air is somewhat cooler and crisper, with winter snows much deeper and longer lasting. Meadows, marshes and many species of flowers enhance the landscape, adding beauty to the rocky lateral moraines that extend out from the canyons.

The view from Scenic Point is truly spectacular with the hazy-blue Owens Valley in the distance, Volcanic Tablelands below, White Mountain Peak (14,246 ') gloriously topping the White Mountains to the east, and Wheeler Ridge right at your elbow to the west. Halfway up the grade, near the 6000 ' elevation sign, is radiator water — not for drinking. During hot summer afternoons it might be best to turn off the air conditioner in your vehicle during this long, high altitude climb to help keep the engine from overheating.

In autumn when golden aspen leaves flutter in the brisk fall breezes, for a nice loop trip out of Owens Valley go up the Sherwin grade to Toms Place and return via Little Rock Creek Road down along the creek. It meets the highway at the bottom of the hill. Rock Creek Gorge and the broad views of Owens Valley below are impressive. There are off-the-road parking areas at good photographic points. The grade is steep in some sections. It must have been an exhilerating trip in old wagons and stages going up to the mines in the early days.

Another trip is via the paved Owens River Gorge Road, off to the right near the bottom of Sherwin grade, and up along the aqueduct pipes on Volcanic Tablelands. The view of the tuff formation reveals how the Owens River eroded and cut through the Tablelands to create the spectacular gorge. You can return to Highway 395 to view the valley below or, if you feel adventuresome, continue north on the dirt and gravel road through the outcroppings and pinyons and join Highway 395 just past Sherwin Summit. Follow the most used and widest of the dirt roads, veering westward.

Indians gathered pinyon nuts from the Tableland and made arrowheads from volcanic glass. In the 1800's prospectors combed the land for paydirt and found some at the northern end of the Tableland, east of Lake Crowley around Banner Ridge. The Clover Patch Mining District was active in the 1890's and again in the 1930's. The quartz veins were almost ten feet thick, with some ore assaying one-half to one ounce of gold per ton. Some mines in this district were called Casa Diablo, Gold Wedge, Wildrose, West Tower, Long Chance and Sierra Vista. A few miles to the southeast both gold and silver were discovered in Blind Spring Hill. Extensive mining occurred in the 1860's through early 1880's. Tungsten came from the Black Rock Mine, and in the 1950's it was the second largest producer in California. Pine Creek Mine was first.

Sherwin Summit Looking South　　MAC

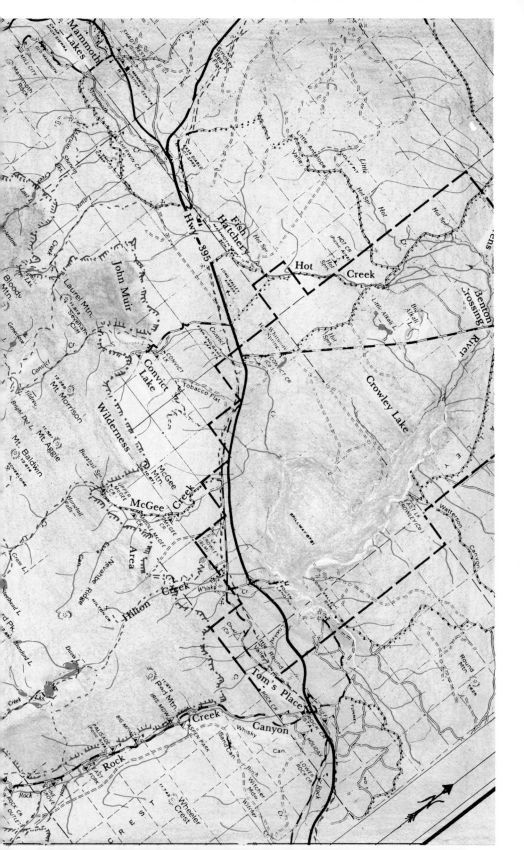

TOMS PLACE
Toms Place, 1934   *Courtesy of Jim Denton*

Hans Lof first had a resort here but in 1919 Tom Yerby, of Bishop, bought the buildings and land and it has since been called Toms Place. This small community boasts a store with ice, groceries, fishing supplies and sundries, a cafe, room and cabin rentals, gas and propane, and telephones. It is a good stock-up place before going up Rock Creek Canyon to the many campgrounds or to fish. In winter a parking area is kept free of snow for skiers.

Across the highway, just to the right, is TUFF CAMPGROUND. The road circles around some houses before ascending to a plateau and heading northwest to reach Long Valley Dam, the outlet for Crowley Lake. A different view of Lake Crowley can be seen here. Unimproved roads which are great for bicycling, continue through the forested lands as far as Casa Diablo Mountain (7912 '). Roads to the east side of Crowley Lake lead to the Watterson Canyon Road and over to Chidago Flat where gold mines were situated.

Jim Denton

ROCK CREEK CANYON   Little Lakes Valley   *Jim King*

When cross-country skiing became popular a few years ago Rock Creek Canyon was opened all year. The roadend up Rock Creek Canyon at Mosquito Flat (10,250 ') is the highest entry into the backcountry of the eastern Sierra. It is higher than Tioga Pass (9941 '). Whitebark pines grow in this alpine environment, some standing upright, buffeted by gales. At higher elevations their gnarled trunks hug the earth.

Up beneath the shadows of Mt. Dade (13,000 '), Mt. Abbott (13,715 ') and Mt. Mills (13,468 ') sits pristine Little Lakes Valley in a deep north-to-south glacial trough. This wonderful fishing country has been visited and appreciated by hikers and photographers since early days. Trails lead up the canyon to many lakes, and over Morgan Pass where pocket meadows are a glorious spectacle of sub-alpine wildflowers in the early summer. Other trails lead south to Pine Creek via Morgan Pass or over Mono Pass (12,000 ') to the famous Recesses, Mono Creek country and the Pioneer Basin lakes. A trail from Rock Creek Lake goes up and over to Hilton Creek Lakes and Hilton Creek Roadend. This route is the easiest way to upper Hilton Creek. Wilderness Permits are required.

Excellent campgrounds are located along tumbling Rock Creek amid cottonwoods, willows, birch and aspens. Some well-placed camp sites nestle among pinyon and Jeffrey pines. In early October the color of the leaves add furthern beauty to this glacial canyon. Check the map and campground chart at the back of the book for specifics.

ROCK CREEK PACK STATION offers complete outfitting for all types of pack trips into the backcountry, as well as day and excursion trips.

ROCK CREEK LODGE offers room and cabin rentals, restaurant, showers, a store with ice, groceries, fishing supplies, firewood, sundries and gas. There are no public telephones beyond Toms Place. In winter, the Lodge has cross-country ski rentals and ski instructions, showers, room and cabin rentals, restaurant and sundries in the store.

ROCK CREEK LAKE RESORT has a cafe, groceries, ice, fishing supplies, firewood, showers, boat rentals, gasoline and propane.

In winter check with the Mammoth Ranger Station for avalanche warnings. They also give free information on how to have a safe winter backcountry trip.

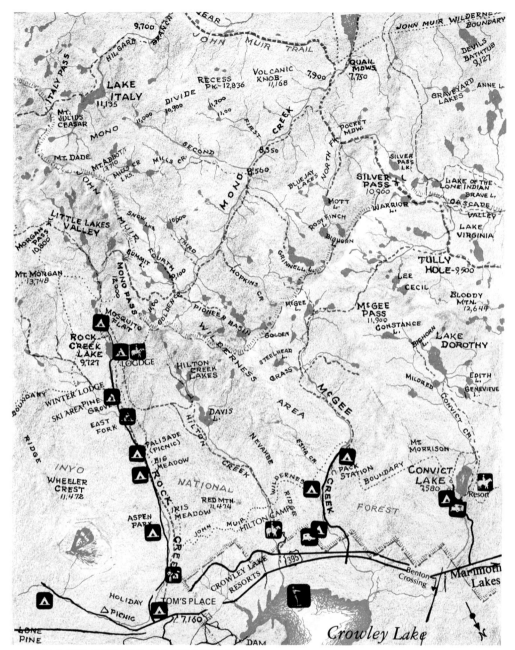

ROCK CREEK COUNTRY

The Rock Creek roadhead at 10,400' is one of the highest in the Sierra. Because of the easy approach to the Mono Creek Basin from the John Muir Trail it is a heavily used area. Firewood is scarce so chemical fuel campstoves are necessary. Be sure to check with the Ranger when you secure your Wilderness Permit for available overnight camp sites. Because of the many lakes and basins, there are places that are not too crowded. For instance in the second Recess area, to get off the beaten track cross-country is possible by following the contour of the land, old abandoned trails and ducked routes.

CROWLEY LAKE

Crowley Lake at the Dam   MAC

Crowley Lake (6781') was named in memory of the Very Reverand Monsignor John J. Crowley, or, as he was better known — Father Crowley or the Desert Padre. He loved this eastern Sierra country and dedicated his life to its welfare.

This reservoir, the largest in Mono County, is part of the Los Angeles domestic water supply and is administered by the Los Angeles Department of Recreation and Parks. In 1932 the Los Angeles Water system was extended to Long Valley, and in 1941 Crowley Lake was completed. The lake is the dominant feature of Long Valley.

Cattle graze contentedly in the grassy meadows surrounding the lake and add a bucolic touch to the high mountain slopes nearby. Crowley Lake has become synonymous with opening day of fishing. Some 30,000 anglers gather around the shore and in boats to start the season. Someone once said that it is the only time to fish Crowley, because by nightfall all the biggest and best fish are taken. Not really! The trout, Sacramento perch (locals call them Crowley Lake Crappie), and catfish do however become sluggish in the warm shallow waters and taste musty late in the summer, so the season is over at the end of July. Water skiing is permitted in the lake and enjoyed all summer, but no swimming is allowed.

Boats can be rented and reserved. Permit fees for private boats or city rentals include inspection and launching. Because gusts of winds from both the desert and mountains are sudden and sometimes extremely strong, no boats less than 12 feet are allowed on the water. That includes rubber rafts and canoes.

CROWLEY LAKE STORE has groceries, ice, drinks, newspapers, books, fishing supplies and information. Licenses can be obtained here. CAMP HIGH SIERRA offers wooded areas for campers with trailers, RV's or tents. They have cabins, a recreational lodge, hot showers, and RV Sanitary Dump Facilities. CROWLEY LAKE RESORT has trailer rentals and housekeeping units.

Continuing north up Highway 395, just past the McGee Maintenance Station, the road climbs up on the moraine to reach the upper end of Long Valley. Before turning away from Long Valley take time to stop and look at the extensive peaceful scenery with Crowley Lake and the High Sierra peaks, McGee Canyon moraine and the White Mountains, with Glass Mountain to the east.

HILTON CREEK

In spring and early summer when the snow melts, new buds and blossoms renew the beauty of this lovely canyon. Hiking is the best mode of travel as the road is short. The sublime Hilton Creek Lakes are a photographer's delight. They are nestled beneath Mt. Huntington (12,405') and Stanford Peak (12,851'). Richard Hilton, for whom the creek and lakes were named, came from Michigan in the early 1870's to settle in Round Valley as a blacksmith and dairy man. He had a milk ranch in Little Round Valley meadow between Toms Place and the Hilton Creek turnoff on Crowley Lake Road. This portion of the old highway 395, El Camino Sierra, from Toms Place up Long Valley, is a pleasant, easy ride for sightseeing or bicycling. Sheep can be seen grazing in the meadow. A new Hilton Creek American Youth Hostel has been opened for year-round use in a renovated cowboy bunkhouse.

MCGEE CREEK CANYON

The McGee brothers were well-liked early homesteaders and cattlemen in Inyo and Mono Counties. The canyon, meadow, creek, pass, lakes and mountain were named for them.

The entrance to McGee Canyon follows around and up along the moraine that extends out into Long Valley. Each mile becomes more spectacular with the color of the gray and red ridges of the surrounding mountain peaks. This gouged-out narrow canyon has avalanche chutes and vertical cliffs all the way up to its head. Campgrounds, picnic areas and a pack station are up in the canyon.

MCGEE PACK STATION offers many trips into the backcountry for families or groups. There are day and dinner rides, junior packer campouts, long backcountry spot trips, and deer hunting. Fishing trips are available up to the lake basin and over McGee Pass to the John Muir Wilderness Area.

The headwaters of McGee Creek rise in half a dozen lakes along the northeast wall of Glacial Divide. Steelhead Lake which is nestled in an alpine cirque is a good, strenuous six-mile hike. Grass lake is a little over four miles and is in a lovely mountain meadow setting. From McGee Pass (11,900') trails lead into the famous fishing country of Cascade Valley and Fish Creek country.

McGee Canyon with Moraine   MAC

GLASS MOUNTAIN (11,123') beyond Crowley Lake is a true volcanic peak with pumice slopes and obsidian outcroppings. This lofty peak is dwarfed by the overpowering mountains on each side of it. Roads lead to the base of the ridge from Highway 120, west out of Benton.

For an extended, interesting loop trip, take the old 1878 stage route between Mammoth Lakes and Benton. Go to Benton Crossing, then down to Watterson Canyon and north past the Banner Ridge where the gold mines were. The road goes to Wildrose Canyon, past Watterson Meadows to Highway 120. This will take you east to Benton Hot Springs and Benton, then west to Highway 395 below Mono Lake. A shorter trip would be to take the gravel road west past Big Sand Flat through the pinyon and Jeffrey pine forest to Wilson Butte and Highway 395.

Back on Highway 395, just after turning the corner out of Long Valley, one of the most awe-inspiring, breathtaking views along the highway can be seen. The unparalleled Ritter Range and Minarets with its jagged crest are on the far horizon. Imposing Mammoth Mountain and the wide open valley on either side of the road are ahead. Mt. Laurel is just to the left.

High Sierra Presbyterian Church   MAC

At the junction with WHITMORE HOT SPRINGS and BENTON CROSSING is the High Sierra Community Presbyterian Church standing alone by the road. The church was erected in 1954 and services are held every Sunday throughout the year.

WHITMORE HOT SPRINGS, a mile off Highway 395, has a public outdoor pool and recreation area operated by the Los Angeles Department of Recreation and Parks. The warm 80° water is fed from the nearby springs which are not unusual in this volcanic land. Further east along the road to Benton Crossing are the shallow Alkali Lakes on a high plateau, and in large meadows cattle can be seen grazing. Terrific views can be had of the eastern escarpment of the Sierra Crest.

BROWN'S OWENS RIVER CAMPGROUND offers good campsites for the spincasters or fly fishermen on the Owens River. There are tables and grills, showers and a store, closed during the winter months.

CONVICT LAKE

H. Remington Slifka

The Indian name for this lovely lake surrounded by colorful rugged peaks, aspens and wildflowers in the high desert environment was "wit-sa-nap". At first the settlers called the canyon and creek Mount Diablo, but when in September 24, 1871 six of the 29 convicts from a prison break in Carson City were caught by the lake, the name was changed to Convict Lake, Creek and Canyon.

After the murder of a mail carrier near the Aurora mining community posses were organized. It was one of the most dramatic shoot-outs and manhunt after a jailbreak in the California and Nevada history. Some of the convicts fled to Bishop where two were hung, three were returned to the Nevada Territorial Prison and one escaped never to be heard of again.

The clear blue cold waters of Convict Lake (7583 ') rests in the glacially carved out basin below Laurel Mountain (11,812 ') and Mt. Morrison (12,268 '), the high peak to the south. Robert Morrison was a member of the Benton posse and was killed by the convicts, so the peak was named in his memory. Fossil stems of crinoid, which were small animals or sea lilies that lived in the shallow waters that covered this part of the Sierra in the late Paleozoic period of time, were found in the dark rocks of Mt. Morrison. They are said to be the oldest in the Sierra.

For a pleasant, easy one-mile hike to a picnic spot on a graveled beach, walk along the north shore of Convict Lake on the Convict Creek Trail leading to Mildred, Dorothy and Genevieve Lakes. The trail follows along the base of the beautiful and rugged Laurel Mountain with its patches of white snow for most of the year.

At the south side of the lake a paved path extends about a half-mile to the parking area for fishermen and day hikers. A fishermen's trail circles around the lake to meet the picnic spot and Convict Creek Trail.

The trail up to Mildred Lake is steep and rocky. The lake lies in a typical U-shaped canyon gouged out by the glacier long ago. It is slowly being filled in with the gravel and silt carried by the waters from above and one day will be only a high alpine meadow. The deep trough of the canyon with the lakes glistening in its basin beneath Red Slate Mountain is magnificent. A trail from Lake Dorothy goes to Lakes Genevieve and Edith before climbing up between Bloody Mountain (12,544 ') and Laurel Mountain where whitebark pines cling to the rocks. The serene alpine Laurel Lakes are nestled below Bloody Mountain and Laurel Creek and Canyon extends north to the Sherwin Creek Road.

CONVICT LAKE RESORT, two miles in from Highway 395 over the moraine, is in a lovely aspen grove with rustic and comfortable cabins completely furnished. They are within walking distance to the lake and creek for fishing. There is a General Store, telephones, boat rentals and a renowned restaurant with a most beautiful view. The resort is open all year.

The campground has some pull-throughs as well as tent pads, in a desert environment or among the willows along the creek. There is a RV Sanitary Dumping Station here.

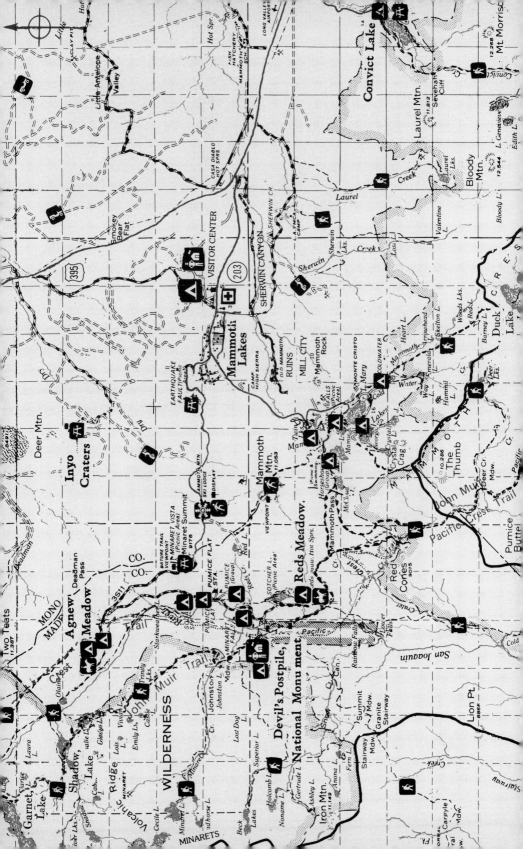

HOT CREEK

MAC

Hot Creek is reached by the gravel road across from Convict Lake Road. It is an interesting ride, passing through dramatic volcanic outcroppings among the sage, rabbitbrush and desert grasses. Fly fishing along Hot Creek is extremely popular although only barbless hooks can be used as the fish bag limit is zero. Here, it is the sport of fly fishing that counts. A Fishermen's Trail leads down to the creek from the parking area.

HOT CREEK GEOTHERMAL AREA is famous for its sulfur or rotten egg smell. It's an unusual place especially in winter, with hot steam rising from the creek while the banks are covered with snow. There is a picnic area, parking and rest rooms. Stairs and railings assist in reaching the creek and the scalding pools of deep blue water, hot steam and lush green banks. Swimming is not encouraged or recommended due to the natural hazards of the extremely unstable ground, slippery rocks and boiling water.

MAMMOTH LAKES FISH HATCHERY   MAC

Beside breeding stock, catchable trout are raised at the hatchery to be stocked in the surrounding lakes and streams. The springs of Hot Creek provide the essential temperature for nurturing these fingerlings so they can grow all year round. Along with other fish hatcheries in the Eastern Sierra enough trout are raised and planted in the lakes and creeks to meet the demand during fishing season.

There are no guided tours here but hatchery employees seem more than happy to answer questions. It is particularly fun when feeding time comes to see all the fish in the holding tanks scramble for their food. Money received from fishing licenses throughout the state of California support the hatcheries and other fish and game programs.

MAMMOTH-JUNE LAKES AIRPORT

This active airport with its large open approach serves the communities of the upper Eastern Sierra via Alpha Air. There's long and short term auto parking available; two charter services and car rentals. Other services at the airport include fueling for private planes and monthly tie-downs for aircraft.

DC-9 Taking Off at Airport   John Anderson

MAMMOTH LAKES
Mammoth Crest & Crystal Crag   L. Dean Clark

Little is left of the old mining camp. Since Dave McCoy set up the first ski tows in 1938 on Mammoth Mountain, and ski races were held by winter sports enthusiasts, the town has never stopped expanding. New roads, new malls and new residences have built Mammoth Lakes into a well established all year resort area. Skiing is good until late June or early July, when fishermen come to try their luck in the lakes. Numerous campsites in the Mammoth Lakes Basin, or Sherwin Creek and near the Visitor Center help to provide good mountain holidays in a pleasant atmosphere under the Jeffrey pine forest cover. All services are available to satisfy visitor needs.

There are six churches of various faiths, Mono County Medical Health Clinic and Hospital, Library, and modern services. The Summer Music Festival; the Fourth of July Gold Rush Days with parade and gaities; the Mammoth Lakes International Arts and Craft Festival; the annual Motocross Race and Tennis Tournament all contribute to the cultural spirit of the present mountain community. Public tennis courts are on Forest Trail Road. The Motocross course is on Sherwin Road. Shady Rest Park has a soccer field, playground, picnic tables and restrooms. For full details and fishing maps read MAMMOTH-MONO COUNTRY by Lew and Ginny Clark, a Western Trails Publication.

Trails around and between the lakes in the forested basin are especailly enjoyable for day hikes or evening strolls among the pines or along the shores. The trails are not too steep, with only short climbs. Flowers prevail in the meadows most of the summer. In autumn the colorful leaves of the aspens add their own beauty.

THE LAKES
TWIN LAKES: Campgrounds. Store. Boat rental (no motors). Handicap Pier. Footbridge between lakes. Forest Chapel. Picnic Area. Scenic falls. Tamarack Lodge.

LAKE MARY: Campgrounds. Store. Yes on boat motors (10 mph max.) Pokonobe Lodge. Crystal Crag Lodge. Wilderness Trailhead.

LAKE MAMIE: Store. Wildyrie Lodge. Boat rental. Yes on boat motors (10 mph max.)

LAKE GEORGE: Campground. Store. Woods Lodge. Boat rental. Yes on boat motors. (10 mph max.) Wilderness Trailhead.

LAKES BARRETT AND T.J.: No boats, motors or facilities.

CRYATAL LAKE: No facilities.

HORSESHOE LAKE: Group camping only, reservations required. Boating. No boat motors. Picnic Area. Swimming on sandy beach. Wilderness Trailhead.

McCLOUD LAKE: No boats, motors or facilities.

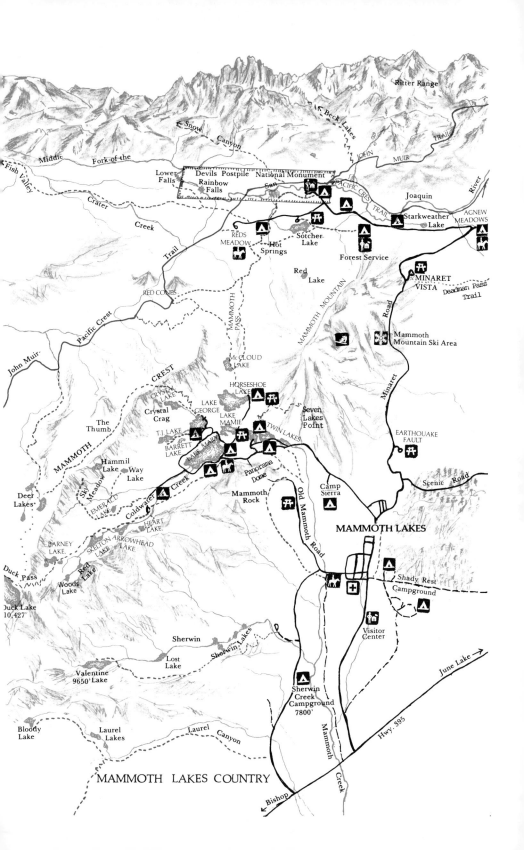

MAMMOTH LAKES COUNTRY

AROUND MAMMOTH LAKES
Rocky Rockwell

MINARET VISTA: A breathtaking canyon vista of the Middle Fork of the San Joaquin River headwaters and the Ritter Range with the rugged Minarets beyond. In the evening watch the sun set behind the craggy Minarets across the valley. Few places provide such a sublime experience or such a sweeping contrast of lush green valley with the towering crests above.

There are picnic tables. Signs provide a self-guiding tour, identifying trees and shrubs, geologic rocks and vista points. The two-and-a-half mile trail leads out along the ridge for a good walk. Take a sweater as it could be chilly. Vista Point is off Minaret Road west of Mammoth Lakes Mountain Ski Area.

MAMMOTH MOUNTAIN SKI AREA: Gondola rides to the top of Mammoth Mountain operate during summer affording fabulous views of the entire Mammoth-Mono country. There's a cafeteria and sport shop.

EARTHQUAKE FAULT: This formation is reached via Minaret Road west of Mammoth Lakes. An exhibit describes the geological break in earth's surface, and a short nature trail leads down to the crack.

PANORAMA DOME: A mile-and-a-half loop trip through the forest provides a fine panoramic view of the entire Mammoth Lakes basin.

PACK STATIONS
Mammoth Lakes Pack Outfit: Operates near Lake Mary. Hourly rides around the forested basin of Mammoth Lakes. Overnight trips to John Muir and Ansel Adams Wilderness Areas, Valentine and Laurel Lakes basin.

Sierra Meadows Equestrial Center: Guided trail rides by the hour or day. Boarding and training facilities. Riding instructions from beginners to advance riders.

Earthquake Fault

L. Dean Clark

126

DEVILS POSTPILE NATIONAL MONUMENT

From Mammoth Lakes the Minaret Road descends to Devils Postpile National Monument, Reds Meadow and Agnew Meadows area through a forest cover on the western slope of the San Joaquin Ridge. Shuttle buses go down to the floor of the San Joaquin River Valley during the summer. By using the bus visitors can enjoy the beauty of this unique valley instead of having to concentrate on driving along the narrow curved road. The pumice and crumbly granite fragments from volcanic action become evident as the valley floor is reached.

There are rustic campgrounds situated along the river, at the Monument, Reds Meadow and Agnew Meadows. Fishing, horseback riding and hiking are predominant sports. Trails lead from the valley floor to backcountry lakes in the Ansel Adams Wilderness Area. Boats are permitted on Sotcher Lake but no motors. Hot Springs are located at Reds Meadow Campground. Ranger programs are provided in the summer.

REDS MEADOW RESORT has cabins, a restaurant and soda fountain, gasoline, groceries, fishing supplies and a pack station. This is the shuttle bus terminal for hikers going to Rainbow Falls.

At Devils Postpile National Monument Headquarters are phones and a campground.

DEVILS POSTPILE

The huge basalt columns known as Devils Postpile were formed in stages over many centuries. The formation is of volcanic origin and had its beginnings in the great earthquake fault that lies along the east side of the Sierra range. Weaknesses along the fracture allowed great flows of lava to pour forth, some of them 1000 feet in depth. As the lava cooled, stress cracks developed in much the same geometric pattern as they do on clay and mud flats when they dry up.

The cracks formed four to seven-sided sections from 20″ to 30″ across. As the cooling process continued, the cracking extended downward to the base of the flow, forming the posts. Later, when glaciers passed over the region the flowing ice cut down the thickness of the lava flows and tore away whole sections. The sheer columns of basalt then became exposed. Evidences of the glacial action are seen in the large piles of broken posts below the main formation, and in the polished surface on the tops of standing posts.

RAINBOW FALLS

The falls, within the National Monument, is considered to be one of the most beautiful in the Sierra, especailly where the sun creates a rainbow mist in the afternoon. A steep short trail leads down to the San Joaquin River below the falls. The many flowers and shrubs at the base are very appealing in the refreshingly cool environment. Take a lunch and camera and enjoy a pleasant day in beautiful surroundings.

L.Dean Clark

IDENTIFYING THE MOST COMMON CONE-BEARING TREES

NAME	SILHOUETTE	CONES	BARK	NEEDLES	RESIDENCE PREFERENCE
PONDEROSA PINE	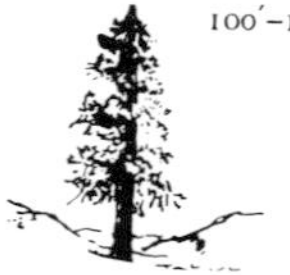 100′–180′ ht. 3′–5′ dia. Trunk smooth, cylindrical, with little taper until crown branches. Limbs tip upward on ends.	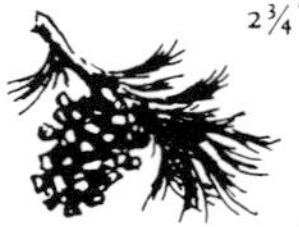 2¾″–5¾″ long. 2″–3″ dia. Oval shape, clustered near end of branches.	3″–4″ thick. Surface divided into broad, shieldlike yellow plates. Surface broken into small, concave, flaky scales.	6″–11¼″ long. 3 in a bundle. Deep yellow-green. Grouped in heavy, brushlike clusters at ends of branches. 	3,000′–5,500′ elevations. Very wide distribution.
INCENSE-CEDAR	 75′–120′ ht. 2¼′–4½′ dia. Crown open and irregular on mature trees. Young have smooth, conical shape.	 1″–1½″ long. ½″ dia. Urn-shaped when green. Sections roll back when ripe.	3″–8″ thick on mature trees. Cinnamon-red, deeply fissured with soft, stringy texture. On young trees is thin, scaly, reddish-brown, flakes off easily.	 ¼″–½″ scalelike leaves covering twigs in tight, overlapping sequence. Very fragrant. Rich, shiny-green coloring	3,000′–6,000′ elevation. Some are 5′–6′ dia. and 125–150′ ht. Those 2′–3′ dia. approx. 300 yrs. A few reach 500 yrs.
SUGAR PINE	 150′–200′ ht. 5′–8′ dia. Flat-topped, long sweeping branches in upper third of tree.	 12″–23″ long. 2½″–5″ dia. Pendent near outer ends of upper branches.	1½″–4″ thick. Medium brown, deeply fissured segments tinged with red.	2½″–4″ long. 5 in a bundle. Blue-green. 	4,000′–8,000′ elevation. North and east slopes of canyons
WHITE FIR	 140′–180′ ht. 3½′–6′ dia. Very massive. Lower 1/3 clear.	3″–5″ long. 1½″–2¾″ dia. Erect on outer tips of limbs near top of trees. 	4″–6½″ thick. Silvery on young trees. Ash-gray to deep brownish-yellow beneath. Young stems have resin blisters.	1″–3″ long. Longest of any fir. Stands out from branch with a twist at its base. Green with whitish tinge. 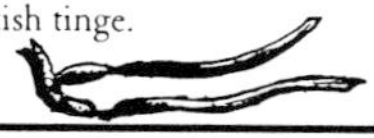	3,500′–8,000′ elevation. 3½′–5′ dia. trees range from 275–450 yrs. old.
RED FIR	 125′–175′ ht. 1½′–5′ dia. Many with broken crowns.	5″–8″ long. 2¾″–3½″ dia. Stand erect near tips of branches. Purplish, edged with brown. 	2″–5″ thick. Deeply fissured and divided by short, diagonal ridges. Outer scales dark red. Inner segments bright red. Surface rough.	¾″–1¼″ long. Four-sided, rounded on top. Attached directly to stem. Limbs form heavy sprays in whorl formation. 	6,000′–9,000′ elevation. Trees 20″–30″ dia. average 225–375 yrs. old.
WESTERN WHITE PINE	 **50′ - 120′ ht. Tall, straight, gently tapered trunk. Upper limbs outward and upward. Similar to Sugar Pine.**	 **4″ - 10″ long. Slender, hang from tips of branches.**	**1″ thick. Surface divided into almost square plates. Dark gray, few loose scales.**	**2″ - 3½″ long. 5 in a bundle. Slender, green. Little shorter than Sugar Pine.** 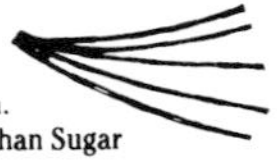	**5,500′ - 7,500′. Found on Alta Peak Trail and Monarch Divide Country.**

Tree	Form & Size	Cone	Bark	Needles	Habitat & Age
JEFFREY PINE	 125'-175' ht. 1½'-4½' dia. Rounded top and many limbs. Large-bodied and straight.	 5"-11" long. 3"-6" dia. Purplish cast.	1½"-3" thick. Reddish-brown, broken into deep plates by narrow furrows. Strong vanilla or pineapple odor.	7"-11" long. 3 in bundle. Blue-green coloring.	5,500'-8,500' elevation. Some age up to 400 yrs. Becomes stunted in high, rocky areas.
MOUNTAIN HEMLOCK	 25'-100' ht. 1'-3½' dia. Limbs close to ground.	 1"-3" long. ½"-1½" dia. Abundant near top.	Young trees: thin and silvery. Mature trees: 1¼" thick, reddish-brown, deeply ridged and furrowed.	½"-¾" long. Grows spirally around branches. Appear thicker on upper side. 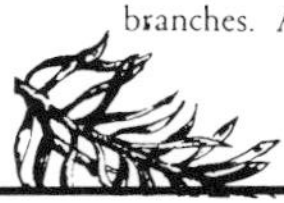	7,700' on up the cool, northern slopes to timberline. Trees 18"-20" dia. and 50'-60' ht. reach ages of 180-250 yrs.
SIERRA JUNIPER	 10'-30' ht. 3'-6' dia. Heavy, twisted trunk.	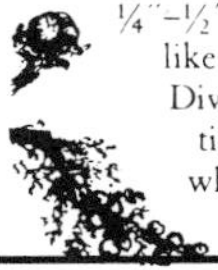 ¼"-½" dia. Looks more like berry than a cone. Divided into three sections. Covered with whitish bloom. Very pungent odor.	2½"-5" thick. Reddish-brown. Long, fibrous ridges of soft bark is easily stripped from trunk.	 ⅛" long. Scalelike, overlapping in clusters of three, similar to incense-cedar. Gray-green.	6,500'-10,000' elevation. On rocky hillsides. Older trees reach ages 500-1,500 yrs. High, rocky ridges
LODGEPOLE PINE	 30'-80' ht. 1-2½' dia. Twisted trunks, often lightning scarred.	 1½"-2½" long. 1"-2" dia. Very numerous.	Very thin. Light gray and yellowish-brown. Very scaly.	1"-2½" long. 2 needles in a bundle. Yellowish-green, often twisted. 	6,000'-10,000' elevation. Ages 100-175 yrs. common.
FOXTAIL PINE	 30'-40' ht. 3'-5' dia. Stands erect. Stout, short branches. Weather-beaten. Some dead limbs.	 2½"-5" long. Dark brown. Finger-shaped. Incurved prickles.	Divided into broad plates. Young trees light gray, smooth. Mature are brown. Old trees orange-brown, furrowed. Lightning scarred.	 1"-1¼" long. 5 in a bundle. Dark blue-green. Short, thickly clustered.	9,000' to timberline. Found on granite ridges.
WHITEBARK PINE	15'-40' ht, 15'-30' dia. in sheltered areas. On open ridges a sprawling, prostrate, shrublike growth. 	 1¼"-3½" long. 1"-2" dia. Oval-shape. Pitchy, thick scales. Purplish.	⅜" thick at base to ¼" on limbs. Dark gray on mature trunk blending to whitish on smooth, outer limbs.	1¼"-2¾" long. 5 in bundle. Dark, yellow-green and thickly clustered near ends of branches. 	9,000' to timberline. 18"-20" dia. are up to 300 yrs. old. 3½"-4" dia. may be 250 yrs. old.

REDS MEADOW and AGNEW MEADOWS PACK STATION

Bob Tanner operates both of these stations where many types of rides can be made from approximately June 15th to October 10th. Pack trips into the Ansel Adams Wilderness Area and Yosemite National Park have become very popular with all ages. Families can enjoy the wonders of the backcountry by walking or riding on the trails while pack mules tote the bedding, cooking and food supplies — with even fresh fruits and vegetables, and portable showers.

It's a six-day trip from Agnew Meadows to Tuolumne Meadows through beautiful 1000 Island Lake area, over Donohue Pass and down the Lyell Fork Canyon. An eight-day trip goes from Reds Meadow to Wawona passing through the lovely southern portion of Yosemite National Park.

One easy way to view Rainbow Falls is to take the wagon ride out of Reds Meadow. A mule-drawn wagon with rubber tires accommodates 15 people at a time. Horses can also be rented for the trip.

Some of the celebrities that Bob Tanner has packed into the backcountry are Art Linkletter, Ronald Reagan, Robert McNamara, Jim Arness and John Wayne. As a matter of fact, back in 1935, John Wayne went down to Rainbow Falls in his first starring role in a black and white film. The Tanners are well-known themselves as for 15 years they have ridden their Leopard appaloosa horses in the Rose Parade in Pasadena. His world champion 20-mule pack train can be seen at the Mule Days in Bishop. Tanner's 125 mountain horses and mules is one of the finest collection in the United States. One of his biggest challenges was when he packed supplies into the June Lake backcountry during the construction of Waugh Lake Dam. It took 4000 mule loads carrying 500 tons of sand and cement — all in 60 days!

Tanner reports that with the conscientiousness of hikers and packers, and the diligence of park and forest services, the mountains are in better shape now than they were 15 years ago. There's less marking of mankind as packers continuously clean up and take out garbage and hikers usually pack out what they take in.

BETWEEN MAMMOTH LAKES TO JUNE LAKES
"THE BURNT LAND"

The first evidences of the tremendous volcanic forces that thrust upward along the Mono Range north of Owens Valley, are the Volcanic Tableland, Glass Mountain, the Bishop Tuff landscape, numerous hot springs and Hot Creek. From Mammoth Mountain north to Mono Lake unique craters and domes can be seen from the highway. Frothy pumice fragments, some boulder size, exploded from the various cones and were scattered throughout the area. This cooled lava froth resembling solid rock can be deceiving. Most of the fragments can float in water. Lava and gray pumicite cover the underbrush, in some places over 3000 feet thick. Pumice Flat, Red Cones, Deadman Pass and Two Teats were also part of the volcanic activity, but cannot be seen from the highway.

MAMMOTH MOUNTAIN was formed by eruptions that piled up thick glassy flows a quarter of a million years ago. Through many years of extensive eruptions the original cone form of the mountain was changed to its present shape. It is not dormant. Some gas vapors still can be seen coming from vents on cold winter days.

JEFFREY PINE FOREST

This is the largest Jeffrey pine forest in the world. These most stately members of the pine family grow in the pumice soil from 75 feet to 175 feet tall and one and one-half to four feet in diameter. The straight, large-bodied trees made excellent mine timbers and were in great demand in the early mining days. The bark is reddish brown and thick, with rough, narrow furrows in young trees, but smoother in older ones. There is a strong vanilla or pineapple smell about them. The cones are large, from three to six inches in diameter, and from five to eleven inches long, with a purple tinge. The end prickles turn inward and do not hurt when handled. Needles come in bunches of three, blue-green, and usually from seven to eleven inches long.

LOOKOUT MOUNTAIN (8352') and BALD MOUNTAIN (9104')

East of Highway 395 are two vantage points that overlook the entire area. They are reached by gravel and dirt roads, with turnoffs marked on the highway.

INYO CRATERS

The two Inyo Craters were formed more recently than the Mono Craters to the north. They are funnel-shaped cones filled with water, making two small, fishless lakes. The rocks that can be seen in the crater wall tell geologists the story of the eruptions. Several million tons of rock debris were spewed out onto the surrounding pumice-covered land. A short trail to the craters winds through a Jeffrey pine forest. The trail can be reached from the Mammoth Scenic Loop Road. Deer Mountain (8796'), just north, is an old cinder cone with no crater at the top.

Inyo Craters   *Rocky Rockwell*

OBSIDIAN DOME (8611')   MAC

The creation of an obsidian dome begins first as an erupted cone. In the center of the cone a volcanic dome of obsidian or rhyolite pushes upward, sometimes partly filling the cone, leaving a moat-like space around the dome, and sometimes completely covering the cone area. When the center dome rises too high and flows over the rim of the cone, it forms a "coulee" as found in Mono Craters.

Pure obsidian is usually black, although it is sometimes a brown and black mixture. Streaks or flakes of white that are found in the black glass was a froth in the hot liquid. When lava cools rapidly glass is formed. Fragments can be sharp as glass and can cut the hand. Indians made arrowheads and spear points from chips of obsidian.

The turnoff to Obsidian Dome is about 15 miles north of Mammoth Lakes. There are foot trails all around the sharp rocks, and picnic places under the pines around to the west and south of the dome.

L.Dean Clark

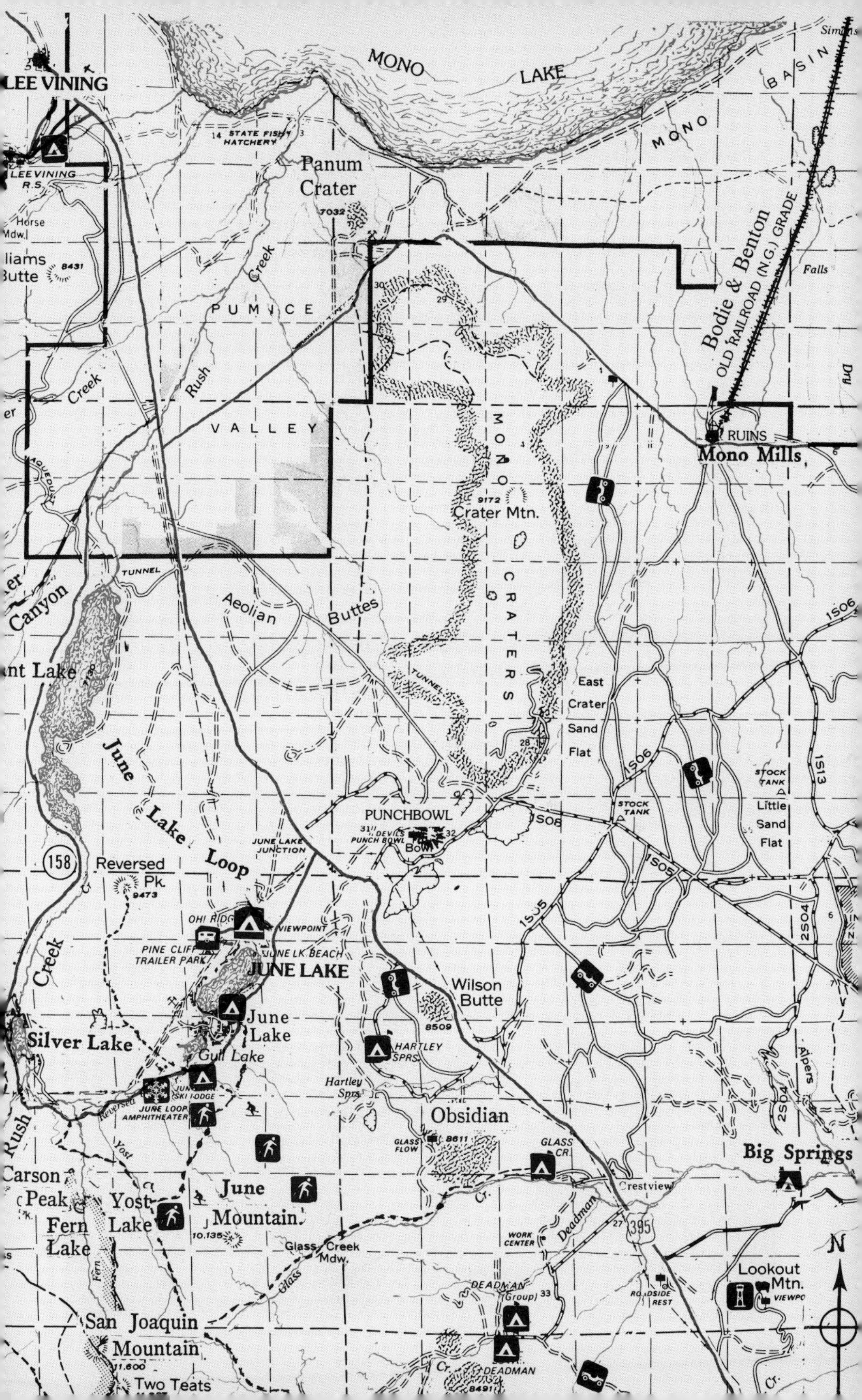

MONO LAKE

LEE VINING

LEE VINING R.S.

STATE FISH HATCHERY

Panum Crater
7032

Horse Mdw.

Williams Butte
8431

MONO BASIN

Bodie & Benton
OLD RAILROAD (N.G.) GRADE

Falls

Dry

PUMICE

Rush Creek

Creek

VALLEY

RUINS
Mono Mills

MONO CRATERS

Crater Mtn.
9172

TUNNEL

Canyon

Aeolian Buttes

TUNNEL

East Crater Sand Flat

June Lake

Lake Loop

158

Reversed Pk.
9473

PUNCHBOWL

June Lake Junction

DEVILS PUNCH BOWL

1S08

Stock Tank

Little Sand Flat

1S06

1506

1513

OH! RIDGE

VIEWPOINT

PINE CLIFF TRAILER PARK

JUNE LAKE

JUNE LK. BEACH

Wilson Butte
8509

Stock Tank

1S05

1S04

June Lake

Silver Lake

Gull Lake

JUNE SKI LODGE

JUNE LOOP AMPHITHEATER

Hartley SPRS.

Hartley Sprs.

Obsidian

GLASS FLOW
8611

GLASS CR.

2S04

Big Springs

Creek

Rush

Carson Peak

Yost Lake

Fern Lake

June Mountain
10,135

GLASS CREEK

Glass Creek Mdw.

WORK CENTER

Crestview

Deadman

27

395

ROADSIDE REST

Lookout Mtn.
VIEWPO

San Joaquin Mountain
11,600

Glass

Cr.

DEADMAN (Group) 33

DEADMAN
8491

N

WILSON BUTTE

Next feature to watch for on the west side of the highway is Wilson Butte, a rhyolite dome formed perhaps less than 5000 years ago. Rhyolite is a fine-grained felsite, light in color, with minerals so minute that they cannot all be identified easily. The almost treeless dome at one time was covered with trees but a violent storm in the early 1900's uprooted them from the rain-sodden pumice soil. At the base of the Butte you can see many of the old tree trunks.

DEVILS PUNCHBOWL

This interesting crater can be reached by a dirt mining road to the east past Wilson Butte that leads up to its rim. This is a small, well-preserved explosion cone. The crater is 1200 feet in diameter and 240 feet deep. At the bottom there is a small obsidian plug 40 feet high and 250 feet in diameter.

Between Mammoth Lakes and June Lake there are several campgrounds: Big Springs, Deadman Recreational Area, Glass Creek and Hartley Springs. Check the campground chart at the back of the book for specifics. There is a Rest Area on Highway 395 with picnic tables and parking to stop awhile and walk under the Jeffrey pines.

MAC

JUNE LAKE LOOP
L.Dean Clark

As shown on the map, the June Lake Loop resembles a horseshoe, as it was original-ly called. But long before the government surveyors named this unusual stream and lake configuration, the Paiute Indians found Reversed Creek Canyon an excellent homeland. The forest provided shelter and fuel and the streams provided fish. They traded obsidian for acorns from the Miwok Indians of Yosemite. The meeting place was near Mono Pass, which today is a principal trans-Sierra trail route.

This horseshoe valley is outstanding geologically and topographically with its four lakes (June, Gull, Silver and Grant) and two creeks (Reversed and Rush). Reversed Creek is so named because it flows toward the mountains and not away from them, as in the usual drainage pattern. Starting at June Lake (7616') the water flows westward to Gull Lake and down to meet Rush Creek and Silver Lake (7223') at the base of the Sierra escarpment. From Silver Lake the waters flow north to Grant Lake before reaching Mono Lake at 6402'.

Standing at the viewpoint on OH! Ridge one looks down at June and Gull Lakes, and Reversed Peak. June Lake Village tucked in among the trees and the Sierra peaks beyond is a spectacle in miniature. A breathless "ooooh!" is in order. This is a year-round resort area. Skiing and winter sports are as popular as camping, hiking, biking, and fishing.

JUNE LAKE VILLAGE is a complete shopping center. In the alpine setting there are sporting good stores, a grocery store, gift shops, laundromat, restaurants and cafes, service stations, and garages. Many lodges and motels operate in winter as well as summer.

On the north side of June Lake below the OH! Ridge summit is PINE CLIFF RESORT and TRAILER PARK. It offers a general store, modern trailer spaces, trailer rentals and storage, laundry and showers. The large June Lake Campground is located beside the resort. Other U.S. Forest Service campgrounds are situated along June and Gull Lakes, and along Reversed and Silver Creeks. SILVER LAKE RESORT has a trailer park, cafe, store, boat and motor rentals, housekeeping cabins and fishing sup-plies. It is one of the earliest resorts in the June Lake area. FERN CREEK LODGE has an Rv Sanitary Disposal, grocery and sporting goods store, modern housekeeping cabins, gas and propane. GRANT LAKE MARINA has trailer accommodations, dump station, showers, cafe, store and marina with boat and motor rentals.

The FRONTIER PACK TRAIN offers backcountry trips into the Yosemite National Park and Ansel Adams Wilderness Area. Many types of rides and tours are available with arrangements personalized to suit each rider's interest and needs.

Around the junction at the southern end of the June Lake Loop Road and Highway 395 is a Mini Mart, gas, California AAA agent, and tow and trailer rentals.

AEOLIAN BUTTES

These buttes, resulting from the oldest volcanic action in the Mono Basin, are over-shadowed by the Mono Craters behind them. An interesting trip can be made by way of a good dirt road that reaches the buttes and other uniquely shaped outcroppings and rock formations.

MONO BASIN

West of the large fault basin called Mono is the Sierra Nevada escarpment, rising over 6000 feet above the basin floor. Deep canyons have been carved out by glaciers, separating the narrow, jagged peaks. Between this escarpment and Mono Craters is the morainal belt. Four different glacial stages can be identified by the moraines left after each glacial epoch receded, modifying the earlier moraines. The large flat plains area of the Basin stretches out eastward far into Nevada. The land is treeless — a desert environment with alkaline valleys, dry lakes and solidified lava flows. But the two most domineering features of Mono Basin are Mono Craters and Mono Lake.

MONO CRATERS

Mono Craters is a ten-mile-long string of volcanic cones, domes, coulees and small explosion pits. The Mono Volcanic Range reaches its highest and most central point where three tower-like domes of equal size are located. The first explosions of gas-charged lava spewed pumice fragments and formed some 20 cones. Then large, solid, cylindral columns of obsidian rose in some bowl centers forming domes of varying heights. At the north and south ends of the Range are coulees that have separated the lava outpourings. The short, thick flows are covered with obsidian blocks. South of the chain is a 'caldera' created when an eruption came at the end of the volcanic cycle. It has a large, flat-bottomed bowl open to the east, with a small cone built up on the north wall. The tops of the obsidian cliffs forming the walls of the calderas are covered by 30 to 50 feet of volcanic ash.

PANUM CRATER is a small, single crater to the north of the Mono Range, reached via Highway 120 on a marked dirt road. It is an excellent example of an obsidian dome rising up in the center of the cone and is separated from the cone rim by a trench. The dome is a jagged jumble of obsidian crags and sharp spires.

Roadside
Grave

MONO MILLS

Highway 120 to Mono Mills (20 miles), leading to Benton, lies on the flat lake plains area of the Mono Basin. The road passes through some scattered and open Jeffrey and lodgepole pine forests in the pumice ground cover. The base of Mono Craters can be seen with its smooth pumice slopes, along with rugged obsidian outcroppings, from the northwest coulee. Side roads lead to Panum Crater, South Tufa Area and Navy Beach. Paths lead down to the beach area on the lake where swimming is allowed. Pit toilets are here. Numerous California gulls fly overhead. The white coloration on the tufa and ground surfaces are from bird residue.

The quiet canyon with only the rustle of wind in the trees at Mono Mills Site can hardly reflect the noisy activity that took place when the mill was operating. The large millpond, flumes, and buildings have all disappeared as has the original forest from which the trees were cut to supply Bodie with wood for the mills and household fuel.

The grade of the old Bodie and Benton Railroad, a narrow gauge spur line, can be seen today only in places out on the desert floor. Like the mill, the heavy locomotives hauling lumber and wood around the lake and up the grade to Bodie are gone. Not all the wood for Bodie was delivered via railroad. Chinese laborers cut pinyon pines and used an eight-horse jerk-line team to drag logs up to Bodie. As they passed the lake they shot ducks they saw and sold them to the miners and railroad men. A large group of Mono Indians lived at the mill and also worked for the railroad. *MAC*

MONO LAKE

MAC

Ancient Lake Russell, at the north of the Mono Range was some 900 feet deep. The 7000′ elevation shoreline marks the lakeshore during the later part of the last glacial stage. MONO LAKE, as it is now called, has no natural outlet and has shrunk in size through the centuries by evaporation. Old terraces, wave-cut cliffs and shorelines tell the story of the lake as we view it today.

As the body of water evaporated it became more saline, saltier than the ocean, and heavy with mineral deposits within the lake. The algae that grow in the saline waters provide food for the brine shrimp and flies. Pupae of the fly were collected and relished by the Indians. The flies and shrimp supplies food for the numerous birds that migrate through these waters. The eared grebe and phalarope come in the spring and two other species of grebe come in the fall, over 8000,000 in all, to dive for the shrimp and flies. Some 50,000 gulls come to Mono Lake across the Sierra Crest from the Pacific Coast to nest each spring when the food supply is plentiful. There are two resident species — the snowy plover and California gull.

Many fresh water springs lie within the lake and when this calciumated fresh water combines with the carbonated salt water of the main lake body a chemical deposit of calcium carbonate coats the rocks, shoals and logs, building up in towers under the water. When the water level dropped after feeder streams were diverted to the Los Angeles Water System in 1941, these tufa towers were exposed. They break very easily. There are two main tufa tower areas: north of LeeVining, and in the South Tufa Area at the south end of the lake. The Mono Lake Information Center in LeeVining offers guided walk tours around the towers and shoreline. At the South Tufa Area there is a self-guided tour and exhibits.

Two islands are in the center of the lake: Paoha, the larger white island, has some hot springs and small craters resulting from ancient volcanic eruptions. In 1908 an oil well was drilled on the slopes of Paoha. After reaching a depth of 1500 feet all that was raised was hot water. Negit, the smaller black island is also of volcanic origin and is a nesting place for thousands of gulls.

MAC

LEEVINING CANYON

Several RV and tent camping areas on the floor of LeeVining Canyon are along the creek among the aspens in a quiet, off-the-road atmosphere. It is a very popular camp for fishermen who enjoy fishing the creek.

Highway 120 leads westward up LeeVining Canyon to Tioga Pass (9941 ') and the eastern entrance to Yosemite National Park. The road, on the north side of LeeVining Canyon is an engineering feet with an elevation change of 3160 feet in six and a half miles. It is closed in winter after the first big snowfall and is usually open by Memorial Day Weekend. Near the top are viewpoints to look back down this impressive canyon and far out to Mono Basin.

TIOGA PASS RESORT has gas, a store that carries many books, postcards and gift items, a cafe which makes a good lunch stop, and cabins for rent along the creek, that is planted with fish regularly.

Campgrounds in the Inyo National Forest are at Saddlebag, Ellery and Tioga Lakes.

Rocky Rockwell

YOSEMITE NATIONAL PARK
L.Dean Clark

The road eastward from Tioga Pass through the park is in real High Sierra country with alpine meadows, avalanche-scraped slopes, close views of picturesque and colorful Mounts Dana and Gibbs. The good two-lane road descends past Dana Meadows, through a forest along the Dana Fork of the Tuolumne River to look up the Lyell Fork Canyon. Terrific views are of the Cathedral Range peaks southwest of Tuolumne Meadows.

At TUOLUMNE MEADOWS is a store, gas, telephones, post office, Visitor Center, a large campground and Ranger Station. The Backcountry Kiosk is on the road to Tuolumne Meadows Lodge and Pack Station. The Lodge has cabins and store, saddle horses and pack station. Trails lead from here south down the John Muir Trail and north on the Pacific Crest Trail to the North Country.

Every Monday morning during the summer season a seven-day walking loop trip to the five High Sierra Camps leaves Tuolumne Meadows for Glen Aulin. This trip can be made individually or with a Park Ranger Naturalist who discusses the environment along the trail and gives campfire programs each night. Services at each camp are not limited to scheduled trips. Family style meals are served at each camp, with overnight accommodations available, advance reservations required. Each camp has a telephone for emergencies and a small store with staple items.

Daily bus service connects Tuolumne Meadows with Yosemite Valley floor.

Many day hikes and walks that require only moderate effort can be made by the family up the Lyell Fork, along the Dana Fork; up Lembert Dome for unusual views of Tuolumne Meadows and surrounding peaks; or up to Dog Lake ascending through a lodgepole forest and small flowered meadows. Take along a picnic and enjoy a day in this most beautiful part of Yosemite Park. Many birds, flowers and animals can be seen along the trails.

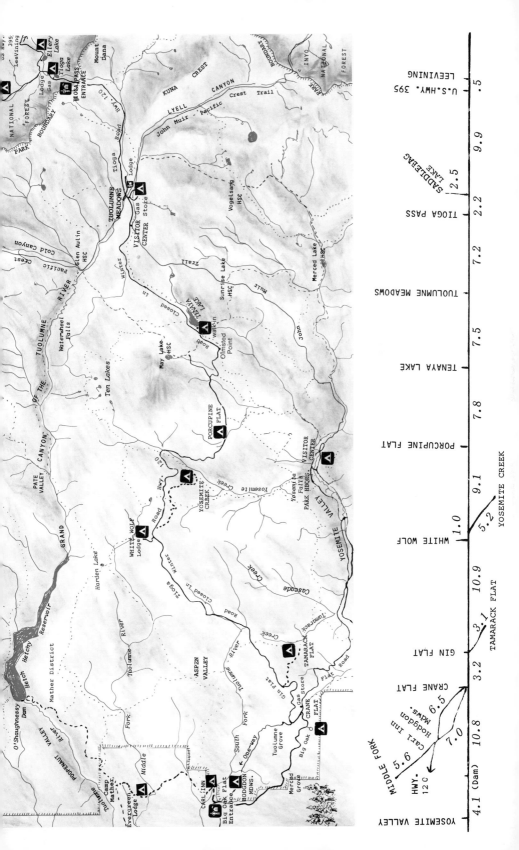

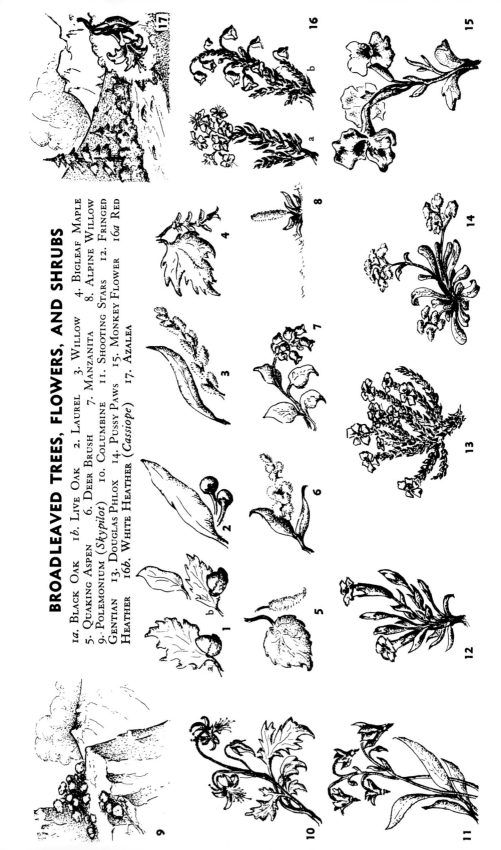

BROADLEAVED TREES, FLOWERS, AND SHRUBS

1*a*. Black Oak   1*b*. Live Oak   2. Laurel   3. Willow   4. Bigleaf Maple
5. Quaking Aspen   6. Deer Brush   7. Manzanita   8. Alpine Willow
9. Polemonium (*Skypilot*)   10. Columbine   11. Shooting Stars   12. Fringed
Gentian   13. Douglas Phlox   14. Pussy Paws   15. Monkey Flower   16*a* Red
Heather   16*b*. White Heather (*Cassiope*)   17. Azalea

SPARROW: (White-crowned Sparrow): Distinguished from other sparrows by black and white stripes on head with one white stripe running back above bill through center of crown. Light grayish-brown on back, underparts light. Seen near thickets in mountain meadows. Has melodious, plaintive song.

BLUEBIRD (Mountain Bluebird): Seen in flight on High Country meadows. Feeds on ground and spends considerable time perched atop a stone singing. Bright blue all over except for a lighter shade on underside. Female usually a paler hue than male.

CHICKADEE (Mountain Chickadee or Short-tailed Mountain Chickadee): His persistent, identifying call of "chick-a-dee" or plaintive "ee-chee-chee" is heard in the High Country. Found on the tiptop twig of tallest trees. Somewhat smaller than a sparrow. Top of head and throat dark; has white line over eye; cheeks and breast are also white.

JUNCO (Oregon, Thurber's, or Sierra Junco): Has quite dark "cape" over head and shoulders; underside is white. Light brown on shoulders and back, center tail feathers black, outer ones white, light-colored bill. Feeds on ground around base of trees. Seen in the High Country at treeline.

ROSY FINCH (Sierra Nevada Rosy Finch): Friendly companion of the high mountain climber. Seen in flocks feeding on snow fields or surface of a glacier. Nests in rocky cliffs along wind-swept ridges above tree line. Bright rosy hue on breast, rump, wings, and shoulders. About the size of a sparrow.

STELLER'S JAY: Large, flashy blue color. Noisy, raucous voice and bold, saucy habits. Lively companion in camp or along the trail. Large feathered crest on head that is dark extending to a blue-black on shoulders and wings. Light blue-gray on underparts. Larger than a robin.

WESTERN TANAGER: His flight in and out of sunlight and shadow is a thing of startling beauty. Often seen at the Mariposa Grove and on floor of Yosemite Valley. Vivid scarlet head, upper back and tail dark, wings black with yellow bars, rest of body a striking yellow. Movements slow and deliberate.

AMERICAN DIPPER: (Water Ouzel): Perches on rocks in midstream, "posts" or bobs up and down when standing. Dives under water for food and propels himself with his wings when submerged. Nests at waterline or behind the spray of waterfalls. Slate-gray, shading to dark on wings and sides of head. Very stubby tail.

AUDUBON'S WARBLER: Has an unusually melodious song heard toward evening. Bluish-gray on underparts; yellow area on crown, throat, on sides near front edge of wings, and on rump. Smaller than a sparrow. Found in areas of oaks and conifers.

CLARK'S NUTCRACKER: (Clark Crow): Usually seen at tree line. Has a noisy cry, quite companionable to people. Pale gray body with dark wings, dark center on tail. Outer edge of tail feathers and rear of wings in white. Size and habits similar to Blue Jay.

Tuolumne Meadows

TRAILHEAD TO THE YOSEMITE HIGH SIERRA

Of the several trailhead centers in Yosemite National Park, Tuolumne Meadows has always been the favorite of back country bound hikers. The Tioga Road provides access at a high elevation, saving a lot of uphill drag needed to get into the high country from trailheads in the western part of the Park. It makes an ideal departure point with main routes leading to the High Sierra Camps, south to the Postpile or Merced River Canyon, and to Yosemite's North Country.

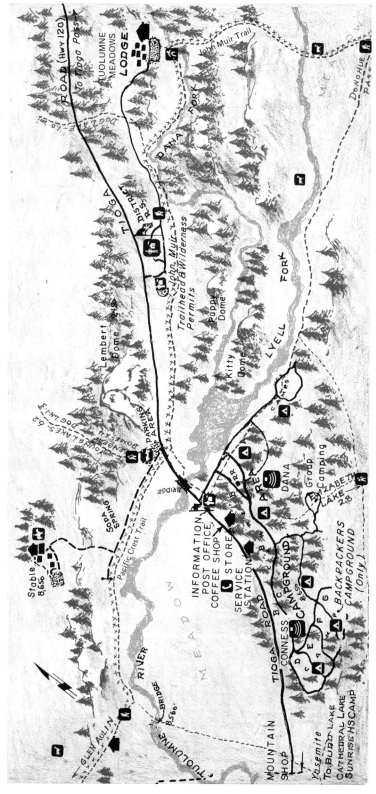

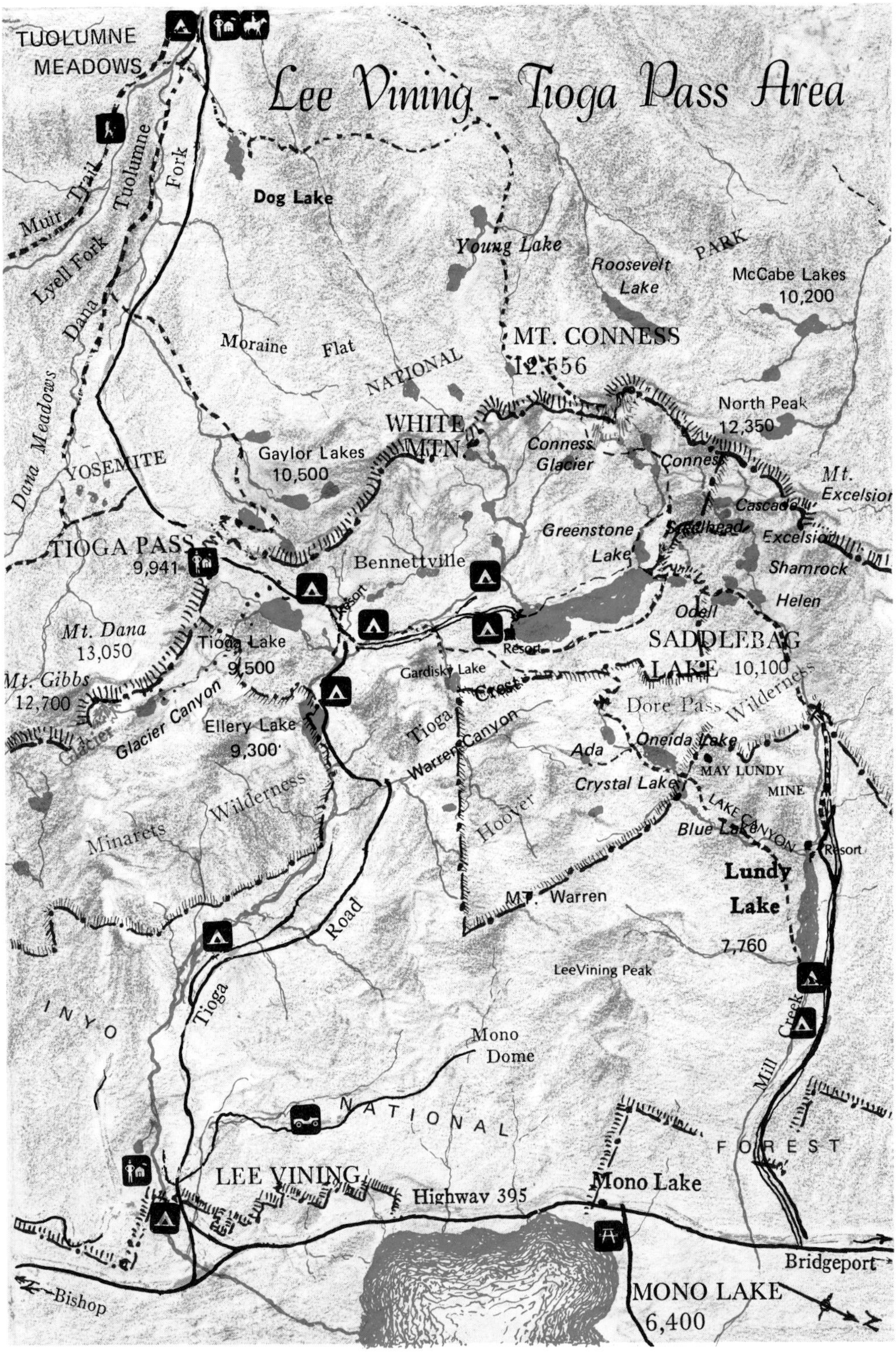

Lee Vining - Tioga Pass Area

TUOLUMNE MEADOWS

Muir Trail

Lyell Fork

Tuolumne Fork

Dana

Dog Lake

Young Lake

Roosevelt Lake

PARK

McCabe Lakes
10,200

Moraine Flat

NATIONAL

MT. CONNESS
12,556

North Peak
12,350

Dana Meadows

YOSEMITE

WHITE MTN.

Gaylor Lakes
10,500

Conness Glacier

Conness

Mt. Excelsion

Cascade

Excelsion

TIOGA PASS
9,941

Bennettville

Greenstone Lake

Saddlebag

Shamrock

Helen

Resort

Mt. Dana
13,050

Tioga Lake
9,500

Odell

SADDLEBAG
LAKE 10,100

Mt. Gibbs
12,700

Gardisky Lake

Resort

Dore Pass

Wilderness

Glacier Canyon

Ada

Oneida Lake

Glacier

Ellery Lake
9,300'

Tioga

Warren Canyon

Crystal Lake

MAY LUNDY
MINE

Minarets

Wilderness

Hoover

Blue Lake

LAKE CANYON

Resort

Mt. Warren

Lundy
Lake
7,760

INYO

Road

Tioga

LeeVining Peak

Mill Creek

Mono Dome

NATIONAL

FOREST

LEE VINING

Highway 395

Mono Lake

Bishop

MONO LAKE
6,400

Bridgeport

LEE VINING (6781')

This is a quaint little community in the shadow of Yosemite National Park and the Sierra peaks, west of awesome, moody Mono Lake. Here you'll find motels, restaurants, service stations, market, trailer parks, gift shops, mini marts and an Indian Trading Post. A city park, one block east of the highway, has picnic tables and a beautiful view of Mono Lake. Mono Lake Information Center, at the center of town, has publications and information on the entire Mono Basin area and offers several interesting tours around the lakeshore.

A mile north of LeeVining there's an access road down to Mono Lake and the Tufa Viewing Area, where you'll find trails and a display. Parking is plentiful down by the lake.

Farther north on Highway 395 along the lake, TIOGA LODGE is open again, with cabins, a cafe and gas. MONO INN RESTAURANT features fine dining five nights a week. At one time this restaurant was extremely popular, specializing in Basque food. People would come for miles around, even as far as Reno, for the tempting cooking and for dancing on the veranda at night. Nearby is the grave of Adeline Carson Stilts, daughter of Kit Carson, the well-known scout and explorer. Adeline came to Mono Diggings with her husband and died at an early age. She was Kit Carson's favorite daughter and he called her "Desert Flower".

MONO LAKE COUNTY PARK is off Cemetary Road on the northwest shore of Mono Lake. It is in a lovely setting with shade trees, a playground, picnic tables, rest rooms, and water. No overnight camping is allowed.

The drive north of LeeVining begins the ascent of Conway Summit, passing through sage and rabbitbrush slopes, and meadows with grazing sheep. Tall, grand Lombardy poplar trees — that look like vine-covered utility poles — are colorful in the fall season. Snow fences that keep the drift off the highway in winter parallel the road. Those interesting, sculptured outcroppings on the way up Conway Summit are an old land formation that was covered with alluvial materials, then eroded away to leave the Rattlesnake Gulch granitic rocks.

Tufa on Mono Lake   *Frank Balthis*

146

LUNDY CANYON

In 1878, when Bodie was in full swing and the demand for more wood was endless, a sawmill was built in Lundy Canyon. Gold was discovered there in 1880 and the lively town had over 500 souls. The mines were small, but good producing ones up Lake Canyon. Total production of these hard rock mines — Lundy, May, Gorilla, and Parrot — was over $3 million. These were not easy placer mines. Ore had to be blasted out by dynamite, making tunnels as miners went deeper into the mountain to get to the precious ore. Cars on tracks hauled ore out to the openings where it was carried away by mule teams. Supplies were brought in on the road up as far as the lake, where the mule teams packed everything up to the 11,000' elevation mine. In springtime, sleds were used for easier hauling.

For more than 15 years Ralph and Bambie Mecey have been the owners of Lundy Lake Resort. This rustic mountain camping and fishing establishment has been popular since its construction in 1935, when Carl and Ellen Miller first built it. There are two old buildings on the property that were in the original town of Lundy — one is owned by the Muir-Hanna family. Tom Hanna, owner of Lundy Mines in the 1920's, married one of John Muir's daughters. The other original buildings were torn down, crumbled from numerous avalanches or destroyed by fire.

There is a store here with ice, books, fishing supplies, firewood, sundries, boat and motor rentals and beer. Hops grow on the front porch entrance to keep the building colorful and cool in the summer. Eleven cabins, eight trailer spaces and 26 tent camping sites lie among willows, shrubs and aspen trees. Showers and laundry are available. The Resort is open from the first day of trout fishing until November 1st, when it becomes a wee bit cold for fishing.

Lundy Lake is about a mile long and lies in the center of a canyon carved out by one of the branches of the Conness Glacier field. Evidences of the glacial activity can be seen in the lower lateral moraines and up Mill Creek at the head of Lundy Canyon, where many ponds are found at the headwaters of North Peak.

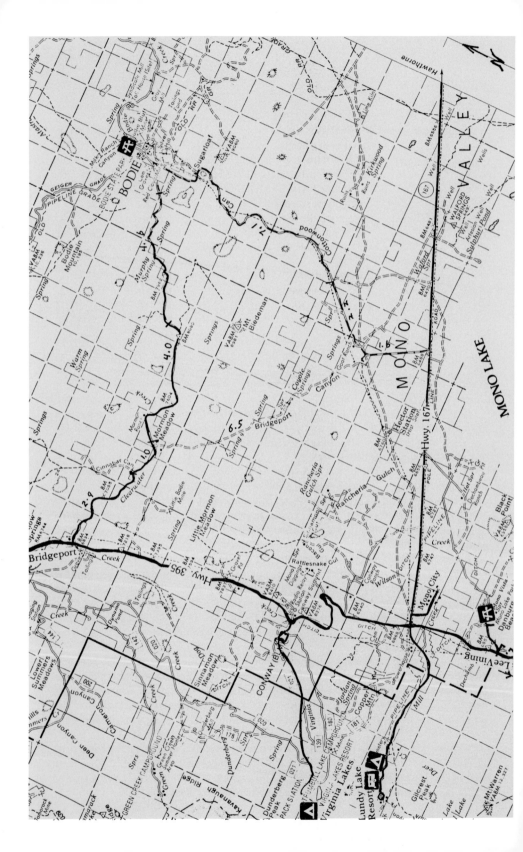

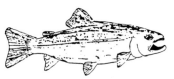

VIRGINIA LAKES

At the Conway Summit a road leads west, ascending Virginia Canyon to reach Virginia Lakes. The beautiful basin within the Hoover Wilderness Area holds a collection of sublime mountain lakes in glaciated granite pockets. The clear, crisp 'high sierra' environs are easily accessible, with a good road approaching the fishing lakes. This secluded valley, surrounded by colorful towering crests of the eastern Yosemite National Park boundary, has lakes stocked with catchable trout all season. VIRGINIA LAKE RESORT has cabins, a restaurant, store with fishing supplies and other camping needs. The campground is at Trumble Lake where fishermen young and old can try their luck and/or skill. VIRGINIA LAKE PACK STATION offers trips into the Yosemite National Park backcountry, and to lakes beneath the Sierra Crest north to the headwaters of Green Creek.

As you continue north along the highway, to the west lie the aspen covered slopes of the lovely Sinnamon Meadows, where Dog and Dunderberg Creeks flow north from Dunderberg Peak and Kavanaugh Ridge. At the bottom of the hill is DOGTOWN, another placer mining site of past glory, which can be identified only by the rock piles along Dog Creek.

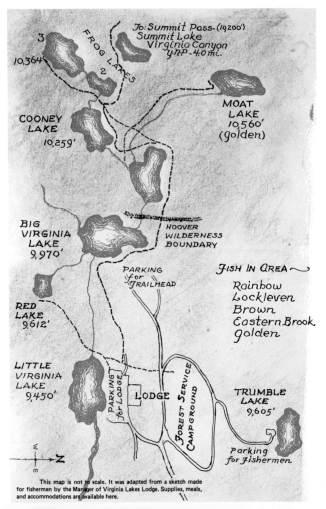

This map is not to scale. It was adapted from a sketch made for fishermen by the Manager of Virginia Lakes Lodge. Supplies, meals, and accommodations are available here.

149

UPPER MONO COUNTY

The highest point in Highway 395 is Conway Summit (8138'), separating the vast Mono Basin from the historic gold fever country of Upper Mono County. The Sierra Crest turns westward here, and extended low hills and meadows reach into the Bridgeport Valley where lakes glisten and cattle graze. At the viewpoint, about halfway up the long grade before turning north, there is a grand, broad view of Mono Basin below, with White Mountains to the east and the Sierra Nevada to the south. This road was used extensively when miners combed the land seeking fortunes. It seems that every little hill and creek was scratched for placer gold. The modern four-lane road was completed in 1962 and named for a pioneer family — Conway — who settled nearby in the 1880's.

At the crest of Conway there's a telephone, Radio Relay Station and the Summit Inn, a restaurant open for evening dining. Up in the hills, east beyond the Relay Station, is the site of Mono Diggings that saw such animated activity in the late 1850's. Nothing remains today alongside Rattlesnake Gulch, where some 40 houses — some two-story — once stood. Because lumber was a premium commodity, whenever a new gold strike occurred and the miners moved to the more lucrative challenge, all the buildings were disassembled and carried away to the next place.

Rattlesnake Gulch near Conway Summit   *Frank Balthis*

TOLL ROADS

Toll roads leading from supply centers to mines were more profitable for their owners than working in the mines. One of the most important toll roads was the Sonora-Mono Wagon Road. This was the first direct route from San Francisco to Bodie in 1878. It took about 40 hours to travel the distance and cost $30.00. The road followed an old emigrant route along the Stanislaus River, and Indian trails over Sonora Pass, stopping at the Leavitt Meadows and Fales Hot Springs Way Stations on the way to Bridgeport and Bodie. When snow closed the road in winter traffic was detoured to the Carson City-Placerville route.

Other roads used by freighters and stages went via Cottonwood Canyon, farther south. The Geiger Grade was shorter out of Bridgeport, but was too steep for freighters. West Walker River Toll Road connected the mines and towns of Aurora, Bodie, Dunderberg, Lundy and Mammoth. East Walker Road to Aurora had stage stations along the present 028 road that are now historical sites.

BODIE MAC

The road to Bodie follows the old toll road from Bridgeport, passing the stage stops of Lower Mormon Canyon, Mormon Ranch and Murphy Springs. From the initial rocky cliff entrance, paralleling Clearwater Creek with its willows and aspens, the road climbs to a high desert plateau interspersed with open meadows. Just before the pavement ends the scenery opens on a wide valley with craggy outcroppings up ahead. At the cattleguard are the first of the mine tailings on the brown desert hills, and in the distance the blue roofs of the Standard Consolidated Mining Company buildings can be seen. Looking over the awesome bleakness of the landscape, so far removed from the conveniences we are accustomed to, one senses that living must have been a severe trial, especially in winter.

Gold was discovered here in 1859 by Waterman S. Bodey (William S. Bodie) but the town developed slowly. In 1864 there were only 20 buildings scattered over the hills. Even by 1870 it was still relatively small. But in 1872 a new vein was found and more miners came. When the Standard Consolidated Mining Company was formed in 1877 the town began to expand rapidly. People came from Aurora, Mono Diggings, Dogtown, Virginia City and San Francisco. The big push was from 1876 to 1884. In 1888 over $18 million had been yielded by the mines. It was the most productive area in the Basin Range Mining District, with over $30 million in gold and 1 million ounces of silver finally taken.

People remained in the town to work the mines even after the big push. In 1893 Bodie became the first mining town to have electricity. A hydroelectric dam and power plant was developed in Green Creek to generate electricity. The 13 miles of poles were placed in a straight line to save time and materials, though local folklore has it that it was not yet determined if electricity could go around corners. Three 500-volt General Electric bi-polar motors ran at 700 rpm, generating power for the Standard Consolidated Mining Company.

Tourism started here in the 1940's. Many buildings had been destroyed in the last big fire in 1932. One of the hazards of mining towns was fire. With dry wood buildings standing in the hot desert sun, the lack of water and equipment, fires started easily and wiped out some towns two or three times. By recognizing the potential historical value of even a partially preserved ghost town, authorities made Bodie a State Historical Park in 1960. What remained was saved from destruction during the 1960's when so many other towns were either destroyed by vandals or carried away — board and brick — by ghost town scavengers.

151

CHINESE AT BODIE

As in many of the western mining towns, Chinese laborers lived and worked in Bodie. They settled close together in a specific area for ethnic and security reasons. They were used, with little or no respect shown them. The East Coast had African slaves and the West Coast had Chinese laborers. Although they were not considered slaves since they were theoretically free, some did "belong" to individuals and were farmed out to work for a company. Charles Crocker imported Chinese coolies from Canton to work for him. They laboriously chipped tunnels in the mines, through the ridges of granite, carried rocks and ore in packs on their backs, and helped build railroads and pipelines.

The native dress of China was worn: a short dark blue cotton blouse that was tight around the neck, cotton breeches, and slipper-type shoes or boots. In the winter the blouse was padded for extra warmth and the cotton topped shoes had wooden soles. Their long hair was worn in a single braid down the back.

The Chinese sold vegetables they grew, dried fish they caught, dressed chickens and hogs they raised and ducks they shot. Trees in the surrounding hills were cut and packed in bundles, which were carried to town on horseback. Charcoal was made where the wood was cut and carried down to Bodie in sacks. It was used in their laundries, in homes for fuel, and in the mills. Instead of using a flat iron heated on a wood stove, the Chinese used charcoal placed in a flat bottomed brass pan to iron their clothes. They also worked in many restaurants and lodging houses.

Although they were industrious, polite, friendly and kind, most of these people were usually mistreated. As scapegoats, whenever there was a crime or town problem, a Chinese was automatically blamed. Children were known to throw rocks at them. They were not allowed to work in the mines until the mine was worked out. Then they could work what was left. Some of the mines around Bodie worked by the Chinese were called: Homestead Mine, Placer Mine, Chinese Camp and China Camp.

To offset the treatment received and to forget the hatred, many Chinese men and women smoked opium. Of course, other members of the community were known to visit opium parlors as well. On Chinese New Years firecrackers were exploded, drums and gongs were beaten, creating great noise and bedlam all around for everyone to enjoy for eight days.

The Orientals saved their money and either sent it back to relatives in China or saved it to buy a return ticket home. Other miners and people of Bodie objected to the money leaving town but the Chinese were not concerned about that. Most had come from Virginia City in 1878, and by 1884 most had left to go to other mining towns or to return to China. Although many Mexicans and Indians lived and worked in Bodie, they were never treated as poorly as the Chinese.

Ernest Hommerding

BRIDGEPORT VALLEY

Continuing north, Highway 395 passes through the gap along Virginia Creek to the Bridgeport Valley. At first it was called, appropriately, Big Meadows. The many square miles of this large, lovely grassy plain is bounded by the Hunewill Hills to the south, the brown Bodie Hills to the east, the Sweetwater Mountains to the north, and at the west by the Sierra Crest, apexing with Sawtooth Ridge and Matterhorn Peak (12,264'). The U.S. Forest Service is south of town, on the east side of the road along Highway 395. Here Rangers can supply information on weather and road conditions, hunting and fishing and otherwise assist the traveler. Wilderness Permits are issued here.

When Aurora, Bodie and the many Mono County mines and diggings developed in the early 1860's, they were scattered throughout the surrounding hills. Livestock feed, meat and lumber were needed. Demand was greater than the supplies coming up from the south through Owens Valley. For this reason the Sonora-Mono Wagon Road was built, as were numerous other toll roads. Bridgeport became a center with freight teams hauling the produce, and lumber wagons coming in from the north and west. Hay wagons rumbled along Main Street and loose sheep, horses and cattle by the hundreds were driven through town, leaving dusty clouds behind them.

Early prospectors realized that the beautiful lush grass in the meadow was excellent feed for both cattle and sheep. Ranching was started early on. The Circle H Ranch founded by Napoleon Bonaparte Hunewill is still operating today as a guest ranch. As activity at the mines subsided, local communities continued to prosper through ranching. Today tourism assists in the economy of Bridgeport.

The Hunewill Guest Ranch was started in 1931 by N.B. Hunewill's granddaughter, LeNore. It is a real working cattle ranch in a real cattle country. Horseback riding is the main feature. Guests are assigned a horse for the length of their stay. Special attention is given to young buckaroos as a children's wrangler offers instructions in riding and entertains them with ranch and western lore on their rides. Fishing, hiking and automobile trips are also included in the agenda.

The most outstanding building in town is the magnificent white Victorian Mono County Courthouse. Designed by John Reed Roberts in 1881, it reflects the influence of New England in its appearance. Handmade bricks were constructed and hauled in from Bodie. The floors of the two-story structure are 1¼" Oregon pine, tongue-and-grooved and highly polished. The 10' wide staircase has a massive newell post with a handrail made of Spanish cedar. When it was built there was a 3000 gallon water tank on the roof to supply local fire hydrants as well as basins in the rooms. It cost $31,000 to build back then.

The Museum for Mono County is in an old schoolhouse, behind the Courthouse. Bridgeport has grocery and sporting goods stores, gift and antique shops, motels, restaurants, service stations and a laundromat.

BROWN (*Salmo trutta*)
(Sometimes called Loch Leven)

large dark spots (some black, some red)
dark

brownish yellow

TWIN LAKES ROAD

The road up to the lakes passes through wildflower-bedecked meadows of the Circle H Ranch. Iris, lupine, sage and mullin punctuate the lush green grass. The road curves around a moraine following Robinson Creek. Doc and Al's Robinson Creek Fishing Resort and campgrounds are on either side of the road along the creek. The setting is perfect but the fish can be stubborn about taking lures or flies. However, the summer days are warm with a pleasant crispness at night — excellent camping weather. But spring comes late and fall comes early.

MONO LAKE RESORT

This fishermens' resort at the west end of Twin Lakes is also a great family vacation spot. It is nestled against one of the most rugged and beautiful settings at an elevation of 7000 ', just 14 miles from Bridgeport. There is fishing, hunting, water skiing and boating with boats and motors available for rent. There is a cement launching ramp and cement piers for private boats. The resort includes a trailer park and camping sites for tents, furnished cabins, coffee shop and cocktail lounge, a good-sized grocery store with sundries, books, magazines, newspapers and even clothing.

TWIN LAKES RESORT

Situated on the lower Twin Lakes, this resort offers lake and stream fishing for the famous brown trout as well as rainbow. There is a complete marina, bait and tackle shop, boat and motor rentals, swimming and picnicking on the waterfront. The General Store stocks everything a visitor might need in the way of groceries, hunting and fishing licenses, sundries and books. A modern trailer park with hookups, laundromat and showers is open for the season.

Courtesy of Mono Lake Resort

154

HUNTOON VALLEY

Leading north from Bridgeport beyond wide-meadowed ranchlands, Highway 395 passes through Huntoon Valley. In the early 1880's Huntoon station was a favorite stop for tired teamsters and travelers on the stages. There were a number of Huntoon brothers who were ranchers, dairymen and saloon keepers. Their sheep ranch was large and sheep still graze in the meadow today.

The road veers west to ascend the Devils Gate Summit and Fales Hot Springs. Be sure to look back at Bridgeport Valley with the Sweetwater Mountains before descending through the gap. In the fall aspens with their golden-leaf display add a colorful touch. As the road turns north again several creeks merge and flow into the West Walker River.

SONORA PASS ROAD — Highway 108

This road over the pass is not recommended for large RV's or trailers as it is narrow, with steep, short curves in some sections. But it is a pleasant drive past the U.S. Marine Corps Training Camp en route to LEAVITT MEADOWS. This sublime valley offers camping, picnicking, fishing and hunting. This country north of Yosemite National Park has miles and miles of beautiful high country lakes and sparkling streams with wildflowered meadows and classic stands of lodgepole pines and white fir. The Pack Station recommends various camping spots and lakes to ride to for either short or extended trips into the backcountry. A store and cafe are open until the snow closes the road.

Signs at Sonora Jctn. MAC

155

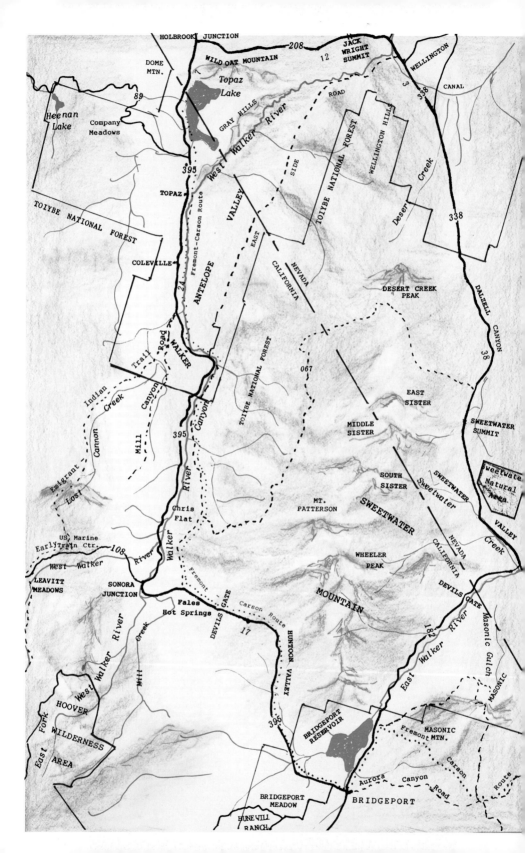

WEST WALKER RIVER
Walker River Headwaters   MAC

At any season the drive along the West Walker River is extremely pleasant. There are campgrounds and many places off the road to park for fishing. When the signs along this road say 25 mph, or 35 mph, believe it. Some of these S curves are sharp. When the road veers westward, the lovely Antelope Valley opens up ahead. Many ranchers came here to settle in the 1860's — the same time as in Bridgeport — to supply feed for livestock. Walker and Coleville were important stage and freight stations for travelers going to and from the mines. Walker has a post office, country stores, trailer park, service stations with propane, laundromat, lodges and Mono County park with handicap facilities and playground. At Coleville Hammerbacher's Cafe and Market has gas and a general store.

MAC

THE HOWITZER

The valley was white with deep snow, cold winds blew and temperatures were below freezing when Fremont, Kit Carson and the other members of the party first entered Bridgeport Valley. These first white men to enter this country had traveled south from Walker Lake, around the hills north and northwest of Bodie to the south end of the Sweetwater Mountains. Here they met a small band of Washoe Indians who traded their pinyon nuts for trinkets and cloth. What made this expedition so exceptional and hazardous was the fact that they were dragging through the snow, with great difficulty, a French, brass short-barreled howitzer. It was mounted on a high two-wheel carriage. The field piece, much esteemed by Fremont, was a valued and versatile mountain gun. It could fire an exploding shell or a ball. The gun barrel was two feet long and two to three inches in diameter.

One of the Washoe Indians offered to guide them north and westward across the Sierra Crest. They went past Devils Gate, Fales Hot Springs and up in the hills paralleling the West Walker River. The temperature on January 28th, 1844 was below zero, the snow was deep under the forest cover and the men's footwear was frozen. In their weakened condition the party staggered onward and stubbornly hauled the cumbersome gun carriage behind them. Finally time came when the howitzer was not worth the lives of the men. They could no longer continue to drag the gun under the adverse factors they were facing, and had to leave it stuck in the deep snow.

This howitzer had been transported ardously over 3000 miles — from the Missouri River, up to The Dalles on the Columbia River down through the Honey Lake country to Pyramid Lake, south to the Carson and East Walker Rivers, around and up the West Walker River country to Coleville. Although a great burden had been lifted from the men, the beseiged company still had to cope with tall drifts of snow, freezing temperatures, hunger and fatigue.

From Coleville they traveled up through Carson Valley, westward slowly trudging across the Sierra at Carson Pass. Kit Carson took time out to carve his name on a tree at the pass that bears his name. Fremont went scouting and climbed a nearby high point, Stevens Peak (10,061'). While he was at the top, the sky cleared and there was Lake Tahoe in its pristine glory. He named it Lake Bonpland, in honor of a botanist.

The brass cannon was found in the early 1860's. Its location had been mentioned in Fremont's notes. From Coleville the gun was taken to Virginia City to be used by the Fire Department. In the late 1880's it was removed and taken to the resort town of Glenbrook, and then to Tahoe City. It now finally rests in the Nevada State Museum at Carson City, a visible symbol of human courage and endurance.

BRIDGEPORT LAKE

This large reservoir has experienced dramatic change in the last few years. It was completely dry at one point and many native fish died, as did fish in the East Walker River. The marina is now closed but the lake is stocked with trout when feasible and can be fished from the shore. Paradise RV Park is on the eastern shore. Lovely views of the Sierra Crest and Sweetwater Mountains can be seen from this side of the valley.

MASONIC

Northeast of Bridgeport is masonic, another of the Mono County mines that had its day in the early 1900's. With all the excitement of Aurora and Bodie there was little activity at Masonic until later. But by 1907 there was a cyanide plant and a 10-stamp mill. Sodium cyanide or a calcium cyanide solution are used in extracting gold and silver from the raw ore. By 1938 the rich veins were depleted and people left. Today only the rodents are inhabitants, gathering nuts from scattered pinyon pines along the gulch. A jeep road leads to this historic site.

ANTELOPE VALLEY

Many of the ranches in Antelope Valley were started in the 1860's when Bridgeport and Huntoon Valleys first cattle and hay ranches were established. It is a lovely ride through this beautiful valley with tall cottonwoods along the West Walker River, before the river turns eastward into Nevada.

Highway 89 junctions at Topaz to go west over the scenic mountainous Monitor Pass (8314') to Marklesville. Established in 1861 by Jacob Markle, the 160 acre claim is now the townsite. The Alpine County Museum Complex includes the Old Webster School. This one-room schoolhouse was built in 1882. The antique school desks are still in place with marked slates and drawings.

TOPAZ LAKE

This popular swimming, boating and fishing lake is half in California and half in Nevada. On the Nevada side along the highway are a number of casinos, some with RV parking. At the north side of the lake is an excellent campground with trailer hookups, showers, tables and fireplaces, playground, marina and telephones. It is an ideal spot for picnicking, fishing or relaxing in a pleasant, scenic place.

At Hollbrook Junction, just north on Highway 395, there's an alternate route south to Bridgeport via Highways 208 and 22. This is a good half-day loop trip either out of Bridgeport or Topaz Lake, riding along the East and West Walker Rivers. MAC

MAC

LOOP TRIP ALONG THE EAST AND WEST WALKER RIVERS

Highway 208 leads east through high desert country with sagebrush and rabbitbrush, yellow and colorful in autumn. There are lovely views to the west in this high open country. After Jack Wright Summit Pass (5483'), the road descends through a canyon to meet Highway 22 and beautiful Smith Valley. The road crosses the West Walker River at the south end of Smith Valley where large hay sheds in the open fields of ranches are to the east.

At Wellington there is an RV and Mobilehome Park in a quiet, bucolic atmosphere with a picnic area under the Lombardy poplars, willows and cottonwoods. Old wagons and a schoolhouse are under the trees. The unique bus depot for school children is enclosed to protect the students on cold, windy or snowy days. This quaint little rural village has a mercantile and hand craft shop.

South on Highway 338, the road passes between Wellington and Grove Hills. These desert mounds are on either side of a long straight stretch up a wash, passing creeks and farm roads. At Dalzell Canyon rugged red rocks and interesting outcroppings add a change to the landscape before the road enters a juniper and pinyon pine forest. There is a lovely section through open range country, with the lofty Sweetwater Mountains to the west and wide views to the south of Bodie Hills.

MAC

After passing the Sweetwater Natural Area on the east side of the road, Sweetwater Canyon and Creek have tall and imposing Lombardy poplars standing like sentinels. This is farmland country and an old gray stone house still stands amid the tawny grasses and willows, recalling gone-by days. At the junction with dirt 028 road east, Highway 182 turns southwest along the East Walker River. This was the livestock drive route out of Bridgeport going to Aurora and Bodie.

A number of old stage station sites are unidentified along the East Walker River Toll Road. After crossing the state border, Devils Gate is a somewhat narrow passage along the willow-banked river before the road comes out to the northern end of Bridgeport Lake and the majestic hazy-blue-colored Sierra escarpment ahead.

To continue the loop follow Bridgeort north along the West Walker River to Topaz Lake and Hollbrook Junction.

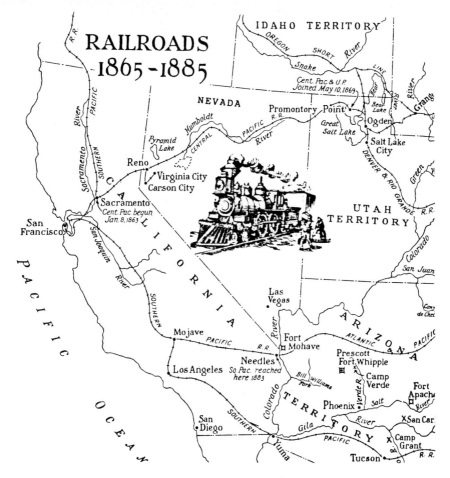

RAILROADS 1865-1885

THE HISTORIC CORRIDOR

When Peter Ogden, Joseph Walker, Jedediah Smith, John Fremont and Kit Carson came into Carson Valley under the shadow of the Sierra, the Washoe Indians' life, as they had lived it, was gone forever. As in Owens Valley, settlers came to raise cattle, hay and crops. Emigrant wagons rolled through the land to cross the Sierra Crest to the San Joaquin Valley. Enough gold samples were found in the many streams to entice people to return. Prospectors roamed the hills in search of precious minerals beneath the sage and rocks. They combed the streams, river beds, and gravel washes. When the ores assayed encouragingly, other miners swarmed the countryside like bees. Then came the Comstock Lode, the grand bonanza.

Not all the wealth was found in river beds and lodes. Towns such as Gardnerville, Minden, Genoa, Carson City, Dayton, Virginia City and Reno were built to accommodate the needs of swarming prospectors and entrepreneurs. Transportation developed from horseback and covered wagon to stagecoach and mule-driven freight teams, then to railroads and highways. Communication by pony express graduated to wire, telegraphy and trains.

Pioneers left a legacy of courage, determination and stubbornness. They endured hardships which are immortalized today. We relive the past by visiting museums, historic buildings, old homes, forts, way station sites, and old ghost towns. From 1844 Carson Valley and Reno became a corridor of American history that Highway 395 now passes through.

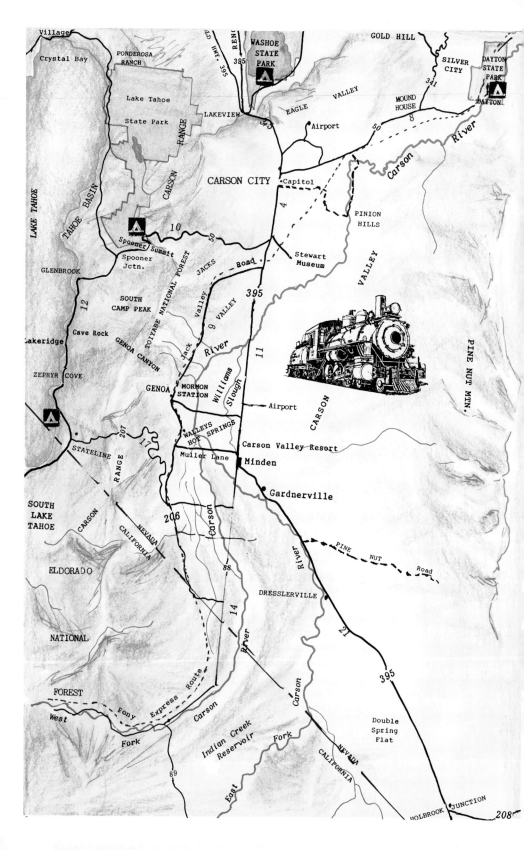

CARSON VALLEY

From Topaz Lake, Highway 395 climbs northward along the Fremont and Carson route, with lovely juniper and pinyon pine forest and meadows on either side of the road. There is a long descent into lower Carson Valley — still a large center for sheep, cattle and hay ranches. The rugged Sierra slopes to the west are an impressive backdrop for this grand broad valley.

DRESSLERVILLE

In 1917 William Dressler gave the Washoe Indians 40 acres of land, in trust with the Nevada Government. If the Indians should leave this land, which is part of the Washoe Indian Reservation, it would revert back to Dressler's heirs. When the white men came, the Washoes' lifestyle changed, as already noted. No longer did they have to gather berries, nuts and roots. They became commercial fishermen, ranch hands and business men. The women helped in homes and on the ranches. When the settlers found that the beautiful Washoe baskets were extremely useful, Indian weavers created new styles to accommodate the demand. They wove baskets over bottles and jugs, and baskets with unique and interesting designs. Weavers were artists and their works were prized. One well-known weaver-artist was Dat-so-la-lee. Some of her baskets can be seen at the Courthouse Museum in Genoa, and at the Nevada State Museum in Carson City.

GARDNERVILLE and MINDEN are now considered the commercial urban center for southern Carson Valley. Gardnerville is known for the Basque restaurants that are popular for "old country" recipes and traditional family-style cooking and serving. Two 'Bed and Breakfasts' are in Gardnerville. The Sierra Spirit Ranch along Pinenut Creek offers many outdoor sports in an open ranch-style setting. The Reid Mansion is a three-story, four bedroom home with formal dining room, large parlor and three porches. The mansion was built in 1910. Bob and Emma Reid, who still live there, are the hosts.

MINDEN, Douglas County Seat since 1915, was a planned community laid out in 1905 around a central town square, with blocks of attractive tree-lined streets surrounding it. Tracks for the southern terminal of the Virginia & Truckee Railroad were extended from Stewart, just south of Carson City, down to Minden. Ranches exported their beef, lamb and dairy products north to service northern Carson Valley and Virginia City. By 1938 the tracks to Virginia City were torn up. the gold boom was over but the need for trains to export products north out of Minden continued. During World War II the line was so busy even the mail and passenger cars were used for freight. Trains ran six days a week at 30 mph until the summer of 1950. As the old engines and cars became wore out, there was no money to purchase new equipment. An era had passed, with no noon whistle to alert the Minden citizens.

At the north end of Minden is the impressive CARSON VALLEY INN, with casinos, convention center, wedding chapel, RV Resort and restaurants. Carson Valley offers many sporting activities for the visitor to enjoy: ballooning, boating, snow and water skiing, snowmobiling, fishing, hunting, tennis, trap shooting and sightseeing.

MAC

ALONG HIGHWAY 206   *Carson Valley*   MAC

As Highway 395 turns north, just past Minden, the superhighway leads straight to Carson City. But, for a pleasant off-the-main-road venture turn west on Muller Lane to Foothill Blvd (Hwy. 206). At the junction of Muller Lane and Highway 206 out in the meadow there is an old stone ruin where some pioneer lived and overlooked the vast Carson Valley to the north and east. A short way up Foothill Blvd. is WALLY'S HOT SPRINGS, which today is a beautifully laid-out resort with restaurant, tennis courts, pool and spa. In the 1870's there was a hotel and bathhouse complex that was very popular. The hot springs were believed to cure "scrofula and rheumatic diseases."

GENOA

Hampden S. Beattie started the first trading post and settlement in Nevada in 1850. He had come to this valley where the Washoe Indians had wintered, enroute to California. The Washoes lived up near Lake Tahoe during the summer. The Mormons had heard of this valley, since part of General Kearny's Mormon Battalion had passed through the Carson River Valley from Placerville (Hangtown) on their return to Salt Lake City in 1848. The Battalion had left Sutter's Fort (Sacramento), and as they progressed eastward through the Stanislaus River country up and over the Sierra, they constructed a road.

A year after Beattie started his successful trading post, his uncles John and Enoch Reese brought in provisions from Salt Lake City to open the Mormon Station. Brigham Young envisioned a western kingdom and organized the Territorial Government of the "State of Deseret", which included present day Utah, Nevada, Arizona and parts of Oregon, California, Colorado and Wyoming. Settlers flocked into the territory — both Mormon and Gentile — to farm and raise livestock. With the increase of inhabitants, there came a need for a government to establish order and record and protect land claims. Judge Orson Hyde, a Mormon, was sent out from Salt Lake City in 1855 to institute law and order as directed by Brigham Young. Hyde renamed the settlement in honor of his original homeland, Genoa, Italy.

In time this natural supply center at the foot of the main pass over the Sierra had need for many services. A grist and saw mill were built; hotels for travelers, a post office and mercantiles were established. Barns, livery stables, blacksmith and harness shops were needed and eventually even printing shops.

Mormon Station   MAC

The Mormons were ordered back to Utah in 1857 to defend Salt Lake City against the U.S. Government troops. There had been some difficulty with recalcitrant ranchers in the Genoa Valley over grazing rights, so the Mormon followers did not hesitate to answer Brigham Young's call. On September 26th, the true and faithful Mormons left their homes, farms, and property and in a procession of 450 men, women and children drove wagons with all the possessions that could be carried eastward back through the desert. When Judge Hyde saw the Gentiles taking over all the Mormon holdings, he left a curse on the valley. Genoa then became a non-Mormon community.

Genoa was the trading center of Carson Valley, and the County Seat until 1915, when the Seat was moved to Minden. It had the first 'squatter government' in what is now known as Nevada, which was in Utah Territory. At the Second Genoa Convention of July 18, 1859, they made a "Declaration of Cause for Separation from the Utah Territory" and wrote a constitution copied from the state of California and fixed proper boundaries. The Territory of Nevada was signed by President James Buchanan on March 2nd, 1861 and became the State of Nevada in 1864. When the transcontinental railroad took over freighting in 1868, the trans-Sierra stagecoaches for passengers and the mule-driven freight teams were no longer necessary, the usefulness of Genoa as a trading center ceased. Reno and Carson City became the hubs of activity. The railroad to Minden took all the freight business while all the mining attention was down at Aurora and Bodie.

GENOA TODAY

This quaint town is a museum with lovely old buildings and homes of a bygone era in peaceful environs. Stroll around the town to visit the antique shops; see the old saloons and restaurants. Many of the original homes and buildings from the 1860's were destroyed in a 1910 fire. However, some were saved and still can be seen.

The Pink House (today a fine restaurant) was first owned by John Reese who ran the Mormon Station. He also had a grist mill and ranch. Historical meetings were held in this house with Judge Hyde and other Mormons when they organized the first government in 1854 and established Carson County as part of the Utah Territory. Many owners have come and gone through the years, changing the house little but keeping up the furnishings and gardens. Today diners can enjoy the house and garden and beautiful antiques in the house.

COURTHOUSE MUSEUM
Courthouse   MAC

The lovely 1865 brick Genoa Courthouse has withstood fire and earthquake and stands today on its original site. The two-story building cost $18,000 to build. Trials held in the courtroom covered divorce, murder, robbery, estate settlements, land claims and other County business until 1916, when the County Seat was moved to Minden. The building was used as a school from 1916 to 1958. Noises of the students were heard in the halls in place of trial testimonies. The Genoa School District deeded the building to the State of Nevada in 1958 when they bussed the few remaining students to Minden.

The Courthouse was opened as a Museum by the Carson Valley Historical Society in 1969. Old oak furnishings of the courtroom were brought back and placed upstairs. In one of the rooms a now silent schoolroom still had its blackboard, slates, maps, text books and desks. The kitchen, originally the District Attorney's office, has a cookstove, hand operated water pump, washboard and butter churn.

Other exhibits in the Museum involve dolls, Washoe baskets, and an Alaskan dog sled that was used to deliver mail to Bodie from Nevada. Strong men wore snowshoes to pull the heavy load over the snowy roads. The Blacksmith Shop has a forge, bellows, tools and a grinding stone. The postmistress in the post office will talk to you, but the jury room is silent and the old jail is bleak.

GENOA HOUSE INN is a charming "Bed and Breakfast". It is an 1872 Victorian home with antiques and old time collectibles, stained glass windows in a rose-colored room, and a spacious porch.

The Masonic Hall was built in 1862; the J.H. Davis Store went up in 1870 and is now an antique shop. Sierra Shadows Restaurant was a century-old barn made into a dining house in 1972. Genoa Community Church — built by volunteer help after fire destroyed the first structure — are some of the buildings worth exploring.

MORMON STATION, a Division of Nevada State Parks, is a restored log cabin stockade and trading post built in 1850. It was the first known permanent structure built by white men in Nevada. There are exhibits of the Mormon way of life in Carson Valley. You may picnic under the trees.

SNOWSHOE THOMPSON

Back in the early days a mail service was established from Placerville over the mountains to Genoa by a special mule-drawn covered wagon that could go rapidly over rough Sierra roads. However, it was of no use for winter deliveries. John A. Thompson, a Norwegian emigrant solved the problem. In the winter of 1856 he built his special "snowshoe-skis", similar to cross-country skis, and carried his mail pouch with letters, necessary medical supplies and assay reports in his backpack. The people of Carson valley no longer felt isolated while Snowshoe Thompson connected them to the outside world with his skis.

He carried ore samples to be assayed from Gold Canyon across the mountain to Placerville, which became the great Comstock Lode. He also transported the type, press parts and paper for the first edition of the *Territorial Enterprise,* which was the first newspaper to be started in Genoa. Later the newspaper was printed in Virginia City.

Thompson ate beef jerky and crackers and snow for water as he swiftly skied across the Sierra. He slept on a soft bed of pine boughs on top of the snow at night, although some nights he skied on with the moon and stars guiding him through. He covered the 100 miles from Carson City to Placerville in three days carrying an average of 100 pound loads, and returned across the Sierra in two days. For nearly 20 years he carried mail and supplies to regions far from the established trails and roads, and maintained a rescue service by locating lost or trapped emigrants in the snow. With his skiing in the mountains he provoked an interest in the sport and in 1866 the first ski club in the United States was the Alturas Snowshoe Club of Plumas County, California.

JACKS VALLEY ROAD

Continuing north on Highway 206, the road passes through the pine-covered Sierra slopes to the west and the lovely wide-spread Carson River Valley to the east. Just past Genoa is the James Canyon Ranch where a fine herd of bison may be seen grazing in the lush meadows. They are shy creatures and should not be disturbed. Horses and cattle also graze in the valley meadows. Highway 206 follows the route of the Pony Express riders who galloped through here on their way to Genoa and on over the Carson Pass (8573') to Sacramento.

STAGECOACHES AND STAGE LINES

In the early 1860's to accommodate the heavy traffic across the Sierra, stage lines were established to carry passengers from San Francisco to Carson City and Virginia City. From San Francisco the passengers and mail heading eastward took the boat to Sacramento, from there a train to Folsom, then boarded the stage for Placerville and over the Sierra. From Hope and Carson Valleys, stages continued eastward along the Humboldt River to Idaho and Salt Lake City. Stages never traveled at night. Meals were served and beds provided at way stations or stage stops. Horses were brushed down, fed, watered and readied for a refreshing start the next morning. Tent shelters were erected about every 12 to 15 miles or between way stations where horses, drivers and passengers could rest.

Passengers were warned that the trip would be extremely hot in the summer while going through the dry desert areas and cold up in the mountains. The rough and rocky roads made the journey a back breaking, jiggley ride at best, over the bumps and ruts in the road. However, in the hot, dry, dusty summer season water wagons, driven by a team of horses, sprinkled water on the road to keep the dust down. In winter roads were cleared of snow by relays of scrapers and drag chains.

By 1862 the toll roads were improved as grades up the mountain were made less steep and smoother. They were made wider, ruts and ravines were filled in with rocks and dirt then compacted together. Passengers could relax more and began to enjoy the beauty of the rushing streams along the road, the grandeur of the Sierra forests, and the magnificence of summit views. The owners of the toll roads charged enough to maintain the roads in both summer and winter. Of course, there were stage holdups with passengers relinquishing their possessions and the strong box of the express company blown open.

Most of the horses used in the stage lines and freight teams were wild mustangs found in the pinyon hills bordering Carson Valley. With sufficient vegetation and numerous streams for water, they roamed free with the coyotes and jackrabbits. They were swift, sure-footed and good mountain horses after being captured, broke and haltered for the teams.

The 'Celerity' or mud wagons were of light weight with a low center of gravity, and had traverse seats to carry about 12 to 14 persons. These wagons were used most often from mountain travel and remote areas as they were better for steep grades and hairpin turns.

The Concord Stage made by the Abbott-Downing Company in Concord, New Hampshire was called the queen of the coaches. It was made of well seasoned hardwood, painted red with gold swirls for decoration. Coach bodies were suspended on thorough braces of thick leathered layers to act as springs, which absorbed the jolts in a swing-and-sway motion along the rough roads. Luggage was carried on top of the coach, held in by an iron railing. A leather covered platform at the rear was for freight, extra boxes and luggage. One seat up in front beside the driver was for "the shotgun". Three upholstered seats on the top could be used for extra passengers if need be. Under the driver's seat was the treasure, or strong box. Concord coaches were for fast freight but were used for all purposes — mail, passengers *and* freight. Horses were changed frequently to travel as swiftly as possible over the roads.

Wells Fargo had many coaches, horses and drivers plus 53 stage stations between Folsom and the railhead at Salt Lake City. The Washoe Express became well known as a carrier of fresh food including butter, eggs and vegetables over the Sierra, returning with gold bullion from the Comstock mines.

Stages used four or six-horse teams as did the freighters with their large, heavy, cumbersome wagons that carried many pounds, and sometimes very heavy mining equipment. In the 1860's when the Comstock mines were developing, some 5000 wagons were engaged in hauling freight from California to Carson Valley and the mines, using the Carson-Placerville route. It took between 10 and 20 days, depending on weather and road conditions. Many teams were strung along the dust-swirling road. Stages often rode behind the freighters which made a very uncomfortable ride for passengers.

THE FERRIS WHEEL

George Washington Ferris, Jr. came west via covered wagon with his family to settle in Genoa. When he grew up he became an engineer and was the designer of many bridges across the country. He heard that for the Chicago World's Fair an attraction was needed that would rival the Eiffel Tower sensation in the Paris Fair. He remembered the waterwheel he had been interested in as a boy at a Mexican mill on the Carson River. The 28′ diameter waterwheel, largest in the west, was used to power a 44-stamp mill that crushed ore from the Mexican Mine up in Virginia City. Raw ore was brought down to Carson Valley in sacks that were placed on special horse-driven ore wagons.

Ferris designed a large wheel that was 25-stories high, capable of carrying 2000 people at a time, taking 20 minutes for one revolution. He scouted around and found a backer who put up the $390,000 needed for him to construct the device. Indeed, it did become the greatest attraction at the 1893 Chicago Fair.

Ferris died in 1895 and never knew his great wheel was moved to St. Louis for the Louisiana Exposition in 1904. It was as great an attraction in St. Louis as it had been in Chicago. Since there were no other major expositions or fairs scheduled in the following years, the wheel was dynamited and sold for scrap. The Ferris Wheel has been duplicated since then to be a standard attraction in many places of amusement.

CARSON CITY (4660')
Courtesy of Nevada State Museum

Christopher (Kit) Carson will always be remembered not only for his illustrious life as a trapper, frontiersman and explorer travelling with John Fremont, but for the places named in his honor: Carson City, Lake, River, Valley, Pass, and Range. He was never able to visit the community bearing his name, although he did see Eagle Valley, at the north end of the present city, when he was driving sheep over the mountains to Sacramento in 1853.

The first settlement in this area was a trading post in Eagle Valley. Some men who were on their way westward to seek their fortune in California decided to stay in Eagle Valley in 1851 to trade and farm. The story goes that one of the settlers killed an eagle, placed the skin and feathers over the door of the trading post and named it Eagle Valley Trading Post. Carson City was founded in 1858. Abraham Curry laid out the township streets and a four-block center square for a plaza where auctions and town meetings were held. The Nevada Territorial Legislature created Ormsby County and selected Carson City to be the capital in 1861, with the first election in January, 1862. When Nevada became a state in 1864, it retained the title. The three-story State Capital building was built in the center plaza area of the town and took two years to build. Curry was able to see the finished building in 1871 on the site he had chosen 13 years previously.

The Classic architecture of the capital building, designed in the form of a Grecian cross, has Renaissance Revival influences decorating the windows and doors. The brown sandstone was quarried at the Nevada State Prison by the inmates. The cupola is painted silver, symbolizing Nevada as the Silver State. The interior is equally impressive with French crystal windowpanes. Marble from Alaska was used for the wainscoting, floors and arches. In 1879 a custom of having portraits made of each governor was started. These are hung on the first and second floors. The building has been added to and restored through the years, but it is the second oldest capital building west of the Mississippi River. The second oldest building in the Capital complex is the State Archives, formerly the State Printing building that was constructed in 1885.

The NEVADA STATE MUSEUM was originally the U.S. Mint building. This, as was true of public and private buildings in Carson City, was made from the brown sandstone at the State Prison quarry. Bricks were made in Genoa at the Adams Brick Works and the wainscoting was sugar pine from the Tahoe Basin. The architect, Alfred Bult Mullett was also influenced by the classical Greek tradition that was so popular after the Civil War. The building was completed in 1869 and the mint started making coins in nine denominations bearing the 'cc' mark. Over $49 million was coined up to 1893 when the mint was closed.

The U.S. Mint sold the building to the State of Nevada in 1933. Since 1941 it has housed many displays of Indian arts and crafts, significant historical artifacts, birds and animals in settings, and an underground mine with mining equipment and the coin press of the original mint.

Carson City is a successful blend of historical and modern day attractions. There are museums, railroad buildings, Capital complex and magnificent mansions to see, and there are parks, pools, brewery, racetrack, and outdoor sporting activities. The Carson Centennial Park and the Eagle Valley East and West Golf Courses also have trap and skeet shooting, tennis courts and picnic areas. Mills Park has a beautiful, green-lawned picnic area under lovely shade trees. From Memorial Day to Labor Day a trip around the grounds in the Carson & Mills Park Railroad delight young and old alike. A physical fitness exercise course is also provided at the park.

The Virginia & Truckee Railroad Museum is next to the Chamber of Commerce and Visitor Bureau Building. Freight and passenger cars have been restored and are on view. There are many types of cars: passenger, baggage, caboose, box, flat and service. All were used at one time on the Nevada tracks of the Nevada Copper Belt, Northern Nevada, The Union Pacific, Southern Pacific, and Tonopah & Goldfield Railroads. Every weekend during summer months the 'Washoe Zephyr', named for the winds that blow across Washoe Lake, runs along the tracks with a gas-propelled engine car, built in 1923.

There are two trailer parks. Comstock Country RV Park at the south end of town is near Highway 50 on Highway 395. This is a new, modern park with pull-throughs, camper and tent sites, laundry, showers, telephones, grocery store and ice. Camp-N-Town is on the north end of town with many sites, showers, laundry and RV supplies for sale.

Two "Bed and Breakfasts" are in Carson City. The Edwards House is a gracious sandstone Victorian home built in 1877, in the center of town. North of town at the Winters Creek Ranch, deer, wild turkeys and eagles can be seen among the ponderosa pines. This inn reflects colonial New England elegance with Victorian furnishings.

Turnaround at V & T RR Museum   *Courtesy of Nevada State Museum*

STEWART INDIAN SCHOOL
1890-1980

ORIGINALLY KNOWN AS THE CARSON INDIAN TRAINING SCHOOL. STEWART INDIAN SCHOOL. OPERATED BY THE U.S. BUREAU OF INDIAN AFFAIRS. PROVIDED VOCATIONAL TRAINING AND ACADEMIC EDUCATION FOR AMERICAN INDIAN STUDENTS FROM THROUGHOUT THE WEST FOR NEARLY A CENTURY.

W.D.C. GIBSON, THE FIRST SUPERINTENDENT, RENAMED THE BOARDING SCHOOL IN HONOR OF U.S. SENATOR WILLIAM MORRIS STEWART OF NEVADA. THE PRINCIPAL FIGURE IN OBTAINING CONGRESSIONAL AUTHORIZATION AND FUNDING FOR THE INSTITUTION.

IN THE EARLY 1920'S SUPERINTENDENT FREDERICK SNYDER INITIATED A BUILDING PROGRAM. STUDENTS WORKED WITH STONE MASONS. SOME OF AMERICAN INDIAN ANCESTRY, TO CONSTRUCT THE HANDSOME STONE STRUCTURES THAT STILL GRACE THE GROUNDS.

STEWART INDIAN MUSEUM
MAC

Just north of Highway 50 leading west to Lake Tahoe is the southern end of Carson City — Stewart. In earlier days this was a station stop on the Virginia & Truckee Railroad. The Stewart Indian Museum on Snyder Street, established in 1982, is on the former Stewart Indian Boarding School campus. All of the 50 buildings are made of native Nevada rocks and were built by students who attended the school. The unique buildings are listed in the National Register of Historic Places. They are administrated by the State of Nevada.

The museum has displays of the former Indian school and collections of Indian arts and crafts. Every third weekend in June there is an arts and crafts show and a Pow Wow held at the Museum. The Trading Post has gifts, souvenirs, publications concerning the museum and the Indians, plus books, postcards, slides and crafts for sale.

PONY EXPRESS

Prairie thunderstorms, lightning strikes in the mountains, hot dry desert air in summer, Paiutes on the warpath, sharp winds, rain-swollen streams, and buffalo stampedes were all part of the Pony Express rider's ride. He rode at gallop or canter past wagon trains and stage coaches, with barely time to wave a greeting. He probably watched installation of the telegraph wires that would eliminate his job. The run from San Francisco, California to St. Joseph, Missouri took ten days. For 18 months — April 3rd, 1860 to October 28th, 1861 the riders crossed eight states through desert, mountains and along rivers.

The first run, 1966 miles, was accomplished in nine days and 23 hours — less than half the time taken by stage, which took 20 days along the same route. The express riders rode day and night covering some 250 miles in about 20 hours in good weather. There were 190 stations along the route where riders changed to fresh horses about every ten miles. The riders usually rode 30 miles before calling it a day. The company had 80 riders, 190 stations as noted, 400 stationmen, and 400 fast horses — for an investment of $700,000.

174

Riders had to be young (under 18 years of age), thin, wiry, weighing not over 130 pounds. Requirements called for courage, stamina, and horsemanship. They were allowed a six-shooter and knife to be used only in defense. No alcohol or use of profanity was tolerated. They were paid $120 to $125 per month. Each wore a red shirt and blue pants, a leather vest, boots and brimmed hat. At first the rider carried a horn to alert the way station men to ready a fresh horse, but experience proved that the rider's dust line on the trail would alert the station man, so the use of the horn was abolished.

Letters were written on thin paper and placed in a leather knapsack called "the mochila". In March of 1861 Pony Express riders carried Lincoln's Inaugural Address to California in the fastest time ever run out of St. Joseph. It took seven days and 17 hours. More letters were sent out of California going east than were sent west. They were mostly letters to congressmen, senators, the president, the war department and, of course, business letters. During the first 15 days of operation some 14,163 letters were received in San Francisco. Many people preferred to use the Pony Express service, which was a private enterprise delivering unopened correspondence, whereas messages sent over the telegraph wires, could be read by anyone.

Most way stations were large and well equipped, but some were made of adobe walls with dirt floors and no glass in the windows. Bunks were built into the walls for beds, and boxes or benches served as furniture. Crude corrals were erected to hold the horses. Eventually the operating company constructed new, better equipped stations and stables, carrying provisions such as ham, bacon, flour, syrup, dried fruit, cornmeal, tea, coffee, but no alcoholic beverages. They also had on hand axes, hammers, saws, stoves, brooms, castor oil, turpentine, cream of tartar, borax, tin dishes, candles, bedding, matches, scissors, needle and thread, and medical supplies.

During the Paiute Indian War the service was shut down for ten days after a rider had been killed during a brisk battle before the Indians retreated. Fort Churchill was built to protect the people using the overland route from further attacks. Telegraph wires were erected from Virginia City to the fort to make a new extended line from California. When the transcontinental telegraph line was completed, the Pony Express was disbanded.

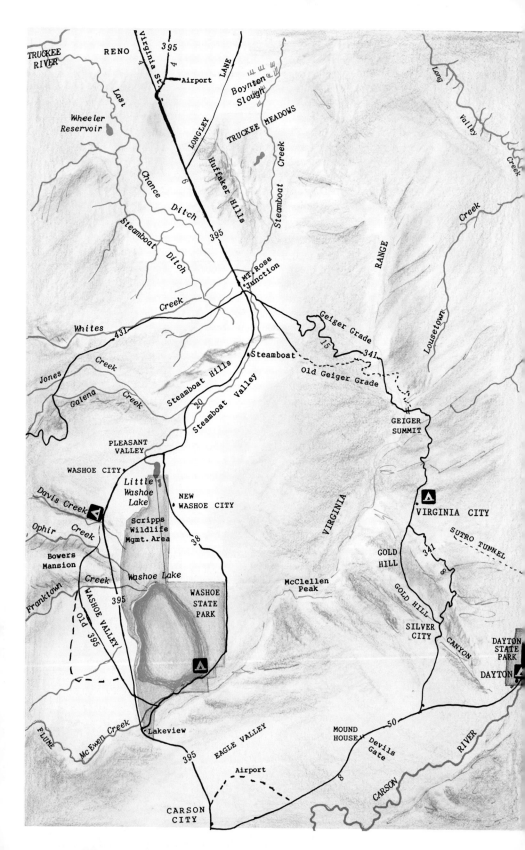

DEVILS GATE

The rugged reef of metamorphic rock was once one of the famous landmarks of the Nevada Territory. In June 1850 John Orr and Nicholas Kelly unearthed a gold nugget nearby, the first found in Gold Canyon. For the next ten years the canyon was the scene of placer mining. One of the first stamp mills in the territory was erected just to the south of Devils Gate. During the brief Paiute War in 1860, the people of Silver City built a stone battlement on top of the eastern summit for protection, and constructed a wooden cannon that could be seen — as a warning. Devils Gate marks the boundary line between Story and Lyons County.

MOUND HOUSE, between Dayton and Carson City was once the terminal point and round house for the Carson & Colorado Railroad and its junction with the Virginia & Truckee Railroad.

DAYTON

Dayton was only a trading post in 1849, situated along the bank where Gold Creek joins the Carson River. It is one of the oldest posts, along with Genoa. For many years the Washoe Indians used this lovely valley as their winter basecamp, fished in the Carson River and held their annual Pine Nut Festivals here. When gold was first discovered nearby in Gold Canyon, prospectors swarmed in and Dayton became a tent village almost overnight.

In 1865, 2500 townspeople worked at farming, freighting or milling Comstock ore. Today this historic town is not as bustling as when Pony Express riders came through and the Sutro Tunnel was being built. A few old buildings still stand.

Dayton State Park is located beside the Carson River beneath cottonwoods and willows in an attractive, pastoral setting. It is an ideal camping area for bird watchers. A nature trail along the river affords ample opportunity to see many migrating birds. A curious aspect of the Carson River is that it flows either north or south, depending on the respective levels of the Humboldt and Carson sinks in different seasons of flood and low water.

... THIS IS ...
GOLD CANYON

Gold Was Discovered at the Mouth of this Canyon Dayton, Nev., in 1849. Yet it Took Ten Years for Prospectors To Work Their Way Up the Canyon to Uncover the Fabulous Silver Lode at Virginia City. By 1863 this Ravine, From Dayton to Virginia. A Distance of Seven Miles, Was A Continuous City of Mines, Mills, Stores, Homes, Restaurants, Offices, Saloons and Fandango Houses. An Endless Stream of Traffic Passed Here Headed for Virginia City. For A Fine Souvenir of Virginia City Get Your Copy of the Territorial Enterprise, Nevada's First Newspaper - Home of Mark Twain Museum

NORTH OF CARSON CITY

On Highway 395 going north out of Carson City the road climbs up to the Lakeview Summit of the Washoe Mountains. LAKEVIEW, had two hotels and stables in 1863. One hotel had been the train station for the Virginia & Truckee Railroad between Carson City and Reno. The sign reads:

"Crossing under the highway are three inverted siphon pipelines furnishing water from the Sierra Nevada watershed to Virginia and Carson Cities. Work was first undertaken in 1873 on the 67-mile box flume and pipeline system with the construction of a maintenance station here. The Virginia and Gold Hill water company's historic water-gathering and transportation complex immediately became world famous.

As early as 1881, Lakeview became a lumber storage area for timber out in the Lake Tahoe Basin. In 1887 shipping activity was accelerated as lumber was fed to the yard by a V-flume originating about present Incline Valley. From there timber products were shipped to the Comstock mines and other points via the Virginia & Truckee Railroad cars. Activity ceased in 1896."

WASHOE STATE PARK

At Lakeview Summit, a road east leads to Washoe State Park which is on the south end of Washoe Lake. There's lovely camping sites under the cottonwoods with sagebrush and shrubs, some with pull-throughs. One nice site is designated for the handicapped with an asphalt pad surrounding the campsite for easy wheelchair access. Cabanas protect campers from the 'Washoe Zephyr', a strong wind that blows across the lake and valley from the west. There are modern flush toilets and an RV dump station. The day use area has a picnic area with barbeques. There are some tables under the cottonwoods on the waterfront. The park offers a sandy beach, fishing, boating and hiking. Two trails are established in the park: the Dune Trail that goes along the Dune Crest and Deadman Creek where many animal, birds and plants can be seen. Migrating birds feed at the lower end of the lake while the Scripps Wildlife Migrating Area at the north end offers refuge for many types of waterfowl during the year. Across the lake Slide Mountain is clearly visible.

MAC

FRANKTOWN ROAD

MAC

The old highway 395, now called Franktown Road, offers an interesting pastoral change from the straight superhighway 395 going north to Reno. Judge Orson Hyde of Genoa established Franktown in 1855, before he left to return to Salt Lake City. Sawmills were erected here and a 60-stamp quartz mill employed many men from the valley. When the railroad was extended from Carson City to Reno in 1869, work at Franktown was no longer needed and the town faded. Driving past the beautiful homes, meadows and cattle grazing in the fields, make this a most pleasant drive.

BOWERS MANSION

The well-preserved Bowers mansion is comfortably sheltered by Lombardy poplars on the Washoe County Park grounds. Sandy Bowers and Eilly Orrum each had a ten-foot claim on the Comstock. After the rich vein in their claims made them both millionaires, they married and built this two-story sandstone building in 1864. The 16-room square house has a large veranda on the ground floor and a balcony on the second. They traveled all through Europe and bought furnishings for the home which, when completed, cost $407,000 — a high price at that time.

Sadly enough, their years of happiness in the lovely home was short. The money ran out with poor investments and bad advice. Sandy died leaving Eilly to struggle with few assets. Not only did she lose her husband, but also her beloved daughter, the mines, the mill and the mansion. She died in poverty in 1903. The State of Nevada became the benefactor. The Bowers created a beautiful reminder of past opulence that was part of Nevada's glorious history.

The well kept Park has swimming and picnic facilities and is open from May to October with scheduled tours through the mansion.

From the County Park, Franktown Road goes up and over the moraine debris left from an avalanche on Slide Mountain that came tumbling down into the valley. The old mill site and town of Ophir are very quiet today. At one time this entire area was a bustling place, with farming, milling, lumbering, and freighting to and from the Comstock mines.

DAVIS CREEK COUNTY PARK

This is another lovely Washoe County park under pines beside a creek. Sites have trailer pull-throughs and a separate area for campers and tents. There are picnic grounds for day use, fishing and swimming in the pond, an RV dump station and evening Ranger programs. Several trails lead up the eastern slope of the Carson Range to Tahoe Meadows. Open from July Fourth to Labor Day. The Junior Ranger Program is for ages 6 to 12.

WASHOE CITY

MAC

After Franktown Road meets Highway 395 the road continues through Washoe Valley to Washoe City which was the first Seat of Washoe County before it was transferred to Reno in 1871. In the 1860's this was a thriving, important community, busy with lumbering and silver mills for the Comstock mine ores.

Today one of the most outstanding attractions is the large fiberglass prospector kneeling on the hillside above the Chocolate Nugget Candy Factory. The 32-foot statue was made in California for a Sparks casino. When the casino was being torn down some years ago, it was brought here to be placed on the old Washoe Indian camping area as part of the Park and Picnic Grounds — a tribute to the prospectors and pioneers of northern Nevada. Three generations have owned and operated the wonderful "richest chocolate in the west" factory.

Highway 395 continues north past Little Washoe Lake and the junction of East Lake Blvd. before climbing over the minor summit to Pleasant Valley, where the Mormons first settled in 1855.

MAC

STEAMBOAT SPRINGS

THESE NATURAL HOT-SPRINGS ARE NOTABLE FOR THEIR CURATIVE QUALITIES. THEY WERE NATIONALLY ACCLAIMED BY PRESIDENT ULYSSES S. GRANT WHEN HE VISITED THEM IN 1879.

EARLY IMMIGRANTS SO NAMED THEM, BECAUSE OF THEIR PUFFING AND BLOWING. LOCATED IN 1860 (BY FELIX MONET); A HOSPITAL, WITH ADJACENT BATHHOUSES WAS SUBSEQUENTLY ADDED BY A DOCTOR ELLIS (1861-1862).

THE COMSTOCK MINING ACTIVITIES, AND THE COMING OF THE VIRGINIA & TRUCKEE RAILROAD IN 1871, CAUSED STEAMBOAT TO BECOME A TERMINAL. HERE MATERIALS FOR THE SILVER MINES WERE TRANSFERRED TO FREIGHT WAGONS FOR THE STEEP HAUL TO VIRGINIA CITY. THE COMPLETION OF THE TRACKS ABOLISHED THE NEED FOR A JUNCTION, BUT ITS RESORT POPULARITY WAS TO REACH ITS PEAK WITH THE BONANZA DAYS.

TO ITS "FINE HOTEL, COMMODIOUS DANCE HALL, AND ELEGANT BAR, CAME THE LEGENDARY SILVER KINGS, POLITICOS, GAMBLERS, AND NEWS CHRONICLERS, ESCORTING THE LOVELY LADIES OF STAGE AND OPERA HOUSE."

WITH BORASCA, ATTENDANCE WANED; FIRES DESTROYED THE LUXURIOUS BUILDINGS, BUT THE THERAPEUTIC WATERS REMAINED, NOT ONLY FOR HEALTH SEEKERS, BUT FOR CONDITIONING ATHLETES—EVEN PRODUCING MINERAL MUDS SOUGHT BY COSMETICIANS AND RACE HORSE OWNERS.

GEIGER GRADE

This was the original Geiger Grade. The one going into Bodie out of Bridgeport was named for this toll road. It was the main route from Truckee Meadows up to Virginia City. From this road there are broad views north to Reno; below to Pleasant and Washoe Valleys. There was a large fire some years ago which burned off part of the forest along the road. This paved road, constructed in 1936, is an easy grade up to Virginia City.

At the Geiger Summit (6799') is the LOUSETOWN plaque which reads:

"North of this marker, a station was established in 1860 on Geiger and Tilton's new toll road from Truckee Meadows. Fine springs, terminus of several wood roads, and a population of teamsters, stock and sheep men were found at Lousetown, Nevada's most unique name. The area included the first Virginia City Railroad surveys, first ice project, and race track with trap shooting and picnic grounds. The first telegraph line to Reno and the largest toll station in the area were in the vicinity of this marker."

View from Geiger Grade   MAC

STEAMBOAT SPRINGS

Fissures and cracks in the earth's surface give off clouds of hot steam. Emigrants coming to California in 1849 camped at the Springs and settlers came to stay around 1860. It has been a popular resort and spa thanks to the hot steamy waters.

MT. ROSE SKI AREA

Highway 27, the Star Route leads gently up the north side of Slide Mountain to reach the popular Mt. Rose Ski Area and the eastern approach to the vast Lake Tahoe Vacation Land.

SIGN ON THE ROAD AT DOUBLE SPRINGS:

> The man who drives
> half asleep
> is now buried
> six foot deep.

181

TAHOE BASIN
Lake Tahoe   *Peggy Warne*

During the Miocene-Pliocene Epoch the western Sierra Nevada and the eastern Carson Range rose skyward when the continental crust broke along fault lines creating towering "fault blocks." The block in between these jagged ranges settled slowly and unevenly, resulting in the Tahoe Basin. This block became plugged at the north end by volcanic eruptions. Subsequent rains and heavy snowfalls filled the basin almost as high as the crests on either side. When the waters found an exit through a low point in the Carson Range, the Truckee River was born. The river cut a deep gorge to the north between the Sierra fault and the volcanic debris, and down the eastern slope of the Sierra, out into the valley to empty into Pyramid Lake. Interstate Highway 80 follows eastward along the river down to Reno and beyond. The waters continued to drain until the lake reached its present level.

During the Ice Age glaciers filled the region between Tahoe City and Crystal Bay at the north end of the lake, raising the water over 600 feet. As the ice melted, some 10,000 years ago, the lake was returned to its former level. High benches and beaches were left on the slopes, and these sedimentary-based benches are structurally weak and unstable, but do make beautiful forest lands.

The highest peaks to the west are Rubicon Peak (9193 ') and Mt. Tallac (9735 '). To the east are Mt. Rose (10,778 ') and Genoa Peak (9150 '). It is interesting to note that the volcanic Mt. Rose is higher than the block faulted granite peaks. Tahoe Lake is 22 miles long, 12 miles wide and some 1650 ' deep. The lake never freezes over as there is a constant water movement from the bottom of the lake to the surface.

Waves from the high waters eroded the volcanic rocks, leaving caves that can be seen at Cave Rock. The Washoe Indians called Tahoe "Da-ow," (Big Lake), where they fished, gathered roots and plants and held their tribal meetings from spring to fall. It was near Cave Rock that the Washoes fought a battle with the Paiutes over the Tahoe hunting and fishing grounds.

This great recreational area, one of America's finest playground and vacation spots, offers unlimited sporting activities: fishing, boating, golfing, tennis, snow and water skiing, snowmobiling, sternwheeling, camping, picnicking, hiking and swimming. One can also tour the lakeshore road to see the magnificent views across the sparkling blue waters and deep green forests that surround the lake.

THE RAPING OF TAHOE BASIN

Initially the lumber and firewood needed for the Washoe and Comstock mines came from massive cutting in the forest north of Lake Tahoe, and from construction of the Central Pacific Railroad. Logs were hauled by ox teams from the forest floor to the sawmill. As demand for more lumber grew the forest around the northern and eastern slopes along Lake Tahoe were stripped. The once beautiful densely forested areas became a slag and stump nightmare. The Pacific Wood, Lumber and Fluming Company in 1876 took out 15,000,000 board feet of building lumber and 75,000 cords of firewood alone.

The 15-mile-long V-shaped flumes were designed by J.W. Haines. They were half-filled with water and smooth on the inside. As timber was placed in the flume water it was carried swiftly downstream. It took some 30 minutes for it to be carried down the -15 miles.

By 1880 ten flumes were scattered along the streams in Sharon, Douglas and Washoe Counties. Some 33,000,000 board feet of timber were flumed down to the mills. It was estimated that 600,000,000 board feet were buried inside the shafts of the Comstock mines. Naturally, it devastated the mountainside. Brush-covered second growth, eroded gullies, dried up streams and smaller mountain lakes resulted. The great rape of the Tahoe Basin forests made a dusty rubble of a pristine forest.

The rail line of the Carson & Tahoe Lumber & Fluming Company switchbacked the lumber from the saw mill up to the Carson Range crest. At Summit Camp lumber was stacked, waiting to be flumed down to the valley mills around the Carson City area. Flumes were held off the ground by wooden supports and trestles were built over gullies and ravines. Lumber yards stretched across the valleys below where sawn planks waited to be shipped to Virginia City via the Virginia & Truckee Railroad.

Courtesy of Nevada State Museum

VIRGINIA CITY

L. Dean Clark

The first rush to Virginia City was in 1857 when the placer mines in Gold Canyon had been worked out and the miners moved up the canyon to Gold Hill. The first assay tests of the "blue stuff" proved to be almost pure silver and gold. News spread fast and "old Pancake" Comstock kept talking about "his mine" so much that the men called it Comstock's mine. Acquaintances of Comstock named him "old Pancake" as "he was even too lazy to make bread, and would never overlook an opportunity for easy pickins." He had bluffed his way into a partnership, claiming that the spring two men who had found ore, were using, was his. The rush was on but with mining, big stakes took big money to extract ore from the ground.

The riches were encased in a great fault line zone. The lode had been developed geologically when hot magma bearing minerals flowed into the massive fault fissures. Silver and gold were deposited in great quantities. The Comstock Lode was two-and-a-half mile long, lying between Gold Hill and Six-Mile Canyon, with the Ophir Mine at one end and the Gold Hill placer diggings at the other. Fifty-seven percent of the Ophir Mine was silver and 43% was gold.

The development of the mines required new methods of extracting ore from great depths. Problems developed that were completely new to the miners' previous experience. The Ophir ore body, which had been only 10 to 12 feet wide on the 50-foot level, increased to 40 to 50 feet in places on the 180-feet level. This was surrounded by materials so soft and unstable that no known method of timbering would permit its extraction without cave-ins.

Directors of the Ophir Company authorized Philip Deidesheimer, a young German engineer, to design a method of timbering. He developed what became known as the "square-set timbering". As explained in Eliot Lord's "Comstock Mining and Miners":

"...to frame timbers together in rectangular sets, each set being composed of a square base, placed horizontally, formed of four timbers, sills, and cross-pieces from four to six feet long, surmounted at the corners by four posts from six to seven feet high, and capped by a frame-work similar to the base. The cap-pieces forming the top of any set were at the same time the sills or base of the next set above. These sets could readily be extended to any required height and over any given area, forming a series of horizontal floors, built up from the bottom sets like the successive stories of a house. The spaces between the timbers were filled with waste rock or with wooden braces, forming a solid cube whenever the maximum degree of firmness was desired."

The miners who worked the Comstock Lode took pride in their work, received top pay and organized a union in 1863. They worked ten hours per shift until the heat and other underground conditions made it necessary to reduce the hours to eight. No non-miner member would work in the mines. Out of 1966 miners in the mines, there were 691 Irish; 543 English; 394 American; 150 Canadians; 44 Scotch; 30 German; 22 Welsh; 11 each Swedes and Italian. The remaining 70 were from various European countries. The average age was 35; average weight 165 lbs.; average height 5'9"; and married. Accidents were considered the risks of the trade and no one was sued for damages in a death or accident. The union and the mining company helped pay for medical expenses, but if a miner was killed, each miner gave the family a day's pay.

Most miners were avid readers. The daily circulation of *Territorial Enterprise* was 745 in 1865. The *Virginia City Union* was read by 190; *Gold Hill News* — 150; *Sacramento News* — 117. The four San Francisco papers had a total of 110 readers. Eastern publications were popular as well. Each month there were 325 copies sold of *Harper's Monthly* and 112 copies of *Atlantic Monthly*. English magazines were popular as were novelists of the day plus such classics as Dickens and Shakespeare. Both Virginia City and Gold Hill had libraries and reading rooms for those who could not afford to subscribe to their favorite publication.

Virginia City was on the entertainment circuit for dramas, noted singers and actresses of the time. Three theatres and Maquires Opera House played to crowded houses. Maquires was changed to Pipers Opera House in 1867. The building is still standing today and is the oldest working theatre in the west. Shows and special events are still featured there.

Courtesy of Mackay School of Mining

SQUARE SET MINING

VIRGINIA & TRUCKEE RAILROAD

The Virginia & Truckee Railroad from Carson City to Virginia City was built in 1869 in only six weeks. From Virginia City at 6205' elevation to Carson City at 4630', the 1575' grade made construction of the line an engineering feat. Hard pushed Chinese worked from dawn to dusk making the steep grade with many sharp switchbacks along the 21-mile track. It was called "the crookedest railway in the United States". On September 28th the last Silver Spike was hammered into the rail. By August 1872 the line out of Carson City was extended to Reno to connect with the Central Pacific Railroad.

One of the attractions at Virginia City is the Virginia & Truckee Railroad Ride, a short run from Virginia City to Gold Hill over the same tracks that presidents, dignitaries and millions of dollars in silver and gold traveled on years ago.

WIRELESS
MAC

Frederick A. Bee built a telegraph line, known as "Bee's Grapevine" from San Francisco to Carson City before the Pony Express. The miles covered by the Pony Express to St. Joseph was without any telegraphic service. From St. Joseph to New York there were "talking wires". The line from California to Nevada in 1869 was a single wire tacked to trees or tall shrubs. Wires were broken innumerable times by storms, or by pioneers who took the wire to repair their wagons. Even though messages could be sent between San Francisco and Carson City, the Pony Express still carried the mail. It was expensive to use the telegraph, so at first only important messages were coded over the lines. Code books with some 45,000 carefully selected words were prepared specifically for the mining industry. This enabled the sender to cover the whole range of language used in conducting the mining business, including those required for participation on the stock exchange floors in large cities. The "talking wires" in Virginia City never stopped talking day or night. Each industrial group had its own code books. They were given only to key personnel and were kept in a safe. In some systems where economy of time, or expense was essential, number systems were used to represent key words that directed action to be taken.

CAMELS

Camels were first used in California when the surveying party of Kiddler & Ives was hired to determine the correct California and Nevada boundary from Mojave to Tahoe. The party had foresightedly envisioned the many changes of terrain along the route and had packed boots, snowshoes, sleds, pack animals, and procured a small herd of camels for desert areas.

Otto Esche imported camels in 1863 and drove them over the Sierra. They caused a great sensation when they arrived in Virginia City. The camels proved to be excellent pack animals for carrying marsh salt and cordwood to the mines over good trails and sandy stretches. However, on mountain roads they bogged down where sharp rocks cut their feet, and the wooden saddles abraded their backs as they heaved along, camel-style, over the ups and downs.

The drivers had no admiration for these beast of burden and took no pride in their care. Camels are stubborn, smelly creatures at best. Other mules and horses became frightened of these strange creatures on the trail. In general, the camels caused runaways and havoc creating more problems than they solved. In 1863 most were auctioned off to Nevada traders. For years fair numbers of them ran wild across the deserts. Nowadays there's a camel race every year the weekend after Labor Day in Virginia City.

ACCOMMODATIONS

In the Virginia City-Gold Hill area there are four historical mansions that are now "Bed and Breakfast" guest inns. Hardwicke House, in Silver City, is near the original silver discovery site. House on the Hill in Gold Hill overlooks Gold Canyon, site of the historic largest gold strike. The Chollar Mansion Bed & Breakfast in Virginia City was built in 1861. The 164-square-foot vault that at one time housed millions in silver and gold bullion is now used to hold wine and cheese for tastings. Edith Palmer's Country Inn, built in 1862, is within walking distance to the heart of Virginia City.

Many fine hotels, motels and restaurants are located in both Virginia City and Gold Hill. The lovely RV Park in Virginia City has spaces overlooking the historic city and mine tailings. Some sites have full hook-ups. They have showers, restrooms, laundromat, market, propane and full security.   *Comstock Lode Tailings*

EMIGRANT PARTIES OVER THE DONNER PASS

When Captain Bonneville sent Joseph Walker, along with some forty trappers, in 1833 to hunt for new beaver streams west of Great Salt Lake, he became more of an explorer than a beaver men. He kept traveling in areas where no beaver could be found. Continuing southward after meeting with the Paiute Indians at Pyramid Lake, he continued along the Humboldt Sink before turning south. He therefore missed the Truckee River and the good pass over the Sierra, which later became the route of emigrant parties and the Central Pacific Railroad.

It was in mid-November of 1844 that the Stevens-Murphy-Townsend Party passed Truckee Meadows and headed westward toward the mountain range. The party ascended along the Truckee River to reach the east end of Donner Lake basin (5935'). Fremont and other early explorers had called the Truckee "Salmon Trout River." The Truckee was named for a French Canadian trapper and mountain men who had been a member of Walker's party, and had previously led emigrants across the Sierra.

Donner Lake is 37 miles west of Reno, lying at the end of a great glacial trough whose waters flow into the Truckee River coming out of Lake Tahoe. The amphitheatre-shaped western wall at the end of Donner Lake presented a formidable barrier for the pioneers. It must have been awesome for them in this lonely bleak lake basin, with raging storms of shifting winds blowing swirling snows around them through the great stands of swaying fir.

The Murphy-Townsend Party went south along the Truckee River on horseback, with their provisions on two pack animals. They reached Lake Bonpland, as Lake Tahoe was called at that time, and passed over the crest and down along the American River to Sutters Fort (Sacramento).

The Stevens party, which remained at Donner Lake, was stalled in a new snow storm that buried the grass so deep that cattle could not eat, thereby threatening the party with starvation. Some of the wagons and three boys were left at Donner Lake, where they built a cabin and killed or trapped game to survive. Two of the boys were able to cross the mountains, but Moses Shallenberger returned to the cabin after being hurt, and spent a lonely winter. In the wagons he found books to read to help him pass the time. He was later rescued and eventually arrived in California.

The main Stevens party, with five wagons, went over the craggy ridge using an ingenious method throught up by Caleb Greenwood, their leader. Using ropes and chains they squeezed the oxen through an impeding fissure one at a time. The men, women and children transported on their backs all the provisions that had been unloaded from the wagons. Then the wagons were hauled up the steep escarpment one at a time. The men lifted the wagons up over the rocks as the oxen up top finally pulled them across the barrier. They were the first party to cross the Sierra with wagons.

The Donner-Reed party of Illinois farmers were well equipped with heavy, lumbering wagons and were oversupplied with provisions that would ensure them a good trip west. They left the east in 1846, and everything was fine until they reached Fort Bridger. Here they followed some bad travel advice which took longer than the established route. The party banished Reed, a leading and much needed member, after he accidentally killed a man. Then they tarried too long at Truckee Meadows before starting up along the river to cross the Sierra. Early snows brought further hardship to the group. The party was snowbound at Donner Lake (7150') and had to remain huddled in improvised shelters all winter. Four months in a frigid, windy, forlorn, lonely place with no food took their toll. Many accounts have been written about their tragic crossing, in which only 45 out of 75 survived the horrendous ordeal through the snow.

Despite the treacherousness of this northern pass, it was to become one of the two main passageways of emigrant parties crossing the Sierra. The Carson Pass, discovered by the Fremont Party in 1843-44, became the well-used southern route.

CENTRAL PACIFIC RAILROAD

There were a great many ideas and suggestions about just where the transcontinental railroad should cross the Sierra Crest. Theodore D. Judah, an engineer who had built railroads in Connecticut and New York, came out to California to construct the Sacramento Valley Railroad to Folsom. Five possible routes were presented to him but Judah liked one that "Doc Strong" wrote to him about. It was a massive, naturally inclined ramp rising unobstructed between the Yuba and Bear Rivers that went all the way up to Donner Pass.

The Central Railroad Company was formed in 1861 and Judah was sent to Washington to secure the federal backing necessary to build the road. Railroad building was so costly that government subsidies were necessary. Usually the lines had to go through such thinly populated areas that they were unprofitable from an investment standpoint, and promoters were not willing to take such a gamble. With the tremendous political clout that the Central Pacific Company presented in Washington, and since no one else was able to challenge them, Judah's route became the designated one. It went up along the American River, over Donner Pass, and down along the Truckee River to Reno before running out across the desert.

The arduous, herculean task of constructing the railbed began in 1863. By 1864, 20 miles were laid; with 20 more in 1865; 30 in 1866; and 47 in 1867. Construction gangs were up in the mountains building the steep grades and dizzying curves around rock precipices. Some 7000 Chinese coolies worked hewing a path out of the solid granite rock. They wore broad straw hats and sloppy pants, hauling wheelbarrows of dirt and rock debris, and scampered away from blasting powder charges.

In the summer of 1868 The Sierra was crossed through a series of tunnels built on avalanche susceptable slopes. The tracks went down along the Truckee River and on to Reno. From Reno the new railroad continued across the desert and met the Union Pacific Railroad at Promentory, Utah in mid-May 1869.

Truckee, 32 miles west of Reno, became an important railroad center with a large roundhouse with enough space for 16 locomotives. By 1880 there were 1000 Chinese, 2000 Caucasians, and 50 Indians living in the mountain town. Reno became the supply and shipping center.

RENO

MAC

1862 — Reno was known as Lake's Crossing when Myron Lake built his toll bridge across the Truckee River. His roadhouse serviced the freighters, horsemen and the many travelers who were on their way to Virginia City.

1868 — Lake made a deal with Charles Crocker of the Central Pacific Company to have the main western Nevada railroad depot here at his farm in Truckee Meadows if Lake would deed lots to Crocker. Lots were auctioned off to over 1000 people. Crocker named the town Reno, after the Union General Jesse Lee Reno.

1870 — The Nevada State Journal began its first daily publications.

1871 — Reno became the County Seat of Washoe County.

1874 — The Mackay School of Mining was established.

1877 — A new iron bridge spanned the Truckee River and became a free passageway.

1882 — Reno now had a commercial district and was a shopping center with a pleasant country atmosphere for its 1400 citizens.

1886 — The University of Nevada was moved from Elko to this thriving town.

1910 — With new growth and industries, the town's population reached 10,000.

1920 — Automobiles brought many people from surrounding areas for social activities and shopping. Reno was also a bustling banking and trading center.

1927 — The Transcontinental Highway Exposition arch spanned across Virginia Street.

1929 — "Biggest Little City in the World" arch was installed, replacing the 1927 arch.

1931 — Gambling became fully legalized, and liberal divorce laws gave Reno new growth.

1963 — A new $100,000 arch was donated by casinos to celebrate Nevada's centennial.

1964 — Reno and Nevada celebrated the Centennial.

1987 — New state-of-the-arts arch spanned Virginia Street and Highway 395.

Many diversified collections and exhibits are on display for the visitor's enjoyment: Harolds Club displays antique firearms, slot machines, music boxes and player pianos and carriages. At the Liberty Belle there is a plaque commerating the first slot machine. On the roof of the building are many interesting old wagons, carriages, coaches, and a covered wagon. Harrah's famous Automobile Collection exhibits vintage, antique and classic cars and other special-interest automobiles, along with the clothing and attire associated with each car. The Mineral Museum at the MacKay School of Mines has collections of geological, mineralogical, mining, and metallurgical interest.

Some of the annual events held here are the International Jazz Festival in March; Reno Rodeo in June; Basque Festival and Nevada State Fair in August; Great Balloon Race, National Air Races and Snafflebit Futurity are all held in September. In the summer there is boating, swimming, golfing, tennis, hiking, camping, picnicking and whitewater rafting. Wintertime is snow time, with many ski slopes to choose from, and cross-country skiing up in the Sierra nearby.

Reno Scenic Drive is a specific route to all the important points of the city including the University of Nevada, the famous downtown Casinos, beautiful local parks and outstanding schools. Signs are posted to indicate the route.

Reno would sparkle with its clean, clear desert air even without all the colorful neon lights that flicker and flash. It's a city that is fun, with entertainment galore. It's new and it's old, it's modern and charmingly quaint with many old historic buildings. There are probably more weddings than divorces. It is spread out and surrounded by many hills, but has easy access streets and freeways. It does its best to live up to its Chamber of Commerce slogan as the "biggest little city in the world".

MAC

Each season presents a special, unique glory to this land — as much in contrast as brilliant sunshine is to gray, storm-laden skies. Its rebirth each spring is a spectacle, with the melting of snows swelling streams and wildflowers on desert slopes and mountain meadows burgeoning. Then comes summer, with its hazy hues, warm tantalizing breezes rustling in the pines, shimmering Sierra lakes dotted with fishermen, and well-travelled dusty trails. Autumn brings a colorful display of aspen, cottonwood, and Lombardies fluttering golden leaves in crisp, cool air and the magic of white-peaked crests against a bright blue sky. All this is followed by a crystal fairy land of winter.

Rocky Rockwell

CHRONOLOGICAL DEVELOPMENT ALONG HIGHWAY 395

With the arrival of Padre Garces in 1776 at Willow Springs and Joseph Walker in 1834, the opening of the west began. Mountain and beaver men, explorers and traders roamed the vast wilderness and by the end of the 1830's the Oregon Trail had already been established as an emigrant route out of St. Louis.

1841 — First emigrant party to California crossing over the Sonora Pass
1843 — Chiles emigrant party crosses Walker Pass by foot after burning their wagons
        John Fremont and Kit Carson cross to California via Carson Pass
1844 — Stevens-Murphy-Townsend party was first to cross Sierra with wagons
1845 — Fremont made his Third Expedition
1846 — The Donner party tragedy
1849 — Trading post started at Dayton
1850 — California becomes a state
        Jayhawkers of the Death Valley party reaches Los Angeles
        Gold was found near Dayton at Gold Canyon
1851 — Settlers entered Eagle Valley
1855 — First Mormon settlement at Genoa and Pleasant Valley
1856 — Snowshoe Thompson backpacked mail across the Sierra by skis
1857 — Mormons returned to Salt Lake City from Genoa
        Initial interest in Virginia City
1859 — Gold found at Bodie
        First cattle drive over Walker Pass
1860 — Gold found at Aurora, Mono Diggings, Masonic and Lousetown
        Ranching began in Bridgeport and Antelope Valley near Topaz
        Pony Express made their first run out of St. Joseph, Mo.
        Freight teams went up and down Owens Valley to and from the many mines
        Paiute Wars at Pyramid Lake near Reno
        "Territorial Enterprise" published in Virginia City
        Square set system of timbering for Ophir mine
1861 — Bishops entered Owens Valley and built their ranch
        First settlers in Lone Pine
        Indian wars in Owens Valley
        Carson City named the capitol of Nevada Territory
1862 — Lakes Crossing spanned the Truckee River at Reno
        Camp Independence was established
        Toll roads were constructed to various mines
1863 — Gold and silver were found in Blind Springs Hill, north of Bishop
        Roads were built over Sonora, Carson, Donner and Ebbett Passes
1864 — Nevada becomes a state
        Bridgeport becomes Mono County Seat
        Camels were introduced as beast of burden at Virginia City
1865 — End of the Civil War
        Cerro Gordo mines began operating
1866 — Inyo County established

1867 — Lone Pine Mint made coins for miners
1868 — Reno established as a city
1869 — Central Railroad met Union Pacific Railroad in Utah
       Railroad tracks were laid from Carson City to Reno
       Nevada mint made their first coins
1870 — Virginia & Truckee Railroad established
1871 — Escapees were apprehended at Convict Lake
1872 — Earthquake epicentered at Lone Pine
1873 — Mt. Whitney initially climbed
1874 — Mackay School of Mining established in Reno
1876 — Town of Rosamond named
       Southern Pacific Railroad extended to Los Angeles
       Bodie was very active from now until 1888
1877 — Indian War over and Camp Independence abandoned
       Stevens Cottonwood flume carried wood to Cartago
1878 — Gold found in Inyo Mountains
       Lundy Mine and sawmill active
1879 — Keeler recharged the Cerro Gordo mines
1881 — Flumes carried wood from Tahoe Basin to Carson Valley
       Bridgeport Courthouse built
1882 — Reno now a thriving community
1883 — Tracks for the narrow gauge Carson & Colorado Railroad was laid
1886 — Independence partially destroyed by fire
1893 — Mining activity at Garlock and Goler
       Electricity introduced at Bodie
1894 — Standard Mountain mines operating
1895 — Yellow Aster Mine began operation
1896 — King Solomon Mine at Johannesburg began operation
       Hamilton's Lida Mine near Rosamond began operation
1898 — Santa Fe Railroad extended from Kramer to Johannesburg
1900 — Cardinal Mine operating
1902 — Valuable ore found at Masonic
1904 — Los Angeles Aqueduct construction began
1905 — Tungsten discovered at Atolia
1907 — First portion of Aqueduct completed
1910 — Southern Pacific extended from Mojave to Owenyo
1919 — Kelly Silver Mine developed at Red Mountain
       Owens Valley farms bought up by Los Angeles Water System
1921 — First resort at June Lake — now known as Silver Lake Resort
1924 — Carson & Colorado Railroad extended to Keeler
1933 — Tropico Mine (the Lida Mine) boom was on until World War II
       Edwards Air Force Base developed
1938 — Mammoth Lakes established first ski tow
1940 — Naval Weapons Center established at Inyokern
1941 — Crowley Lake was made a reservoir for Los Angeles Water System
1960 — June Mountain ski lifts built
       Bodie becomes a State Park
1966 — Laws deeded to Bishop by Southern Pacific Railroad
1969 — Alabama Hills Recreation Area established
    In the 1970's and 1980's tourism became a major industry with visitors enjoying year round recreation — backpacking, camping, fishing, hunting, touring, skiing, sledding, or just enjoying the beautiful lakes, meadows and mountains.

CAMPGROUND & TRAILER PARK DIRECTORY

MOJAVE DESERT

OFF I-15 - RIDGECREST

HWY. 14 - INYOKERN

OWENS VALLEY

LONE PINE AREA

INDEPENDENCE

	SEASON	TENT/RV SITES	GROUP	MAX.SIZE	STOVE/GRILL	TABLE	DISPOSAL STA.	HOOKUPS	STORE	SHOWERS	LAUNDRY	PROPANE	FISHING	HORSES	BOAT RENT/MARINA
Rodeo Fairgrounds (2220')	all yr	5	(Check in by 5 PM)												
Saddlebutte State Pk. (2400')	all yr	50		30'	✓	✓	✓								
Sierra Trails RV Park (2700')	all yr			(Mobile Home Park with overnight spaces)											
Red Rock Cyn. State Pk. (2600')	all yr	50		22'	✓	✓	✓								
Chimney Creek (5900')	all yr	36		22'	✓	✓			✓				✓		
Kennedy Meadows (6100')	all yr	39		22'	✓	✓			✓				✓		
Troy Meadows (8000')	5-11	63		22'	✓	✓							✓		
Diaz Lake (3700')	all yr	47		22'	✓	✓							✓		✓
Lone Pine (6000')	all yr	43		22'	✓	✓			✓				✓		
Portage Joe (4500')	all yr	15		22'	✓	✓									
Sierra View Mobile Pk. (3700')	all yr	12						✓		✓					
Tuttle Creek (5120')	5-10	85		22'	✓	✓			✓				✓		
Whitney Portal (8100')	5-10	44	yes	16'	✓	✓							✓		
Independence Creek (4000')	all yr	25		22'	✓	✓							✓		
Gray Meadows (6000')	4-10	52		22'	✓	✓							✓		(some cabanas)
Onion Valley (9200')	5-9	17		16'	✓	✓							✓		

Handicap Site

	SEASON	TENT/RV SITES	GROUP	MAX. SIZE	STOVE/GRILL	TABLE	DISPOSAL STA.	HOOKUPS	STORE	SHOWERS	LAUNDRY	PROPANE	FISHING	HORSES	BOAT RENT/ MARINA
INDEPENDENCE – BIG PINE															
Ft. Independence (3900')	all yr	51			✓	✓	✓			✓					
Goodale Creek (4100')	5-10	62		22'	✓	✓							✓		
Oak Creek (5000')	all yr	24		22'	✓	✓							✓		
Tabose Creek (4200')	all yr	45		22'	✓	✓							✓		
Tinemaha Creek (4100')	all yr	45		22'	✓	✓							✓		
BIG PINE AREA															
Baker Creek Co. Cpgd. (7700')	all yr	50		22'	✓	✓							✓		
Big Pine Creek Cpgd. (7700')	5-10	33		22'	✓	✓			✓				✓		
Big Pine Trailer Pk. (7000')	4-11	35		22'	✓	✓	✓	✓		✓			✓		
Big Pine Triangle (4000')	4-11	30			✓	✓									
Cedar Flats Co. Cpgd. (7200')	5-10		yes												
Grandview (8000')	5-10	26				✓									
Sage Flat (7400')	4-11	27		22'	✓	✓							✓		
BISHOP AREA															
J-Diamond Mobile Pk. (4150')	all yr	28						✓		✓	✓				
Schobers Park (4100')	5-11	160	yes		✓	✓		✓	✓	✓					
Shady Rest RV Pk. (4150')	all yr	25						✓	✓	✓	✓				
BISHOP CREEK AREA															
Aspens Meadows (8400')	5-11	24		22'	✓	✓							✓		
Big Trees (7500')	5-11	9		22'	✓	✓							✓		
Bishop Park (7500')	5-11	20		22'	✓	✓							✓		

Location	Season	Sites		Max Length							
Forks (7800')	5-10	9		22'	✓	✓					✓
Four Jeffreys (H) (8100')	4-10	106		22'	✓	✓	✓				✓
Haebeggers Resort (8300')	4-10	48		22'	✓	✓		✓			✓
Intake Two (7500')	4-11	14		22'	✓	✓					✓
North Lake (9500')	5-10	9		22'	✓	✓					✓
Sabrina (9000')	5-10	21		22'	✓	✓		✓	✓		✓

BISHOP, NORTH

Location	Season	Sites							
Highlands RV Pk. (4500')	all yr	130		✓	✓	✓		✓	
Millpond (4200')	all yr	80		✓	✓				✓
Pleasant Valley Co. Pk. (4200')	all yr	200		✓	✓				✓
Horton Creek (4950')	5-11	53		✓	✓				✓
Paradise Resort (4960')	4-10	20		✓	✓		✓		✓

MONO COUNTY

ROCK CREEK AREA

Location	Season	Sites		Max Length				
Aspen Group (8100')	5-10		50	16'	✓	✓		✓
Big Meadow (8600')	5-10	11		22'	✓	✓		✓
East Fork (H) (9000')	4-10	133		22'	✓	✓		✓
French Camp (7500')	4-11	86		22'	✓	✓		✓
Holiday (7500')	4-11	33		22'	✓	✓		✓
Iris Meadow (8300')	5-9	14		22'	✓	✓		✓
Lower Rock Creek (6600')	4-11	5			✓	✓		✓
Mosquito Flat (10,000')	6-9	19		22'	✓	✓		✓
Palisade (8700')	5-10	5			✓	✓		✓
Pine Grove (9300')	4-10	11		22'	✓	✓	✓	✓
Rock Creek (7500')	4-10	22	50	22'	✓	✓		✓
Rock Creek Lakes (9600')	6-10	86		22'	✓	✓	✓	✓
Tuff (7000')	5-10	34		22'	✓	✓		✓

CROWLEY LAKE — MAMMOTH LAKES

	SEASON	TENT/RV SITES	GROUP	MAX.SIZE	STOVE/GRILL	TABLE	DISPOSAL STA.	HOOKUPS	STORE	SHOWERS	LAUNDRY	PROPANE	FISHING	HORSES	BOAT RENT/ MARINA
Browns Owens River Camp (6800')	6-10	100			✓	✓							✓		
Crowley Lake Cpgd. (7000')	5-6	47		22'	✓	✓	✓		✓				✓		✓
Crowley Lake Tr. Pk. (7600')	all yr	100			✓	✓	✓	✓					✓		✓
McGee Creek Cpgd. (7600')	6-10	28		22'	✓	✓							✓		
Mcgee Creek RV Park (7000')	5-10	37			✓	✓							✓		
Convict Lake (7500')	5-10	88		22'	✓	✓	✓		✓				✓		

MAMMOTH LAKES AREA

	SEASON	TENT/RV SITES	GROUP	MAX.SIZE	STOVE/GRILL	TABLE	DISPOSAL STA.	HOOKUPS	STORE	SHOWERS	LAUNDRY	PROPANE	FISHING	HORSES	BOAT RENT/ MARINA
Camp High Sierra (8400')	6-9	40		22'	✓	✓			✓						
Coldwater (8900')	6-10	78		22'	✓	✓			✓				✓	✓	
Horseshoe Lake Group (8900')	6-9		6	22'	✓	✓								✓	
Lake George (9000')	6-10	37		22'	✓	✓			✓				✓		✓
Lake Mary (8900')	6-10	100		22'	✓	✓			✓				✓	✓	✓
Mammoth Mtn.RVPk. (7860')	all yr	138		22'	✓	✓	✓	✓		✓	✓	✓			
New Shady Rest (7800')	5-11	96		22'	✓	✓									
Old Shady Rest (7800')	6-9	66		22'	✓	✓									
Pine City ((8900')	6-10	112		22'	✓	✓			✓				✓	✓	✓
Pine Glen Group (7800')	6-9	21	150	22'	✓	✓									
Sherwin Creek (7600')	5-10	87		22'	✓	✓							✓		
Twin Lakes (8700')	6-10	97		22'	✓	✓			✓				✓		✓

DEVILS POSTPILE AREA

	SEASON	TENT/RV SITES	GROUP	MAX.SIZE	STOVE/GRILL	TABLE	DISPOSAL STA.	HOOKUPS	STORE	SHOWERS	LAUNDRY	PROPANE	FISHING	HORSES	BOAT RENT/ MARINA
Agnew Meadows (8400')	6-10	36	4	22'	✓	✓							✓	✓	
Devils Postpile Natl.M. (7560')	6-9	23		22'	✓	✓							✓	✓	

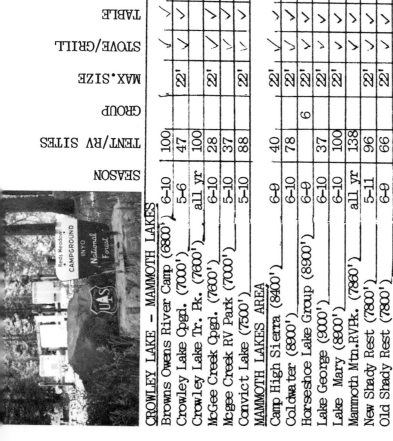

Location												
Minaret Falls (7600')	5-10	27	22'	✓							✓	
Pumice Flat (7700')	7-10	17	4	22'	✓						✓	
Reds Meadow (7600')	7-9	54	22'	✓	✓					✓	✓	
Upper Soda Springs (7650')	7-9	25	22'	✓						✓	✓	

"BURNT LAND" MAMMOTH LAKES – JUNE LAKES

Location												
Big Springs (7300')	6-10	24	22'	✓	✓							
Glass Creek (7600')	6-10	30	22'	✓	✓							
Hartley Springs (8400')	6-10	20	22'	✓	✓							
Lower Deadman (7800')	6-10	30	50	22'	✓	✓						

JUNE LAKES

Location												
Golden Pine RV Pk (7600')	all yr	32		✓	✓	✓	✓	✓	✓		✓	
Grant Lake Resort (7300')	5-10	140		✓	✓	✓	✓	✓	✓	✓	✓	✓
Gull Lake (7600')	5-10	12	22'	✓	✓						✓	
June Lake (7600')	5-10	22	22'	✓	✓						✓	
Oh! Ridge (7800')	4-10	148	yes	22'	✓	✓						✓
Pinecliff Resort (7800')	5-10	180		✓	✓	✓	✓	✓	✓			✓
Reversed Creek (7500')	5-10	17	22'	✓	✓						✓	
Silver Lake Cpgd. (7300')	5-10	65	22'	✓	✓	✓	✓	✓			✓	
Silver Lake Resort (7300')	4-10	75		✓	✓	✓	✓	✓	✓	✓	✓	✓

LEEVINING CANYON

Location												
Aspen Grove (8000')	5-10	50	50								✓	✓
Big Bend (6780')	5-10	18									✓	
Ellery Lake (9500')	6-10	13		✓	✓						✓	
Junction (9600')	6-9	12	22'	✓							✓	
LeeVining Creek (8000')	5-10	90									✓	
Saddlebag Lake (10,000')	6-10	20		✓							✓	
Tioga Lake (9700')	6-10	13									✓	

YOSEMITE NATIONAL PARK

	SEASON	TENT/RV SITES	GROUP	MAX. SIZE	STOVE/GRILL	TABLE	DISPOSAL STA.	HOOKUPS	STORE	SHOWERS	LAUNDRY	PROPANE	FISHING	HORSES	BOAT RENT/ MARINA
Porcupine Flat (8700')	6-9	86			✓	✓						✓	✓		
Tuolumne Meadows (8600')	6-10	370		20'	✓	✓	✓		✓				✓	✓	
White Wolf (8000')	5-9	87		20'	✓	✓	✓		✓				✓	✓	
Yosemite Creek (7300')	6-9	75			✓	✓							✓		

LEEVINING, NORTH

	SEASON	TENT/RV SITES	GROUP	MAX. SIZE	STOVE/GRILL	TABLE	DISPOSAL STA.	HOOKUPS	STORE	SHOWERS	LAUNDRY	PROPANE	FISHING	HORSES	BOAT RENT/ MARINA
Best Western Lodge (6780')	4-10	6					✓								
Mono Vista Tr Pk. (7300')	all yr	27								✓					
Mill Creek Co. Pk (8000')	5-10	100			✓	✓				✓	✓		✓		
Lundy Lake Resort (8200')	5-10	15			✓	✓		✓	✓	✓	✓		✓		
Trumbull Lake (9500')	6-9	44		22'	✓	✓				✓			✓		✓
Virginia Ck. SetImt. (6800')	4-11	10			✓	✓		✓	✓	✓	✓		✓		
Willow Springs (6800')	4-10	19			✓	✓		✓	✓	✓	✓		✓		

UPPER MONO COUNTY
BRIDGEPORT AREA

	SEASON	TENT/RV SITES	GROUP	MAX. SIZE	STOVE/GRILL	TABLE	DISPOSAL STA.	HOOKUPS	STORE	SHOWERS	LAUNDRY	PROPANE	FISHING	HORSES	BOAT RENT/ MARINA
Buckeye, (7000')	5-10	69		22'	✓	✓							✓		
Honeymoon Flat (7000')	5-10	47		22'	✓	✓				✓			✓		
MonoVillage Resort (7000')	5-10	370			✓	✓		✓	✓	✓	✓		✓		✓
Paha (7000')	5-10	15			✓	✓				✓			✓		
Paradise Shores TR. Pk. (6500')	4-10	42					✓	✓		✓	✓		✓		
Robinson Creek (7000')	5-9	45				✓							✓		
Twin Lakes (Lower) (7000')	5-10	17		22'		✓		✓			✓		✓		
Twin Lakes Resort (7000')	5-10	16				✓		✓	✓	✓	✓		✓		✓

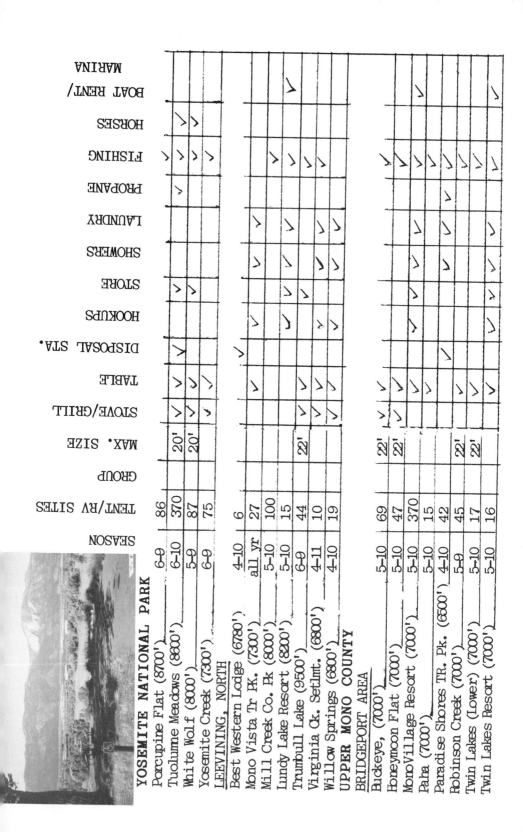

WALKER RIVER AREA

Facility	Season	Sites	Max Length
Leavitt Meadows (7000')	6-10	18	16'
Sonora Bridge (6800')	5-10	13	22'
Chris Flat (6000')	4-10	15	22'
Bootleg Cpgd. (6600')	4-10	62	22'
Topaz Lake RV Pk. (H) (4800').	all yr	50	
Topaz Lake Park (5100')	3-10	54	
Holbrook Jctn. (4800')	all yr	46	

HISTORIC CORRIDOR

CARSON CITY AREA

Facility	Season	Sites
Camp-N-Town (4600')	all yr	74
Carson Valley Inn (4500')	all yr	60
Comstock Co. RV Pk. (4600')	all yr	150
Davis Creek Co. Pk. (4700')	all yr	63
Dayton State Park (4600')	all yr	15
Oasis Trailer Haven, (4600')	all yr	20
Virginia City RV Pk. (6800')	all yr	90
Washoe State Pk. (4600')	all yr	49

RENO AREA

Facility	Season	Sites
Bally's Resort (4500')	all yr	450
Chrism's Tr. Pk. (4500')	all yr	50
Reno KOA, (4490')	all yr	248
Reno RV. Pk.,(4600')	all yr	46
Reno River Edge RV Pk., (4500')	all yr	164
Shamrock RV Pk., (H) (4400')	all yr	129
United Campground, (4600')	all yr	150

Index

A

Aberdeen, 71,83
Adelanto, 10,17
Aeolian Buttes, 136
Agnew Meadows, 121,125,130
Alabama Hills, 63,68,71
Ancient Bristlecone Pine Forest,
        1,90,92,93
Antelope Valley (Mojave), 17,36,49
Antelope Valley (Mono), 156
Atolia, 17,21,23,41

B

Bald Mountain Lookout, 131
Barnes,Charlotte, 72
Baxter Pass, 71,73,74
Bed & Breakfast, 165,173,187
Benton, 1,73,92,94,95,137
Benton Crossing, 113,119
Big Pine, 1,10,71,86,87,88,92,93,96,
Big Pine Creek, 71,86,88
Big Pine Lakes, 88,100
Big Pine Volcanic Field, 71,83
Birds, 143
Bishop, 1,10,11,73,92-99,106,108
Bishop Creek, 96,99,100
Bishop Pass, 88,103
Bodie, 1,8,137,148,151,153
Boron, 17,20,41
Boundary Peak, 92,94
Bowers Mansion, 176,179
Bridgeport, 1,11,156
Bridgeport Lake, 156,159
Bridgeport Meadows, 156
Bridgeport Valley, 153
Burcham, Dr. Rose L., 28

C

Cactus Flat, 50,55
California City, 17,36,41,42
Camels in Virginia City, 187
Camp Independence, 71,80,81
Campgrounds, 34,44,50,63,71,78,84,85,
        87,88,91,96,100,102,108,109,
        114-121,124,125,127,133,135,
        139,144,145,147,149,155,173,
        176,177
Campground & Trailer Park Directory,
        195-201
Cantil, 17,32,41
Cardinal Mine, 104
Carson City, 1,8,11,73,166,167,172,173,
        176,177,178,186
Carson & Colorado Railroad, 73,94,95,
        97,105,107
Carson Pass, 188
Carson Range, 164
Carson River, 1,165,166,177
Carson Valley, 165
Cartago, 55,59
Cave Rock, 164,182
Central Pacific Railroad, 186,191
Cerro Gordo Mines, 44,50,55,58,59,62
Chalfant, 73,92,95,99
Chalk Cliff, 92,96
Charcoal Kilns, 55,60
Chimney Meadows & Peak, 50
China Lake, 17,41
Chocolate Factory, 180
Cinder Rock (Red Hill), 53
Coleville, 156
Convict Lake, 116,120,121
Conway Summit, 11,148,150
Coso Junction, 50,53

Coso Range, 50,55,66
Cottonwood Creek & Lakes, 60
Crater Mountain, 71
Crowley Lake, 1,113,116,117
Crowley Memorial, 41,47
Crystal Crag, 121

D

Dalzell Canyon, 156
Davis Creek County Park, 179
Dayton, 1,177
Dayton State Park, 164,176,177
Deep Springs Lake & Valley, 91,92,93
Deer Mountain, 121
Dehy Community Park, 75
Desert Plants, 19
Desert Rails, 107
Desert Tortoise Natural Area, 17,41,42
Devils Gate, 156,176,177
Devils Postpile National Monument,
     121,124,127
Devils Punchbowl, 133,134
Diaz Lake, 50,55,61
Dirty Socks Mineral Hot Springs, 50,
     55,56
Dogtown, 149
Dolomite, 55
Double Springs Flat, 164
Dunmovin, 10,50
Dyer, 92,94

E

Eagle Valley, 164,172,176
East California Museum, 76,77
Eastern Sierra Interpretive Assn.,
     61,63,71
Edwards Air Force Base, 17,35,36
El Dorado National Forest, 164
El Paso Mountains, 17,31,32,41,43,46
Emigrant Parties, 47,48,188

F

Fales Hot Springs, 156
Ferris Wheel, 171
Fish Hatchery, 71,82,113,123
Fish Lake Valley, 92,94
Fish Slough, 92,96
Fish Springs Valley, 1,71,85
Flowers, 142
Fossil Beds, 55,56,57
Fossil Falls, 50,53
Franktown Road, 176,179
Freeman Junction, 17, 41,47
Fremont, John C., 20,188
Fremont - Carson Route, 156
Fremont Peak, 17,20
Fremont Valley, 17,41

G

Gardnerville, 1,164
Garlock, 17,31,32,41,43
Geiger Summit, 176,181
Genoa, 1,164,165,167,168,169,179
Gilbert Pass, 92,94
Glacier Lodge, 71
Glass Mountain, 119
Gold Canyon, 176,177
Gold Hill, 164,176,186
Golden Trout Wilderness Area, 60,63
Goler, 17, 31,41
Goodale Creek, 71,74
Grant, 50,54

H

Haiwee Reservoir, 50,53
Hamilton, Ezra, 35,37,38
Hilton Creek, 113,116,118
Historic Corridor, 162 - 191
Holbrook Junction, 156,159,161,164
Homestead, 49

Hoover Wilderness Area, 156
Horseshoe Meadows, 60,63
Hot Creek, 113,122
Howitzer, 156
Hunewill Ranch, 153,156
Huntoon Valley, 155

I

Incline Village, 164
Independence, 1,10,71,73,74,75
Indians, 12-15
Indian Campaign, 80
Indian Creek Reservoir, 164
Indian Wells Valley, 17,41,49,50,52
Inyo Craters, 131
Inyo Mountains, 60,64,66,71,72,92
Inyo National Forest, 71,74,88
Inyokern, 17,41
Isabella Lake, 17

J

Jack Wright Summit, 156
Jacks Valley Road, 164,169
Jawbone Canyon, 17,41
Jeffrey Pine Forest, 131
Johannesburg, 1,17,23,26,41
John Muir Trail, 64,74,79,103
John Muir Wilderness Area, 63,71,74,
        88,100,113,116
Joshua Trees, 43
June Lake, 1,8,11,133,135

K

Kearsarge Mine, 78
Kearsarge Pass, 74,79
Keeler, 50,55,58,59,73
Kelly Mine, 22,27
Kennedy Meadows, 50,52
Keoughs Hot Springs, 96
Kern River, 50,54,63
King Solomon Mine, 26
Kings Canyon National Park, 88
Klondike Lake, 86,96
Koehn Dry Lake, 17,41,43
Kramer Junction, 1,10,17,20,36,41

L

Lake Sabrina, 100,102
Lake Tahoe, 8,164,182,183
Lakeridge, 164
Lakeview, 176,178
Lancaster, 1,17,34
Laws, 73,96,106
Leavitt Meadows, 155,156
LeeVining, 1,11,133,145,146
LeeVining Canyon, 139
Little Lake, 1,50,52,53
Little Lakes Valley, 115,116
Little Pine Creek, 71
Little Washoe Lake, 176
Lone Pine, 1,10,50,55,59,61,62,63,65,
        66,69,72,73
Long Valley, 117,119
Lookout Mountain, 133
Los Angeles, 1
Los Angeles Aqueduct, 41,44 50
Lousetown, 176,181
Lower Rock Creek, 96
Lundy Canyon & Lake, 145,147,148

M

Mammoth Lakes, 1,8,11,113,121,123,124,
        125,126,138,148
Manzanar, 70,71,73
Marklesville, 159
Masonic,156,159
Maturango Museum, 33
Mazourka Canyon, 71,77
McGee Creek, 113,116,118
Mill Pond Park & Road, 96
Minden, 1,164,167
Mining Days Railroad, 73
Mojave, 1,17,34,36,39,40,41
Mojave Desert, 16-53
Mono City, 148
Mono Country, 111-116
Mono Craters, 132,133,136,137
Mono Diggings, 150
Mono Lake, 1,8,111,145,148
Mono Lake State Park, 146
Mono Mills, 133,137
Montgomery City, 95

Montgomery Pass, 73,92
Mormon Station, 164,167,169
Mound House, 73,164,176,177
Mt. Rose, 181,182
Mt. Rose Junction, 176
Mt. Whitney, 1,61,63,64,65
Mt. Whitney Station, 72
Muller Lane, 164,165

N

Naval Weapons Center, 33,49,50
Nelson, Mary & Richard, 37
Nine Mile Canyon, 50,52
North Fork Creek, 71,74
North Lake, 100

O

Obsidian Dome, 132,133
Oak Creek, 71,79
Olancha, 1,110,50,54,55
Owens Lake, 54,55,59,62,63,64,66,73
Owens River, 1,71,92,93,99,113
Owens River Gorge, 96,112
Owens River Wild Trout Area, 108,109
Owens Valley, 1,8,50,54-110
Owenyo, 71,72,73

P

Pacific Crest Trail, 64,74,79,103
Pack Stations, 87,102,110,111,115,
    118,126,135,149
Paiute-Shoshoni Museum, 96,99
Palisades Glacier, 86,88
Palmdale, 1,17,36,39
Panum Crater, 136,137
Pearson, Lucy, 51
Pearsonville, 17,41,50,51
Pine Creek, 96,100,110,112
Pioneer Basin, 116
Piute Pass, 100
Pleasant Valley, 176,180
Pleasant Valley Reservoir, 96
Ponderosa Ranch, 164
Pony Express, 164,174,175,177,186
Poverty Hills, 85
Pumice Flat, 121
Pumice Valley, 133

R

Rainbow Falls, 127,130
Ranch Lands, 105
Randsburg, 1,8,10,17,22,23,28,29,30,41
Rattlesnake Gulch, 150
Red Mountain, 17,22,41,71,85
Red Rock Canyon, 17,20,41,44,45
Resorts, 52,71,87,135,139,146,147,148,
    154,159
Reds Meadow, 127,130
Reno, 1,118,167,176,190,191
Rest Areas, 59,53,134
Ridgecrest, 1,33,10,
Robber's Roost, 41,46
Rock Creek Canyon, 96,111-116
Rosamond, 17,35,36,39
Rose Valley, 53
Round Valley, 96,109
Rowena, 108,109

S

Saddlebag Lake, 144
Saddlebutte State Park, 17,34,36
Sawmill Creek Road, 83
Sawmill Pass, 71,74
Shephard Pass, 71,79
Sherwin Canyon, 121,124
Sherwin Summit, 11,96,111,112
Silver City, 164,176
Sixty Lakes Basin, 17,74
Schmidt, Burro, 46
Snowshoe Thompson, 169
Soledad Mountain, 17,36,39
Sonora Pass Road, 1,11,155,156
South Lake, 88,100,103
South Lake Tahoe, 164
Southern Pacific Railroad, 26,32,34,72
Sportscar Raceway, 38
Square Set Mining, 185,187
Stagecoach & Stagelines, 170
Steamboat Springs, 181
Steamboat Valley, 176
Stewart Indian Museum, 174
Swansea, 55,58
Sweetwater Creek, 156
Sweetwater Mountain, 156,161
Sweetwater Natural Area, 156,161

T

Taboose Creek Road, 71,74,84
Tahoe Basin, 1,164,178,182
Tanner, Bob, 130
Tehachapi Mountains, 17,34,36
Tinemaha Reservoir, 71,85
Tioga Pass Road, 141,145
Toiyabe National Forest, 156
Toll Roads, 150
Toms Place, 1,11,96,111,113,114,
Topaz, 1,11   116
Topaz Lake, 156,159
Trail Crest, 63,64
Trailer Parks, 135,154,159,
                165,173,187,
                195-201
Tree Chart, 128-129
Trona Pinnacles, 17,33,41
Tropico Hill & Mine, 17,36,38,39
Tule Elk, 85
Tungsten Hills, 96
Tuolumne Meadows, 140,141,144,145
Twin Lakes Road, 154

V

Virginia & Truckee Railroad, 73,165
        183,186
Virginia City, 1,8,71,164,176,184-187
Virginia Lakes, 148-149
Volcanic Tablelands, 92,96,112

W

Walker, 156,157,160
Walker, Joseph, 28
Walker Canyon, 156
Walker Pass, 17,41,48
Walker Lake, 1,71
Walker River, East & West 1,8,157,158
Wally's Hot Springs, 164,166
Washoe City, 180
Washoe State Park, 164,176,178
Washoe Valley, 176,180,191
Wellington, 156,160
Westgard Pass, 60,64,91
Willow Springs, 17,36,37
White Mountains, 60,64,66,68,92,95,96,
White Mountains Circle Trip,93   111
Whitmore Hot Springs, 119
Whitney Portal, 60,61,63,64
Wireless, 186
Wilson Butte, 133,134
Winnedumah Monument, 71,77
Wyman Canyon,92

Y

Yellow Aster Mine, 23,24,25,28
Yosemite National Park, 140-144

Z

Zephyr Cove, 164

Indian Basket Collection   *Courtesy of East California Museum*

IN APPRECIATION . . .

I am especially indebted to Richard F. Dempewolff for editing and giving valuable suggestions for this publication . . . and to MAC who supplied many photographs of scenes along the highway to use on the covers and in the book. I would like to express thanks to the following people who gave time and information to make this book as accurate and up-to-date as possible:

Dorothy Alcorace, Eastern California Museum

Raymond Andrews, Paiute-Shoshone Museum

Teri Cawelti, Mammoth-June Lakes Airport

Jack Cockran, Alpha Air, Bishop Airport

H. R. Denniss, Keough's Hot Springs

Wayne Frye, Geologist, U.S.Forest Service, Bridgeport

Shirley Giovacchini, Genoa Courthouse Museum

LeNore Hunewill, Hunewill Circle R Ranch

Jamie Hurly, Ridgecrest Daily Independence

Ed Johnson, Stewart Indian Museum

Peggy Lyons, Mono Village Resort

Connie & John Magee, Magee Graphics Corp.

Dorothy Matthew, Benton Library

Ralph & Bambie Mercey, Lundy Lake Resort

Bill Michael, Eastern California Museum

Marilyn Muse, U.S.Forest Service, Bridgeport

Mary & Richard Nelson, Willow Springs

Robert A. Nylan, Nevada State Museum

Erin O'Connor-Henry, U.S.Forest Service, Bridgeport

Larry Osborne, Carson City Chamber of Commerce

Stanley Paher, Nevada Publications

Geraldine Pasqua, Paiute-Shoshone Indian Museum

Lynne Ragar, Ridgecrest Chamber of Commerce

Richard R. Scott, Inyo & Mono County Brands

Lois Stroke, Genoa Courthouse Museum

Bob Tanner, Reds Meadow Resort

Larry Weatherford, Edwards Air Force Base

Edward Zolkowski, EZ Nature Books

Contributing Photographers:

John Anderson	Jim Denton	Lee Roeser
Frank Balthis	Barbara Gray	H. Remington Slifka
Tom Blair	Ernest Hommerding	Peggy Warne
L. Dean Clark	Jim King	Bob Wheir
Cliff Dennell	Rocky Rockwell	Jim Wilson

OTHER PUBLICATIONS BY LEW & GINNY CLARK

YOSEMITE TRAILS
A revised, up-to-date complete guide to all the trails and roads in Yosemite National Park with 5-color Topo and 4-color maps, day hikes, where to camp, wildlife notes with sketches, Trail Profiles showing elevation and mileages between points. Many photographs. 6" x 9". 144 pages. $8.95.

JOHN MUIR TRAIL COUNTRY
A detailed, illustrated book with maps, photographs and sketches of the John Muir - Pacific Crest Trail country between the lower Kern River on the south to Emigrant Basin to the north. The Clarks describe trails to explore, lakes to fish and what to see along the way. 6" x 9". 144 pages. $8.95.

MAMMOTH - MONO COUNTRY
A revised edition on the most beautiful year round resort area with many maps in color for the backpacker, fisherman, day hiker and mountain enthusiasts. Numerous sketches and photographs, 5-color Topo maps, wildlife notes, bicycle information and Campground and Trailer Park Directory. 6"x9". 96 pages. $7.95

HIGH MOUNTAINS & DEEP VALLEYS, The Gold Bonanza Days
Ghost towns from Calico to Virginia City; Death Valley; and the Basin and Range Country are all described with colorful maps, sketches and photographs. This book is a must for desert, ghost town and history buffs. 6'x9". 196 pages. $9.95.

GRAND CANYON COUNTRY
The land and environment of this great region are described with trail notes and auto tours that include the cultures of the Hopi and Navajo Indians and sites to visit of the ancient Anasazi dwellings. Wildlife notes and sketches. Many photographs. 6'x9". 144 pages. $7.95.

SEQUOIA - KINGS CANYON TRAILS (ready for spring 1991)
A complete guide to these two National Parks with 5-color Topo and 4-color maps. Both the eastern and western approaches to this magnificent country of towering crests,. granite slopes, sparkling lakes are included... story of the giant sequoias, day hikes and winter activites with sketches and photographs. 6"x9". 144 pages. $9.95.

CATCH 'EM & EAT 'EM, a Fish Cookbook
Over 200 recipes for fresh and salt water fish with ideas for baking, broiling, barbecue and camp cookery, casseroles, left-overs, Southwest and party fare, salads and soups, with many helpful hints and numerous sketches. Colorful cover. Spiral bound. 128 pages. $6.95.

GINNY CLARK

Some years ago Ginny Clark left New York to check out the west and never returned east to live. The 'printers ink' became ingrained in her blood at her first job as file clerk for Readers Digest. Before the western trek she worked for such notable publishing houses as Harper & Row and Thomas Y. Crowell gaining expertise in the book business. before she married she worked for the San Francisco Chronicle and Stanford University Press.

The honeymoon trip down the John Muir Trail awakened her appreciation for the awesome beauty of the Sierra Nevada. The Clarks explored most states along with Canada and Mexico as well as raising three children. The desert was their 'home' as much as the mountains.

In 1976 Western Trails Publications was started to publish their guides. After Lew Clark passed away Ginny continued the work they had planned together. Their books reflect the concern for the care that needs to be taken to preserve our heritage through the understanding of our surroundings. The GUIDE TO HIGHWAY 395, Los Angeles to Reno, the latest book describes the road they had traveled so often and love so much.

For more information on these publications write:
WESTERN TRAILS PUBLICATIONS, Box 1697, San Luis Obispo, Ca., 93406